Changing Identities in Higher Education

What does it mean, personally and professionally, to be an academic, a student, an educational developer, an administrator or a manager in higher education today? *Changing Identities in Higher Education* attempts to answer such questions. Throughout the pages, readers are invited to look through the lens of a historical process of construction, deconstruction, and reconstruction, three movements that are seen at the heart of any identity dynamic.

In this timely and innovative book, scholars from the UK, Europe, North America and Australia explore their own sense of identity, reflecting both on their research and scholarly interests and on their work experiences. Through a combination of the analytical and the autobiographical, the synoptic and the particular, the book offers a rich and nuanced set of fresh insights into identities in higher education today.

Taking the form of a debate, and helping to take forward current thinking on identities in higher education, *Changing Identities in Higher Education* helps to widen the contemporary space for debates on the future of higher education itself. The book is organised into three parts:

- Part I offers an essay each on a set of identities within higher education (academic, student, administrative/managerial and educational developers).
- Part II includes responses to Part I from authors speaking from their own professional and scholarly identity perspective (manager, sociologist and so on).
- Part III offers perspectives on the identities of students, provided by students themselves.

For its original, dialogic form and varied content, this book is of interest to all those concerned in current debates about the state and nature of higher education today. It makes especially useful reading for students of higher education, lecturers in training, academics and managers alike. It is also of significance for all social theorists interested in questions of identity.

Ronald Barnett is Pro-Director for Longer Term Strategy and Professor of Higher Education at the Institute of Education, University of London.

Roberto Di Napoli is Senior Lecturer in Educational Development at Imperial College London.

Key Issues in Higher Education Series
Series Editors: Gill Nicholls and Ron Barnett

Changing Identities in Higher Education

Voicing Perspectives

Edited by Ronald Barnett
and Roberto Di Napoli

Routledge
Taylor & Francis Group

LONDON AND NEW YORK

First published 2008
by Routledge
2 Park Square, Milton Park, Abingdon, Oxon OX14 4RN

Simultaneously published in the USA and Canada
by Routledge
270 Madison Ave, New York, NY 10016

*Routledge is an imprint of the Taylor & Francis Group, an informa
business*

Typeset in Times New Roman by Prepress Projects Ltd, Perth, UK
Printed and bound in Great Britain by Biddles Digital, King's Lynn

British Library Cataloguing in Publication Data
A catalogue record for this book is available from the British Library

Library of Congress Cataloging in Publication Data
   Changing identities in higher education: voicing perspectives/edited by
Ronald Barnett and Roberto Di Napoli.
      p. cm. – (Key issues in higher education)
   Includes bibliographical references and index.
   ISBN 0–415–42605–7 (hardback)
   1. Education, Higher–Social aspects. 2. Group identity. I. Barnett,
Ronald, 1947– II. Di Napoli, Roberto.
   LC191.9.C43 2007
   306.43′2–dc22

                                                            2007004688

ISBN10: 0-415-42605-7 (hbk)
ISBN10: 0-203-94490-9 (ebk)

ISBN13: 978-0-415-42605-4 (hbk)
ISBN13: 978-0-203-94490-5 (ebk)

In ricordo della madre e del padre di Roberto

Contents

Illustrations

Figures

Tables

Acknowledgements

We wish to thank Ms Heather Fry and the Centre for Educational Development, Imperial College London, for their support for this project, especially for hosting the preliminary meeting among authors in May 2005.

Contributors

Ronald Barnett is Pro-Director for Longer Term Strategy at the Institute of Education, University of London, where he is also Professor of Higher Education. Among his books are *The Idea of Higher Education, Realising the University in an Age of Supercomplexity* and *Beyond All Reason: Living with Ideology in the University.* He is also the Editor of *London Review of Education.*

Dr **Roberto Di Napoli** is Senior Lecturer in Educational Development at Imperial College London. Among other things, he is co-editor (with Loredana Polezzi and Anny King) of the volume *Fuzzy Boundaries? Reflections on Modern Languages and the Humanities* (CILT, 2001). His most recent scholarly interests include academic identities, the changing nature of doctoral studies, and the theory and practice of higher education. He works as a consultant for the Institue of Education, University of Barcelona, Spain.

Alison Ahearn teaches in both civil engineering (construction law) and educational development at Imperial College London.

Dr **Denise Batchelor** is a Reader in Educational Development at London South Bank University. Her research interests lie in the area of student voice and academic identity, and she is particularly interested in philosophical perspectives on learning, teaching and student support.

Victor M. H. Borden is associate vice president for university planning, institutional research, and accountability at Indiana University and an associate professor of psychology (IUPUI) with adjunct appointments in higher education (IU Bloomington) and informatics (IUPUI). He is a past president of the Association for Institutional Research (AIR). His primary research interests are in the areas of institutional and program performance assessment and improvement.

Oliver Broadbent is completing the final year of his degree at ENPC, Paris under Imperial's 'Year Abroad' scheme and is the 'foreign correspondent' for the student newspaper, *Livic.*

Robert Burgess is Vice-Chancellor of the University of Leicester and Chair of UCAS, the Research Information Network, the UUK/Guild HE enquiry on Measuring and Recording Student Achievement and Teacher Education Advisory Group. He is a member of the British Library Board and a Trustee of the Higher Education Academy and has written widely on social research methodology and the sociology of education.

John Collins completed his MEng degree at Imperial College London in

2005–06. John has stayed on as the elected president of the Imperial College Union.

Gerard Delanty is Professor of Sociology and Social and Political Thought, University of Sussex. He was previously Professor of Sociology, University of Liverpool. He is the author of numerous papers and ten books in addition to being editor of seven volumes on various issues in sociology and social theory. His publications include *Challenging Knowledge: The University in the Knowledge Society* (Open University Press, 2001) and the *Handbook of Contemporary European Social Theory* (Routledge, 2005).

Gunnar Handal is Professor Emeritus at the Institute for Educational Research at the University of Oslo, Norway. He has worked in the field of higher education for decades. His recent research has been on research supervision and student transition from studies to work life. He has been teaching faculty development courses and has been a consultant for educational development projects in higher education.

Allison Gonsalves is a PhD student in the Department of Integrated Studies in Education at McGill University. Her dissertation investigates how gendered practices and social relations in science are perceived in lived experience, and examines the implications this has for the formation of a scientific identity and persistence in doctoral science education.

Marian Jazvac-Martek is a faculty lecturer and PhD candidate in the Department of Educational and Counselling Psychology at McGill University. Her research focuses on academic identity development in relation to graduate student attrition.

Ray Land is Professor of Higher Education and Director of the Centre for Academic Practice and Learning Enhancement at the University of Strathclyde in Glasgow. His current research interests include the practice of academic development, theoretical aspects of digital learning, and the emerging framework of threshold concepts and troublesome knowledge.

Susan Lapworth is Academic Registrar at Brunel University, having previously worked in a number of other UK higher education institutions in administrative and managerial roles. From 2003 to 2005 she undertook the MBA in Higher Education Management at the Institute of Education, which sparked a more academic interest in contemporary issues in the management of universities. She is currently undertaking further research in this area.

Lynn McAlpine, a Professor of Education at McGill University, Canada, publishes internationally on educational development and is co-editor of the *International Journal for Academic Development*. She recently received awards for significant contributions to higher education research from both the American Educational Research Association and the Canadian Society for Studies in Higher Education.

Dr **Laura Miller** has worked at a number of London universities as a lecturer and research fellow. Her background in sociology and social psychology has led to her exploring the pedagogic aspects of her role in both contexts, and she has carried out ethnographic research into interactions in university lectures and seminars. Recent research has focused on contemporary forms of racism and exclusion and new strategies for democratic engagement. She is about to leave the university environment (perhaps temporarily) to take up a research post exploring e-democracy for the Hansard Society.

Eirini Spentza completed her MEng degree at Imperial in 2005–06. Eirini has stayed on to do a PhD in fluid mechanics.

Marilyn Strathern is William Wyse Professor of Social Anthropology, University of Cambridge, and Mistress of Girton College. Her principal fieldwork was in the Highlands of Papua New Guinea and her public service includes serving on the Nuffield Council on Bioethics. Her most recent book is *Kinship, Law and the Unexpected* (CUP, 2005), a treatise of sorts on 'the relation', and her most recent research work deals with the ramifications of interdisciplinarity.

Peter Taylor is Assistant Dean (Learning) in the Faculty of Education of the Queensland University of Technology. This work reflects his long-term involvement in and leadership of pedagogical innovation. In turn, that involvement has also been the major stimulus for much of his scholarly work, including a range of publications exploring learning, innovation and change and their impact on both students and staff in higher education.

David Watson is an historian and Professor of Higher Education Management at the Institute of Education, University of London. He was Vice-Chancellor of the University of Brighton (formerly Brighton Polytechnic) between 1990 and 2005. His academic interests are in the history of American ideas and in higher education policy. His most recent books are *Lifelong Learning and the University* (1998), *Managing Strategy* (2000), *New Directions in Professional Higher Education* (2000), *Higher Education and the Lifecourse* (2003), *Managing Institutional Self-Study* (2005) and *Managing Civic and Community Engagement* (2007).

Celia Whitchurch has held senior management roles at the Universities of Birmingham and London. She is currently Visiting Research Fellow in the Department of Management at King's College London, and is undertaking a major study for the UK Leadership Foundation for Higher Education on *Professional Managers in UK Higher Education: Preparing for Complex Futures*. She is a Fellow of the Association of University Administrators, was the founding Editor of the Association's journal, *Perspectives: Policy and Practice in Higher Education* and is Associate Editor of *Higher Education Quarterly*.

Introduction

Roberto Di Napoli and Ronald Barnett

This book's own identity

Perhaps, before all else, a book about identity should declare its own identity. Among its many connotations, identity is always located. One cannot have an identity in the abstract. Identity is formed or ill-formed in a certain situation. How, then, do we see this book's situation?

We offer this volume, first, as an addition to the developing literature on identities in higher education. We aim especially to situate its explorations in the context of more general debates about identities. Second, we want to stimulate thinking about the identities of a number of groups *within* higher education today (not only academics but also managers, students, educational developers and so on). Third, we have encouraged contributors who belong to one or more of these groups to explore their own sense of identity, in terms both of professional and scholarly interests and of practice. Through this combination of the analytical with the autobiographical, and the synoptic with the particular, we believe that we are presenting here a rich and nuanced set of fresh insights into identities in higher education today.

Genesis

As the editors of this volume, we have been interested, in our own scholarly work, in issues of identities in higher education. This common interest ignited the idea of a volume that could bring together and help to take forward current debates on identities in higher education. In so doing, such a book might just widen the contemporary space for debates on the future of higher education itself.

We resolved that the book should include the voices and perspectives of scholars, managers and students involved in higher education, as well as practitioners and/or researchers. We chose writers who either had a particular interest in identity issues in higher education or were known as scholars who could contribute particularly well to the theme of the book because of their specific professional position. Additionally, we wished to have an international set of contributors, so that a cross-national range of perspectives could come into view.

Our main hope of this book, therefore, was that it should offer a synoptic, but fluid, picture of how the current nature of higher education may be understood as a site of many identities-in-the-making, by seeing higher education from the different vantage points of some of the many academic and professional groups that make up its life. At the same time, we hope we have shown some of the complexities that characterise the identity of each group.

The historical background

In the last thirty years or so, higher education in Britain has undergone some seminal changes that have altered its nature, scope and aims. Up until around three decades ago, there was a shared perception that the British higher education system had a rather stable structure, in terms of its scope and aims. Universities, at least in the UK, were (technically) elite institutions whose main aims were the pursuit of knowledge and, subsidiarily, the formation of professional cadres. More broadly, higher education was perceived as a fairly compact system, at least in its intents, which revolved around a binary division. This division was essentially one between the traditional, elite universities, whose main aim was seen as research, and the former polytechnics, whose task was to prepare students for specific professions, through good teaching. (That neither account in fact served as an accurate description of the two sides of the binary line is a point we may bypass here, where perceptions are rather more important.)

Within this binary division (as it was perceived), a tacit consensus more or less governed the higher education sector for a generation. The sector was perceived as having a compact and collective character that worked towards tacitly agreed aims. Because of this consensus, little systematic reflection was conducted on the character of the system (that is, between Robbins (1963) and Dearing (1997)). Identity tensions were largely registered at the level of the disciplines.

The post-Robbins consensus started visibly to break down during the 1980s, with the advent of Thatcherism, as successive governments began to take an interest in university life, looking for more accountability to the taxpayers. Moreover, universities were urged to enter the market in order to generate additional income to meet the increasing demands on the system. Concurrently, there was a thrust towards making universities sites for the production of practical, professional knowledge with immediate applicability in the 'real' world. These governmental pressures instigated a form of auto-reflection, on the part of the whole higher education system. Each university had to rethink its own purpose and activities (teaching, research, and so-called 'third stream' activities) in order to spell out in some detail its distinctive 'mission'.

The quality regimes that developed in the early 1990s further sharpened this sense of auto-reflection. This was achieved, first, through various forms of 'quality assurance' (with a 'light touch' eventually emerging) and, more recently, through the discourse of 'quality enhancement' (arguably still struggling to emerge). These trends were accompanied by the swift development of a mass system that was promoted by a national policy framework (in the UK) of egalitarianism and opportunity. Taken cumulatively, all these changes made impossible any previous sense of a consensus on the nature, aims and scope of higher education.

There have been several consequences of these trends. While the UK university system witnessed, in 1992, the end of the binary system, the growth of the audit and quality regimes, from the early 1990s onwards, fractured the higher education system in significant ways, putting an end to the consensual set of understandings that had characterised it until then. Established academic identities and senses of self were brought into question. Academics, whose traditional sense of identity might have been framed by the notion of 'academic freedom', were obliged to re-think their roles in higher education. Wider phenomena such as massification, accountability and marketisation aided these dislocations of identity.

It is, in our view, against such a reading of the recent history of UK higher education that the contemporary picture on academic identity has to be understood.

Framing of this book

This volume turns on two key concepts within the context of higher education: identity and voice.

Identity

Arguably, amid all the changes that we have just summarised, spaces for academic identities actually widened and new kinds of academic identity emerged. In order to bring about the new agenda, a number of actors who had worked 'silently' behind the scenes until then (such as administrators and librarians) were given more voice and space in redefining, along with academics, the nature, aims and scope of higher education. The wider groups have increasingly made their influence felt on the life of universities, contributing, in a proactive way, to its change. The life of universities has therefore become shaped significantly by the perceptions and agendas of groups, including students, beyond those employed to conduct teaching and research.

At times of change and turbulence, each of the many groups has been trying to define itself, its role, its domains and boundaries in relation to the others. Perhaps paradoxically, as the state has sought a larger role in shaping higher education, more space has been accorded to the sector, albeit within an overarching policy framework. Accordingly, the many groups of players at the local level within and across institutions have found themselves with space in which to work at their role, status and agendas. Processes of identity deconstruction and construction have gone hand in hand in the formulation of the new order. The overall identity of higher education today seems therefore to be a patchwork of *communities of identity*.

These communities are by no means fixed. On the contrary: a continuing but arguably new process of identity construction is under way within higher education. Each group, within and across universities, has started to try to mark out anew its own identity, thus contributing to this construction a better awareness of its members' roles and space. Obviously, now that it is under way, this process is never to be fully completed. In turn, the nature of academic identity is both contested and subject to a dynamic, if complex process. As the contributions to this volume testify, the contestation is taking place not just across institutions, but within institutions and within groupings. The professional managers, the academic developers, the students and the academics themselves each, as groups, bear witness *within themselves* to the multiple interpretations being given to academic identity.

We see identities, therefore, as a historical process of construction, deconstruction and reconstruction, three movements that we see at the heart of any identity dynamics. This theoretical position informs the entire book.

Voice

In this book, we also wanted to give voice to many of the groups that make the new higher education order. The concept of voice implies, first and foremost, space for airing one's opinions, thoughts and ethical concerns within the fragmented space of the current higher education system. Having a voice means being empowered to express oneself within a complex power space in which certain views – if only unwittingly – may be marginalised and rendered semi-detached from 'the real world'. In turn, this book aims at providing a space for such voices by being inclusive and dialogic. The hoped-for result is a modulation of voices that express themselves, their views, concerns and hopes, in the spirit of dialogue and understanding.

Obviously, the voices in this book do not pretend to have any final say on the nature and aims of higher education. They are rather the personal perspectives of a number of scholars and practitioners involved in rethinking the education systems in which they are immersed, in different capacities and roles. Opinions and thoughts, while well informed and embedded within different situations across higher education, remain such. However, we hope that these voices will contribute to the current debates about the new identity (or, indeed, identities?) of higher education, in Britain and elsewhere. Voices can modulate thoughts and thus help towards the framing of a higher education whose overall character gains strength through its very plurality.

Structure

The book's structure consists of three parts:

The first part offers a set of essays each on a set of identities within higher education (academic, student, administrative/managerial, educational developers and so on).

The second part includes responses to Part I from authors speaking from their own professional and scholarly identity perspective (manager, sociologist, anthropologist and so on).

The third part offers perspectives on the identities of students, provided by students themselves.

For the contributions in Part II, we encouraged writers to embed their contributions in their own personal and professional narratives, so offering an illustration of the issues in part from immediate experience. In this way, we have sought to produce a book in which identities are not only discussed in conventional research and scholarly idioms but in which these reflections also come alive through the personal narratives of some of the authors. We have tried to encourage the emergence, in the book, of lived, 'warm' identities rather than 'cold', 'objectified' ones.

From the start, we were keen to give the book a sense of co-construction, between the authors and ourselves as editors. Once a number of authors had accepted our invitation, we organised a meeting that was attended by some of them. During this meeting, the concepts of identities and voices were explored in their different facets in a debate that also encouraged our own thinking about the volume. Thus, for instance, we decided to have an early chapter on knowledge identities, as we came to feel that this was paramount in setting the scene for the examination of all other identities.

On knowledge

Our thinking here – in making that particular decision – was that shifting conceptions of knowledge can be conceived as one of the origins of many current changes in the identity of higher education. As Marilyn Strathern illustrates in her Preamble, knowledge remains, surely, as the fundamental dimension of universities and of academic life, but what counts as knowledge is changing, or at least widening, and, in that latter process, is becoming more disparate. As knowledge has come to be increasingly fissiparous, in turn, its stakeholders have multiplied. Knowledge production today is perceived as being the domain not only of academics but of managers, private sector organisations, national bodies, educational developers, professional groups and so on. Conversely, this increase in the number of stakeholders contributes to shifting knowledge definitions, thus making its nature increasingly contested. Accordingly, knowledge identities in universities are liable to proliferate or, at least, become more fluid.

On students

In the course of this project, too, we came to be sensitive to the absence of student voices, as we had originally scoped the volume. This prompted us to create the third section, which would not only be dedicated to this end but would be written by students from different institutions, at different stages of their career (undergraduate in one case, postgraduate in the other).

Other possible voices

Suggestions were made, too, about including also the voices of other professional groups like educational technologists, librarians and so on. No doubt, this would have made our project more complete. However, eventually, editorial considerations about the structure and length of the book discouraged us from pursuing such an aim, worthwhile as it would doubtless be.

Inside stories

In his Postscript, David Watson attempts to make sense of the complexity of identities in higher education today. Using three conceptual vantage points ('vocabulary', 'hierarchy' and 'story-telling'), Watson offers a synoptic view of the whole book, as he perceives it from his own standpoint as an ex-vice-chancellor. The result is an overview of the current higher education system (especially in the UK), as evidenced in its inside stories.

The end product is a volume that claims no exhaustiveness in the treatment of its theme but offers a variety of stories related to it. It also offers something of a dialogue on the unfolding nuances that identities are displaying in higher education today.

Preamble

Chapter 1

Knowledge identities

Marilyn Strathern

This whole collection presents identities and roles in higher education in such a way as to throw light on issues that practitioners take for granted, take in their stride – or grumble about endlessly. Above all it endorses the point that higher education is for many the world within which they must work out their lives. The privilege it offers academic practitioners in particular is the in-built opportunity to use professional knowledge to reflect on one's own conditions of existence. Perhaps this comes most readily to social scientists, and their colleagues in the humanities, but it is not confined to them.

In this chapter I bring social science into view through a specific discipline, and thus comment on a disciplinary dimension of academic identity. People's identities are in part forged in the kind of knowledge practices that different disciplines engender. This is not just in terms of shared bodies of knowledge, but rests in the manner in which material is collected, evidence appraised, work criticised and results validated. Assessment of a kind is central. I cannot conceal my disciplinary identity as a social anthropologist nor its particular practices in this regard. At the same time, much of what I say resonates with many of the perspectives offered in the following chapters.

In starting with disciplines, I move to the promise that interdisciplinary endeavour seems to hold these days. The topic is interesting if only because here the traditional virtues of assessment, including appraisal and criticism, seem to run aground. In reflecting on some reasons why this is so, I proffer a contrast between two approaches to educational and research development, one of which stresses the different kinds of identities that disciplinary and interdisciplinary work engender, the other of which would see practitioners managing both identities together. The value of the exercise lies less in the suggestion itself, however, than in the route it takes, and the manner in which substantive knowledge figures in the argument.

Disciplines: generating heat

Callon (1998) takes up an old anthropological contrast between hot and cold societies in a new way, reflecting on changing pressures on the way knowledge is used. In 'cold' situations, calculated decisions can be taken with relatively stable measurements of outcomes. He instances the pollution of a watercourse by a chemical factory: sensors are already calibrated, analytical procedures codified, and protagonists know how to calculate the costs before the experts are called in. 'Hot' situations, by contrast, arise from the unpredictable criss-crossing of diverse factors, as in the turmoil of BSE[1] where, arguably, a simple economy (to save money by reducing the temperature for processing animal feeds) led to havoc and tragedy. Unforeseen events are commonplace; heat comes from the mix of *incommensurate* knowledge bases. A network of specialists and non-specialists, diverse interests, policies and research outcomes somehow have to be combined, for as fast as calculations are required the very instruments of measurement have to be created and agreed upon. Hot situations, he argues, become increasingly prevalent as controversies cross boundaries of discipline and skill and it gets increasingly harder to cool them down, that is, reach consensus on how to measure, in this case, what is safe. Hot situations, registered routinely in information overload, are complex phenomena. The challenge of this kind of complexity to specialists (such as anthropologists) and to the university system (which produces almost all and employs many of them) has become a familiar shadow of disciplinary identity and higher education alike.

It is not to be avoided. 'Supercomplexity' is the term Barnett (2000) gives to a heated-up world as it looks from the university. He sees an urgent need to embrace it and its uncertainties: to at once heat things up further – generate more uncertainty – and enable people to live with the heat, moving through the uncertain and unpredictable with cooling shields of self-reflexivity. 'Supercomplexity is the world into which the graduates of universities will go; it marks out the experiences they will face of continual challenge and insecurity' (Barnett 2000: 167). Expertise as such can no longer claim authority – there are simply too many knowledges. This is more than the multiple vision of postmodernism. The supercomplex graduate has to grasp *unpredictable intersections* of knowledges that fold in on one another. Here Barnett reminds the university of its own educative aspirations, to encourage self-reliance, flexibility and adaptibility, its claim to hold up to society new and counter frames of understanding, and adds a new one. If it can adopt the collective responsibility of attending to supercomplexity, it stands a chance of producing people unafraid either of uncertainty or of making daring interventions. This will require academics, diversified through their relationships with the wider community, working with one another in 'epistemological pandemonium'.

---

1 Bovine spongiform encephalitis ('mad cow disease'). 'By turns we hear from vets, farmers, manufacturer of animal feed, proponents of Thatcherite deregulation . . . outraged members of the public, the media, prions . . . The controversy lurches first one way, then the other – because nothing is certain, neither the knowledge base nor the methods of measurement' (Callon 1998: 260–1).

But haven't we met supercomplexity elsewhere? Suppose we probe inside disciplines themselves. Here I describe my own, imagining that similar probes may be done into others. One overlooked and currently maligned skill often relegated to the past is that of the anthropologist's 'holistic' approach to data.[2] However shaky present-day anthropologists would say the theoretical basis of holism was (conceiving such entities as whole societies for a start), imagining holism as an ethnographic goal increased the possibility of tracing through the events that lead to unpredictable outcomes. How so? Because of the simple rule of thumb that nothing was too insignificant to record. So the ethnographer would always record more than was in the line of sight of his or her direct interests. This rule of thumb could also detect 'hot' situations. For the heterogeneous data that resulted required interpretation, and interpretation in turn required multiple approaches based on different orders of knowledge (economic trends, semantic domains, religious values), or clusters of them (the relation between biological and social phenomena, between historical and presentist accounts). These well worn divisions demanded that data was modelled in terms of intersection. Additionally, then, anthropological knowledge thus worked on problems through creating matrices that drew on potentially conflicting specialisms within itself.

In short, out of all the ways of navigating a supercomplex world, this discipline has travelled some interesting routes, as I imagine other disciplines have theirs. Anthropology creates for itself incommensurable orders of facts that constantly demand translation and comparison. It offers real-world exemplars to work on, taking a society's own orientations as given, while encouraging reflexivity through cultivating divergences of understanding, hoping that practitioners will learn how to create hot mixes they can handle. Anthropologists take their identity from this, fine-tuned for many through a second identity with the particular field site in which they are quite arbitrarily caught up (cf. Corsín Jiménez 2004). Here, if truth be told, an anthropological field site can be anywhere – but it has to be somewhere.

Disciplines: different ways of cooling heat

You would have supposed, then, that anthropologists might have been at least a little open to the audit practices that, running through most public service provisions, found a field site in UK higher education some twenty years ago. I refer to evaluations of teaching and research through what became the Quality Assurance Agency (QAA) and the still active Research Assessment Exercise (RAE). Incommensurable orders of facts are created and then compared (depending on the exercise, committee agendas, paper trails, student ratings, mission statements, and published outputs, selection of the research active, research strategy, funding income, and so forth). This is all with the aim of describing – before assessing

---

2 Its premise is that one can give a 'rounded' or 'whole' account of society because there is a sense, in terms of their functioning, in which societies are rounded and whole. The ethnographer on the ground thus collects all and any kind of data, regardless of specific research questions.

– whole institutions in terms of their teaching and research functioning. Assessment is made in the light of their own orientations. So why do anthropologists join so many other academic practitioners and grumble that their identity is being assaulted?

Audit encourages just the skills Barnett sees within the university system, though as outcomes not so much for individuals as for the system as such. Audit hopes to galvanise that system into consciously promoting such skills and learning, to be reflexive about its own practices. It thus adds a layer of activity that claims to be independent of disciplinary content: the QAA is judging not the discipline itself but its effective management for the purposes of teaching, while the RAE is designed to measure research accomplishment, and in such a way as to allow peer review to deal with content. At its best, this hands-off approach to disciplinary substance is just that. But, at its worst, the distance conceals substantive demands of its own. Audit is in effect about creating a certain kind, its own kind, of knowledge. The auditing remit is simple: how does the system *know* it is performing properly? The performance in question is not of students and teachers and researchers but of the university as an organisation and of research as product. Let me speak briefly of teaching and the QAA as it was instigated in 1997. For, if in the UK we have since moved on from the early days of the QAA, higher education institutions have taken (had to take) on its mantle themselves, and a backward glance is salutary.

The QAA's learning and teaching audit wanted the organisation to demonstrate its organisational capacities of not just good practices but specifically those good practices that show the organisation in action. How does a university keep track of itself; how does it meet its own aims and objectives; how does it guarantee the learning outcomes it promises; how can it demonstrate the procedures by which it *knows* that this is what it is doing? Evaluation is needed. Students' work must be marked in relation to specified learning outcomes; if skills are imparted, the system must be able to point to where these are assessed. And only a paper trail can measure the measurements. The paper trail makes transparent a genealogy of decision-making, implementation and outcome, in short, at once mimics and instantiates management procedure. Focus on the measurable and recordable deletes anything imponderable and unpredictable. For only some activities will count as organisational 'good practice', above all communication (do different parts of the organisation communicate with one another?) and feedback (are there good channels for recording response to decisions taken?).

Was this knowledge worth having? In some situations, yes. But it was also a diversion. In a climate of performativity, observes Barnett, processes receive low marks. He means those processes by which the university should instead have been gearing up for an age of supercomplexity. The balance-sheet approach concerned with outcomes is insufficient to the point of actively discouraging institutions from looking to their responsibilities (see also Mills 2004: 27).

Academics' expressions of identity assault speak to another danger: that teachers collude with learners in the triple fantasy that communication is by nature transparent, that specifiable skills are the desirable outcome and that substance (types and bodies of knowledge) does not matter. One problem with the QAA kind of knowledge is that skills are conflated with performance indicators: the skills are *all* performance-positive. Doubt and uncertainty, not by any stretch of the imagination performance-positive, may mould modes of being (in Barnett's phrase) but will not show up as skill-related. Yet 'flexibility' is nothing without uncertainty to give it an edge, 'confidence' is shallow without doubt, 'reflexivity' cannot develop if there are no crises to work it against, 'communication skills' are untried until there is a dilemma to solve. Above all, 'clarity' depends on the kind of puzzle that gets the intellect into knots before it begins to release comprehension. Yet where is the discussion of how to evaluate the crises and dilemmas that study inculcates, the puzzling obscurities students tussle over, the time it takes problems to be worked through? Sometimes such situations speak of desperate dead-ends; but sometimes they motivate just the kind of mind-work that will enable the student to handle the unpredictable. The point is that we don't know in advance! If the QAA's intention was that teachers should banish unpredictability from the curriculum, what then of the mission to prepare students for a real world where they have to be uncertain and still act, have doubts and still know what to do, encounter the unforeseen and carry on?

Substance matters. There are different ways of presenting complexity to the imagination, and they are not all equally good. If you imagine hot conditions for teaching and learning blowing like a blast from a furnace, the thought follows that the stokers must keep the fire going while themselves needing personal cooling devices. If instead you imagine hot conditions like soup in winter, then its warmth will limber you up; cold soup would stiffen the muscles and cramp the stomach – until, that is, summer comes and the positive and negative values are reversed. The former imagining (Barnett's model) suggests one may need to know how to be hot and cold *at the same time*: the calculations intersect unpredictably. The latter (the QAA's model) creates one-way measurements: how far along the scale of being *either* hot *or* cold you are, the unpredictable element being instead in the hands of auditors who determine what season of the year it is, and thus which is desirable. To my mind, only one of these apprehensions of complexity has substance worth spending time on.

The feeling of identity loss some of the authors in the chapters to follow depict, and challenge, may come in part from the tacit nature of much disciplinary practice, often mute in relation to the fundamental skill of assembling substantive 'knowledge' (materials, data, information) appropriate to one's tools. Yet explicit procedures of quality evaluation often seem to increase rather than diminish the sense of disciplinary loss. So many practitioners swing from embracing disciplines to instead embracing interdisciplinary approaches. Indeed, 'interdisciplinarity' has new value these days in the eyes of some (mission-statement writers, research council policy-makers) as a means to impart 'heat' to what are seen as 'cold. subject areas. However, in the spirit of the above remarks, this resembles the QAA model (hot or cold); perhaps by contrast, then, Barnett's model holds an alternative promise (hot and cold). If one can advocate *both* interdisciplinary *and* disciplinary endeavours, then each should heat and cool the other in interesting ways.

Interdisciplinarity: reconfiguring assessment

So we have not quite finished with disciplines yet. It would be mischievous for academics to suggest that the QAA is based on values at arm's length from their own. It is very much part of the higher education field: we share identities here (Brenneis 1994). Auditing and evaluation find analogues in disciplinary work itself and, in the anthropological case I describe, in the very social practices that research in particular may reveal. The case assembles some substantive knowledge, the results of research, to make the point.

There is a moment in the course of Fijian gift-giving when the givers' side 'subjects itself to the gift-receivers' evaluation, and quietly hopes that the other side will respond positively' (Miyazaki 2004: 7). Motionless, the givers' spokesman holds out the object until a recipient steps forward and takes it. 'In this moment of hope, the gift givers place in abeyance their own agency, or capacity to create effects in the world' (ibid.). Hesitation, vulnerability, opens up in the very act of handing over. Now, once recipients accept the gift, they may immediately deny the importance of gift-giving among people and offer the item to God. At the moment at which the giver's hope is fulfilled by the recipients, it is replaced by a second hope that God's blessing will fall on everyone. It is this replication that Miyazaki takes as his problematic. People cease to emphasise their own actions and look to others for their response. Fijian participants thus experience the fulfilment of their hope as the capacity repeatedly to place their own agency in abeyance. Hope recurs. Miyazaki sees a parallel in the anthropologist's hope of an adequate analysis and the possibility of fresh knowledge. The Fijian gift contains an unexpected significance in the account given of it: the anthropologist called that hesitation a moment of evaluation.

Risk assessment is all about managing possible outcomes by measuring impact, as are protocols of audit and accountability, or any policy process where evaluation is a crucial step in the chain of scrutiny that leads from fact-finding to decision-making. However, for academic practitioners in research, evaluation is simultaneously a management *and* a research tool. Evaluation is after all central to the research processes that choose what shall be kept or discarded, that elect the next route to take, that sort poor data from rich. That kind of scrutiny is second nature to the researcher, often deploying a primary one: the researcher's disciplinary identity. Disciplines offer frameworks for criticism. The perspective offered here comes from practices in the humanities and social sciences.

Disciplinary criticism is not quite the same as self-evaluation for the purposes of better management. No doubt managers (and researchers acting as managers) are told to be critical of themselves and of others in order to improve things. Yet the desired outcome is already specified, in the goals of the organisation in question, and goals work best when everyone agrees on them. Researchers (and managers acting as researchers), on the other hand, criticise retrospectively, in relation to the canons of their discipline. A discipline is a body of data, a set of methods, a field of problematics; it is also a bundle of yardsticks, that is, criteria for evaluating outcomes, maintaining standards and recognising originality. Knowing that canons often change, and outcomes are uncertain, enhances rather than detracts from this. It follows that there is no *desired* outcome – only the hope that there will *be* one. I can criticise Miyazaki's concept of the gift, but there is no ideal version to strive for. Rather, the aim of criticism is to multiply (divide) the outcomes of any one particular argument. In fact disciplines seek out disagreement as points of growth. The academic researchers' hope that there will be an outcome to their labours is given a specific impetus: in looking to colleagues for criticism, they look for life. For their instruments of self-renewal, the papers they write and the books they generate, allow disagreement to remain, so to speak, unclosed. The disagreement, the opening out to further futures, can be left just as that.

Perhaps this points to one way in which Power's (2004) recent agenda for uncertainty, and thus for renewal, is already built into disciplinary practice. However, these days academics often feel that they cannot leave renewal to take its own time. One must strive for it. Disciplines thus have to give evidence of their vitality (one of the points of QAA and RAE), and above all perform their accomplishments: 'knowledge' must be conveyed in a widely communicable mode, as information or evidence (as in evidence-based policy), that can be put to use as driving ingredients of the knowledge economy. Knowledge pressed into the service of ends such as problem-solving expresses such vitality in turning its back on the authority of the discipline to embrace the interdisciplinary. Interdisciplinarity that shows an openness to different fields also works as a sign of a willingness to subordinate disciplinary interests to finding common solutions. What, then, of assessment? What, then, of the critic?

In that willingness, something interesting happens to evaluation (Strathern 2004). Interdisciplinarity evoked as a measure or yardstick of vitality obscures attempts to apply evaluation procedures to itself. The result is 'the lack of available criteria to assess interdisciplinary work on its own terms' (Mansilla and Gardner 2003: 1). Asked about outcomes, researchers rely on indirect indicators such as publications or patents or whether an interdisciplinary team applies for funding a second time. 'Measures that directly address epistemic dimensions of interdisciplinary work (e.g. explanatory power, aesthetic appeal, comprehensiveness) [are] rarer and less well articulated' (2003: 1–2). In the management view, interdisciplinarity runs into some of the problems that bedevil attempts to justify government support for the creative arts as a contribution to public well-being (Selwood 2002). What impact do cultural programmes have? How can evidence of impact be captured within the frameworks of specific projects? Attempts at qualitative assessment of the success of individual programmes have tended to focus on the directly observable, for example surveying participants for the satisfaction they register. How otherwise does one demonstrate that some difference has been achieved?

Now, among the reasons that demonstration is so difficult is perhaps the way the single outcome, the effect of collaboration, is impossible to measure against its own multidisciplinary, and thus multiplying, *origins*. Evaluating interdisciplinary endeavour is not the same as evaluating the degree to which a problem is solved. There is little against which to measure the effectiveness of interaction itself when the whole point was that there was no pre-existing relationship, only diverse starting points, and the subsequent product (the singular outcome) was always a hope for the future.

By the same token, the evaluative genre most prevalent in research, criticism, becomes equally obscured in interdisciplinary contexts. Here it is for the opposite reason: it is the expectation of multiplying *outcomes* that compromises the ability to criticise. The agreed upon (disciplinary) canon can be no measure of the new combinations and cross-overs that point to future growth. For those who advocate interdisciplinarity as good in itself, and thus as an alternative to disciplines, disciplines and their critical apparatus simply 'get in the way'.

Interdisciplinary collaborations, then, must be promising innovation and creativity by means other than criticism. Instead of generating disagreement and multiplying future possibilities by informed comment from within a defined field of knowledge, interdisciplinary conversations hold out the hope of fresh combinations as sources of synergy. Combination can be performed over and again. Although pinpointing the effects of interdisciplinary endeavour seems doomed to failure, hope regenerates exactly as Miyazaki argues for the Fijians' constant return to the issues of land compensation. This focus on land arises out of the Fijian experience of colonisation. Repeated efforts are made to present their claims, yet each new effort requires putting to one side their knowledge about what happened the previous time. As the ethnographer says: 'How have Suavou people kept their hope alive for generation after generation when their knowledge has continued to fail them' (Miyazaki 2004: 3). They simply return to the same points of departure. The desire for interdisciplinary synergy seems of the same ilk.

Interdisciplinarity: the future of assessment (and the critic)

I proffer one suggestion for carrying our thoughts forward (being disciplinary and interdisciplinary at the same time). It springs directly from the substance of anthropological knowledge but does not stay there. The suggestion is how we might use a disciplinary insight about social relations to configure a model for interdisciplinary collaboration.

Let us look at the researcher's faculty for criticism more closely. It is a social faculty. In that Fijian moment of hesitation as the gift is given but not yet received, and agency suspended, could we not say that the giver *desires* to be divided from the receiver, to be recognised as a separate social person? Now the capacity that the division (re-)enacts is the very capacity that persons have to separate themselves in the first place not from an other but from their own selves. This is a social act before it is anything else. Anthropologists divide themselves off from anthropologists, multiply their positions, precisely because they have common origins. The same could be said of the whole company of disciplines that make up academia.

It is worth expanding the point briefly. Divisions are obviously at work in the way disciplines propagate: they segment and breed through cleavage, whether by the recognition that old categories no longer hold things together or through acrimonious wranglings that open up rifts. Here division operates as a form of multiplication, a mode of generating new forms. However, division can also be the impetus to intellectual colonisation. Each scholar may see something of value in the other but wishes to appropriate it for their own agenda, that is, it already no longer belongs to the other person alone, just as my rendering of the Fijian gift takes it away from its location in the ethnographer's account. Yet again, in contemporary exhortations to interdisciplinarity, division becomes a sign or a marker for failure to communicate, for failure to create a wider community, whether that includes the public or other disciplines. Disciplines are accused of failing to cross the divide between esoteric and common knowledge.

However, the divisions a critic envisages are none of these. Rather, they are (seen to be) *created in the course of interaction* itself. The critic has a different relation to the discourse under scrutiny from the proponent of it; united by an interest in a particular work, the interdependency between critic and proponent means that they are specifically divided from each other by the problems they conceive. The impetus to divide ourselves from ourselves is a social one. Those second selves emerge as others, a movement recapitulated in the yielding of one's own agency to the one who is now othered.

When the Fijian gift-givers' spokesman fell silent, he placed their agency in the hands of the recipients who would reveal its effectiveness. There is power play in this creation of uncertainty (cf. Ericson 2005). For 'they experienced the fulfilment of their hope as the capacity repeatedly to place their own agency in abeyance' (Miyazaki 2004: 106). What we should note here is that regardless of hope for renewal we can recognise hope for *engagement*. Such hope also feeds into the interactions of critics. Indeed, we could think of critics as those whose willing suspension of agency, a division of self from self, allow themselves to be *captured* by someone else's work. Critics find themselves drawn into other people's agendas. Engagement does not multiply; it does not to look to standards and requires no evaluation. To argue with an idea is to be captured by it. In this kind of engagement, one can be captured more than once.

Here is a kind of hope for interdisciplinary endeavour. The very idea of traversing disciplinary boundaries speaks of possibilities that lie in being captured by another's concerns. For it also makes visible the interest of those who are identifiably 'other' to one's own discipline. The anthropologist has been here before: engaging one's interest in 'other people's' agenda is as crucial to the enterprise of fieldwork-based research as it is to the writing afterwards. In interdisciplinary work, I see for the anthropologist a replication of his or her hope in the ethnographic moment (cf. Miyazaki and Riles 2005: 328). Each interdisciplinary encounter points to fresh encounter in a terrain only uncertainly mapped. The imperfect grasp, the constant shortfall of knowledge, conversations that never get beyond very primitive communication, hold out the hope that one can always re-engage. This has little to do with performance or products, much to do with process.

Coming back over and again to a substantive account (here, Fijian ethnography), whether to agree or disagree, makes the possibility of re-engagement 'critical'. A new problem is conceived. We return to an observation offered at the outset: precisely because anthropologists never exhaust the information they collect, ethnography has the remarkable capacity to outlive the particular uses made of it.

There is one caveat. From thinking of future engagement predicated upon the hope for it, it is a short step to asking how to best manage it or build such hope into research protocols. I do not think we should. Re-engagement needs to be *re*-engagement, and a matter for the future that the present should leave undefined. Yet how can one not plan ahead; how can one not make a virtue out of engagement? One way might be by imagining that one has to protect (cherish) the process as though it were knowledge to be protected from itself. Presumably knowledge best not acted upon is best put into abeyance. So perhaps the answer is to not treat these observations *as knowledge* at all. Perhaps rather than the faculty for hope (hope for engagement) we might just want to say that engagement is a faculty. This would make everything very simple. For nothing more is implied beyond each act of engagement, insofar as each contains the possibility of re-engagement without specifying what it would be. The future is grasped as indeterminate, uncertain. It is simply the possibility of renewed engagement that is (already) enacted in the present – the idea that one can meet again, come back to the data, revisit the analysis. We just need to keep that as routine as possible.

Acknowledgements

I am grateful to both editors for their invitation, and to Ron Barnett for his inspiration. This draws on two earlier reflections: an editorial in *Anthropology Today* (February 2001); and the Huxley Memorial Lecture (*Journal of the Royal Anthropological Institute*, March 2006), from a project, 'Interdisciplinarity and Society', undertaken jointly with Andrew Barry and Georgina Born (ESRC grant RES-151-25-00042) as part of the ESRC Science in Society Programme led by Steve Rayner.

Part I
Perspectives

Part I consists of four chapters. As mentioned in the general introduction, these are in the form of essays, written by scholars who have a special interest in the identity type they explore (academic, student, academic developer and administrative managers). Each chapter offers an original classification of identity types *within* each of the groups in question while, together, the chapters demonstrate the dynamism that characterises the contemporary development of 'identity' across higher education. In turn, the chapters constitute the base for the responses in Part II.

In 'Being an academic today', Peter Taylor deals with issues surrounding the contested notion of 'academic' by referring to three different contexts: the Finnish, the Australian and the British. In each of these, academic identities are experienced in different ways: on the one hand, with a degree of regret for a 'golden past' and the apportionment of blame for the end of this to academic managers (in the Finnish and Australian cases); and, on the other hand, as the opening up of possibilities for rebuilding traditional conceptions of 'academic identity' (in the British case). Of course, the author does not take any of these positions as representative of the whole higher education system in each country. Rather, a mixture of them is possible, to different degrees, in different contexts.

Taylor argues that academic identity is, therefore, a highly contested and contextual notion, which deserves analysis within the specific environments that nourish them. This dynamic view of academic identity is reflected in the 'being' in the title of the chapter. Ideas of process and transience between past, present and future are used by the author, in the concluding part of the chapter, to propose some possible alternative (academic) identity options.

Denise Batchelor, in her chapter entitled 'Have students got a voice?', offers a philosophical analysis of the notion of 'student voice' in the current higher education system in the UK. 'Voice', which is construed by the author as an ontological entity of openness and understanding, gives important insights into possible ways of what a student identity may be and/or mean today. The author argues that, in the current educational climate dominated by market and managerial discourses, contradictions arise in the interplay within the institutional marketing language and the promises it holds.

While students are invited to make their voice heard through complex evaluation systems, the progressive eroding of time and space for students, as a consequence of depleting resources, runs counter to the flourishing of the development of student voices. Such a flourishing, according to Batchelor, should be based on principles of understanding, curiosity and dialogue. The author argues for the widening of students' intellectual and emotional spaces, in a plea for a type of higher education that is more akin to cultivation than to production.

In 'Identities of academic developers', Gunnar Handal examines different realisations of the identities of academic developers, that is, those members of staff who, within an institution, assist in policy and educational changes (like staff and educational developers). Such identities are analysed by the author both 'internally', from the vantage point of the academic developers themselves, and 'externally', through the lenses of faculty and an institution as a whole. Through the use of theories of 'community of practice', Handal unpacks different notions of the identity of academic developers.

Adopting a number of apposite metaphors, he creates a set of ideal groupings into which different ways of being an academic developer can be accommodated. Two main orientations characterise this set of groupings: of the academic developer as 'change agent' (in his/her role as guide, expert) and as 'midwife' (in his/her role as interpreter, collaborator). After examining each orientation, and raising the idea of the role of academic developers as 'jesters', he arrives at what he sees as a possible optimal formulation of the role of an academic developer, that of 'critical friend'. This metaphor allows Handal to argue for a particular way of being of academic developers as supporters of staff but also as critical agents of academics' concerns, assumptions and activities. Finally, the author urges the strengthening of the overall identity of academic developers through activities aimed specifically at their own professional enhancement, though scholarship and research.

Finally, in 'Beyond administration and management', Celia Whitchurch, following empirical research undertaken with senior and middle-level administrators and managers, investigates the complex identities of these groups. The author distinguishes the groups she is interested in (which include, among others, professionals in finance, estates, human resources, registry and the secretariat) and that of academic managers (such as deans and vice-chancellors).

Whitchurch proceeds to offer a framework for distinguishing types of professional administrators and managers. This consists of four major categories: 'soft administration' (characterised by the voice of 'generosity'); 'hard administration' (whose voice is that of 'justice'); 'soft management' (which voices 'negotiation'); and, finally, 'hard' management' (the voice of which is that of 'opportunism'). Whitchurch argues that these groups have evolved out of changes in the British higher education system from the beginning of the 1990s, when the market and accountability started reshaping the overall ethos of British universities. Such changes have brought with them an enhanced role for administrators and managers. This has created the necessity of dialogue and understanding between administrators/managers and academics.

The author concludes by arguing in favour of identities that are in line with the complex world in which they are immersed. These should contribute to a greater harmony within institutions both through acting as filters between internal and external clients and by contributing to organisational research and development.

Chapter 2

Being an academic today

Peter Taylor

Identity work is ongoing work. It is work that is constituted by history and by the conditions within which we live and work, including the conflicts and tensions within specific workplaces. In this chapter, I focus on three themes born out of the tensions evident in academic identity and academic work in this post-millennial time. Specifically, I refer to (a) a prevailing negative climate within universities as workplaces characterised by a view that former golden times have been lost; (b) a sense of personal loss on the part of individual academics; and (c) a perceived shift from a culture of science to a culture of research that demands that knowledge be 'capitalised' to realise its value. I want to indicate that I am neither endorsing nor dismissing these developments. Rather, I seek to explore how they arise and how they contribute to contemporary academic identity formation[1] as an ongoing, troubled and conflictual domain.

My exploration is introduced by a brief discussion of the history of the idea of 'identity' itself. This is done not simply because of the importance of that context, but because so much of this history appears to be absent from current discussions of identity formation. Put bluntly, much of the current discussion of the decline and fall of universities and academic work is based on myth. Having said that, I also suggest that there are real matters of the intensification of academic work and a sense of personal grieving that demand attention. These are explored more fully through the introduction of three studies of academic identity, two from European contexts and one from an Australian context. These studies show the themes at work in academic identity formation worldwide.

---

1 This discussion assumes, and is therefore limited to, Western cultural contexts and their traditions. I am aware that others, such as Nandita Chaudhary (2003), provide alternative readings of how notions of self are viewed differently from a non-European perspective.

The idea of identity

The idea of identity has its own history. Donald Hall (2004) provides a very useful overview of that history, suggesting that 'one's identity can be thought of as that particular set of traits, beliefs, and allegiances that, in the short- or long-term ways, gives one a consistent personality and mode of social being' (2004: 3).

In essence, Hall suggests that there are four 'stages' in the historical development of the Western concept of identity. The first spanned the time up to the mid-seventeenth century. This was a time much influenced by Greek philosophy, and followed by Christian precepts. It gave us a view of identity as outward-focused, expressed in terms of issues of stability and tradition, and the need to align it with larger truths and moral purposes, especially religious truths and purposes. From this perspective, identities are 'taken on' through shared practices that demonstrate faithful acceptance of given truths. This perspective was challenged in the seventeenth century by the writings of René Descartes, and his well-known dictum – 'I think, therefore I am'. For Descartes, it is thinking about, and reflecting on, the sources and standards of knowledge that are key challenges for every individual. In this second stage, identities are forged through work on the self, rather than 'taken on' from some external authority.

The third stage drew on the work of Hegel and Freud. This work involved a shift from a focus on reason 'as a drive towards the totalization and unification of human experience' to a focus on issues *other than* [individual] *reason*' (Schrag 1997: 8, emphasis in original), including the non-rational, the subconscious and the emotional. As a result of this work, identities came to be seen as co-constructions. In the fourth stage, discussions of 'identity' became thoroughly politicised and embodied. This was based on the work of postmodern philosophers, such as Lacan, Kristeva, Bosch, Foucault and Butler, who focused on the relationship between an individual's sense of existential fragmentation and the need to assert some level of 'self-unified identity' (Hall 2004: 83). For the postmodern philosophers, identities are always 'under construction' in contexts that are characterised by indeterminacy, partiality and complexity. This sense of identity is well captured in the following.

> [I]dentity' is . . . a constructed entity, both individually and collectively. It is born of multiple conflicts, and [has a] . . . a collective dimension [that] gives rise to conflicts. It is by definition dynamic and nourishes a complete mythology in political history, whether that be of class, race or religion, whether it reposes upon a desire for cultural authenticity, the need for belonging and recognition, or upon exclusion, intolerance, enmity and sometimes the project of annihilating a real or imaginary enemy.
>
> (von Busekist 2004: 84)

Von Busekist draws attention to the practical nature of identity, rather than something that is inwardly informed and inwardly felt and focused, engaged as it is with conflict and emerging, as it does, out of conflict.

In summary, these four 'positions' distinguish identities that are:

- 'taken on' through shared practices that demonstrate faithful acceptance of given truths;
- constructed through individual thought and reflection based on doubt and scepticism, rather than uncontested dogma and tradition;
- co-constructions, with an individual's 'traits, beliefs, and allegiances' reflecting non-rational processes and commitments;
- continuously 'under construction' in contexts that are characterised by indeterminacy, partiality and complexity.

In keeping with the view that former cultures and paradigms continue to influence and have value for later generations (see Taylor 1999: 79–80), *each* of these positions remains viable today. In fact, the postmodern perspective acknowledges that an individual can draw on all of these philosophical traditions in context-responsive ways. Thus, a person can 'demonstrate faithful acceptance of given truths' in a context where they choose to defer to the dogma and tradition associated with some external authority, while in other contexts they actively contest and oppose particular dogmas and traditions. Thus, a person's 'identity' is likely to include traits, beliefs, and allegiances that are epistemologically inconsistent, yet afford particular 'real world' benefits in terms of opportunities and actions that reinforce a sense of self.

Amongst many others, Manuel Castells (1997) suggests that identity is a source of meaning for individuals. On the other hand, he sees roles as 'defined by norms structured by the institutions and organizations of society' (p. 7). The relative importance of the multiple roles that each person undertakes 'depends upon negotiations and arrangements between individuals and these institutions and organizations' (p. 7). Castells argues that, while roles involve accommodations with specific contexts, identities are ultimately 'internalizations' and, because of this, 'identities are stronger sources of meaning than roles . . . In simple terms, identities organize meaning while roles organize functions' (p. 7). For individuals, roles give rise to context-specific opportunities to express, and even to develop, personal identity.

Before turning to explore the stories that represent a sense of what it means to be an academic today, I want to link my focus on identity with other discussions of *voice*. Social scientists tend to refer to voice as the informants' voice, intimately connected with culture and personal meaning and identity. It is also suggested that interview transcripts and oral histories provide contexts within which identities are rehearsed. Put differently, remembering and sharing aspects of personal experience and perspective are themselves creative, rather than objective acts – they tend to portray respondents as they want 'others to see them' (Errante 2000: 21). As Errante understands it, 'oral history events become occasions in which the identities of *both* narrator and historian are practised' (p. 26, emphasis in original).

This means that there are reasons to hear and to read accounts of academic life with some caution. We need to accept that identities are continuously 'under construction', and that those constructions are linked to the need for personal meaning. When informants share their sense of who they are and what their current experiences mean to them, they do so in ways that are collaborative acts of identity formation, involving both the researcher(s) and the respondent(s). And they often speak in ways that belie any overarching sense of indeterminacy, partiality and complexity in that formative process.

Tales from the academy

Although there is no such thing as a standard academic career, most academics aspire to a career within academe, and that aspiration is underpinned by a conception of academic identity. Versions of identities, whether achieved, aspired to, or mourned, are evident in much of the contemporary discussion of academic work. I want to share three examples from that literature. The examples are selected for two reasons. First, taken together, they imply that this discussion is not a localised discussion, given that each draws on surveys of different nation-based groups of academics. Second, they explore different contexts for academic work, using different analytic tools. In this respect they illustrate diversity within the global academic community. These stories represent a disposition to academic work and academic identity that is indicative of a fundamental pessimism about the present and the future, and this is so whether or not others, including senior managers, politicians and industry partners, see things more optimistically. The stories do not analyse the factors that give rise to this sense of loss and the related pessimism, but underline its centrality in academics' self-portrayal.

Finnish academics

Lili-Helena Ylijoki (2005) provides an account of academic work in Finland. She does so through an analysis of focused interviews of 23 senior researchers based in three different academic environments: a scientific research facility located within a department of physics; and, in a second university, both a work research centre (WRC) and a department of history. Her analysis explores the academic nostalgia expressed by her respondents. For the researchers in the scientific research facility, 'in the golden past researchers could follow the internal logic of the field and meander where the research seemed to lead them' (p. 563). In the discomfort of the present, research activities, because they are externally funded, are often also externally directed. This research is held to be focused on 'product development'. This is indicative of a shift from autonomous basic or pure research to user-led and product-focused client investment. As one of her respondents comments:

> In fact freedom is not the same as what it used to be earlier, since we have to be more responsive in terms of what we are doing with the money society gives us when we run this research business here.
>
> (p. 564)

She concludes that these academics are yearning for a golden age that valued 'risk taking and profundity as opposed to market-oriented values and practices' (p. 565). It is interesting to note that academics mourn the loss of risk-taking at the very time when universities are being encouraged to adopt a consciously entrepreneurial approach to their activities, especially their research activities. This raises questions around the nature of the risks associated with entrepreneurship in comparison with the risks associated with relatively unfettered intellectual pursuits (McWilliam 2005).

For Ylijoki, the WRC researchers yearned for a past, real or imagined, when they could undertake both research funded by external bodies and their personal research – usually 'working on a licentiate or doctoral thesis' (Ylijoki 2005: 566). Later the author indicates that the time restriction associated with funded project work (where a limited budget is tightly linked to specific and time-based outcomes) crowds out even the most fundamental academic work, such as self-directed reading and writing. Thus, she argues that 'the inability to promote one's own interest creates anxiety and disappointment'. In turn, there is a loss of 'personal sense and meaning of the work' (p. 567). The author suggests that there is a problematic conflation of academic goals and personal development, and this leads to 'a sort of identity crisis both at the unit and the personal level' (p. 567).

The academics employed in the department of history have a primary focus on teaching, whereas there is a research focus in the other two settings. Ylijoki (2005) focuses on the impact of a loss of the time these historians have to undertake personal academic work – time 'to read, think and write in peace' (p. 568). In the current environment 'all the time they have goes into teaching and into administration' with a resulting 'decline of freedom and autonomy in work' (p. 568). It is worth noting that Ylijoki's account changes from claims that 'all of the time is lost', to 'less and less time is available', to the claim of 'an extensive growth in the workload and to the decline of freedom and autonomy in work' (p. 568), and thus appears to be somewhat inconsistent. Nevertheless there is no doubting the sense of loss expressed by her respondents. For example, one academic expressed the sense of loss thus: 'I imagined that I would be able to realize big dreams and now I realize that I'm reading students' theses' (p. 569). Although one can question why this person regarded reading students' theses as an unexpected aspect of academic work, Ylijoki identifies the 'mutually contradictory ideals and morals between the disciplinary culture of historians and the externally imposed demands' (p. 569). Her discussion gives importance to the ethics, values and ideals of the field, to a moral order that is seen to be in danger of disappearing, and to the diminishing opportunity her respondents perceive 'to socially construct their academic identities in a positive light, to maintain their self-respect and to find coherence and continuity in their way of being historians' (p. 570).

Australian academics

Don Anderson, Richard Johnson and Lawrennce Saha (2002) provide a similar story of changes in academic work through their government-sponsored survey of Australian academics. Their data was collected through an online survey of academics from 12 of the 38 publicly funded Australian universities. In all, 2,075 usable responses were received – a 50 per cent response rate. The survey invited respondents to rate (on a five-point scale) 40 topics in terms of three issues: their 'importance in your work'; the 'extent it has changed in the last two decades or since you became an academic'; and 'whether that change is for the better or worse' (p. 10). There were also 12 questions on the respondent's background, as well as provision for written comments after each question and at the end of the instrument. The authors note that '[n]early all respondents added some written comment to their multiple choice responses'. The total 'amounted to over 600 A4 pages' (p. 10).

In their study, Anderson *et al.* (2002) identify a number of issues that appear to resonate with similar studies, irrespective of their national focus. First, there is a sense that the academic community is looking back 'to a former golden age', exemplified by the 1959 Murray Committee report into Australian universities, an era when governments provided most of the income for universities. According to the authors, 'the Murray Committee's report is still alive in the memories and folklore of many current and recently retired academics' (p. 1). This was a time when:

> Universities were left very much to run their own affairs, determine what courses they would offer, how they would teach them, whom they would admit as students, how they would organise their internal admin-istration, whom they would appoint as staff and what duties would be expected of staff.
>
> (p. 1)

Now governments provide less than 50 per cent of the funding of many universi-ties. Universities are now 'much more energetic in seeking funding wherever it can be found; much more rigorous in scrutinizing the performance of their staffs; [and] much more rigorously accountable to Government' (p. 3). In terms of ac-ademic work roles, 'new tasks, new technologies, and new accountability and bureaucratic procedures have been added to the traditional academic responsibili-ties. Nothing has been taken away' (p. 8). I return to this issue.

Anderson *et al.* (2002) report that older academics are more likely to indicate both that things have changed, and that these changes have been 'for the worse'. The former is to be expected – anyone who has been employed in a field for a long time is likely to have experienced more change than someone who has entered that field more recently. On the other hand, as with Ylijoki's study, they report a pervasive sense that the for-the-worse ratings indicate a sense of loss particularly in relation to autonomy and academic freedom. This loss is related to the demands of the additional work which occupies the discretionary time needed to exercise autonomy. This increasing workload is also seen to have a negative impact on the quality of the attention that they can give to issues of great importance to respondents, such as 'contact with students', which they indicate to be the most important of the 40 topics they rated.

Another general trend involves a tendency for respondents to blame university managers for their sense of loss. Here the notion of loss is linked to the disappearance of collegiality and collegial decision-making, displaced by managerialism and corporatism. Again, long-term academics recognised and resented this trend more than others. Anderson *et al.* (2002) observe that the 'separation of management roles from academic roles has had a dramatic effect on the ways that academics see themselves, and more specifically, the ways they perceive their own relationships with those who manage universities' (p. 50). This statement acknowledges that academics have always had some responsibility for institutional management, but points to the growth in the nature and scale of that work in contemporary university operations. Later the authors note that the qualitative comments are 'scathing, cynical and abusive' such that 'few academics showed signs of sympathy, and even those who did, portrayed university managers as victims of their own environment' (p. 53). They point to the potential crisis in the relationship between academic managers and academics-as-workers that these comments pose for universities as organisations.

UK academics

The work of Jacquelyn Allen Collinson (2004) provides a third example from the literature. It reports an exploration of the working lives and identities of academic staff employed as contract researchers in 11 English and Welsh universities. Her interviews reveal 'the shifting and complex nature of occupational identity amongst researchers, contingent upon an amalgam of biographical features such as educational or professional socialization and previous work experiences' (p. 316). Importantly for this chapter, her work highlights the influence and continuity of the biographical resources that each individual brings to any occupational context.

Allen Collinson (2004) identified three distinct patterns of biographical heritage in her interviews of 61 social science researchers. I will comment here on two of these patterns. The first and smallest group of researchers shared a heritage of 'practical' professional or occupational experience. 'These "practitioner researchers" frequently constructed the "practical" self in opposition to the category of "academic"; a role with which they manifestly did not identify' (p. 317). They expressed a sense of moral purpose focused on social justice and political change.

The second group shared a biographical heritage of socialisation within the academy, and more particularly within the social sciences and humanities. Their heritage was 'grounded in prolonged disciplinary socialization based on a set of academic values . . . the pursuit of truth, academic honesty, acceptance of reasoned criticism, open transmission of knowledge, and a belief in academic quality' (Allen Collinson 2004: 318). This self-image was overlaid by a disciplinary perspective whose strength reflected the intensity and duration of the period of socialisation. For example, the notion of 'reasoned criticism' is itself to be under-stood as involving a discipline-specific approach to academic work rather than a more generalised attribute.

The story illustrates how biography is informed by context. Allen Collinson (2004) describes how some respondents 'confessed' to 'essentially opportunistic motives' in their use of time and 'gave precedence to self-identities external to the research work' (p. 318), with the implication that opportunities for personal and professional gain were being sought outside the academy. She also indicates that, where they were able to collaborate, they did so very generously 'in order to gain further contracts and to fend off the perennial spectre of unemployment' (p. 321). This work presents academic identities as both multiple and contextually malleable, yet always including elements of biographical continuity. The point here is that those who feel that their employment is marginal to the academy do not necessarily leave, but find ways of re-investing in their own personal and professional lives.

Identities and themes in the three stories

It is clear from the three cited reports that academics have available a range of roles and identity positions.[2] The work of both Ylijoki (2005) and Anderson *et al.* (2002) introduce the theme of the loss of the 'golden age'. This includes a loss of a culture characterised by professional autonomy, academic freedom and collegi-ality. Particularly in the latter report, Australian academics are seen to blame this sense of loss on their academic managers. In terms of identity, these reports imply that respondents have largely 'taken on' beliefs in autonomy and freedom. This claimed belief represents a core element of their expected career as an academic. It is interesting to see that these beliefs are claimed in ways that at times imply alignment with notions of individual thought and reflection, as suggested by the very personal ways in which this loss is experienced. Thus, while the 'taken on' elements of academic identity align with early Greek philosophy, the reference to rationality indicates that Enlightenment ideals of social progress and betterment remain central to academic identity.

The theme of loss of 'a golden age' is paralleled by a sense of personal loss. Ylijoki's respondents express this in terms of both personal anxiety and disap-pointment, and a loss of personal fulfilments. Anderson *et al.* (2002) report very similar responses. These are clear indicators that academics are grieving the loss of their anticipated career. During this, there is a tendency for activity to be seen as increasingly meaningless, and for the grieving person to simply 'go through the motions' with little purpose and even less sense of accomplishment. Universities cannot afford to have staff remain in this state. Rather, leaders should provide time for activities that invite collective introspection and reflection. The purpose

---

2 It is interesting to note that some of those positions eschew the reference to 'academic', as indicated in the work of Allen Collinson (2004). Thus, the available positions are not limited to the academy.

of such activities is to allow academics to reconnect old purposes with new activities and circumstances. I will explore this possibility later.

Although the phenomenon of blaming can be associated with grieving, it can also speak to a failure of leaders to connect academics to the relatively rapid changes in universities' internal operations that have resulted from changes in the external context. This issue has been discussed at length by a range of authors, including Ramsden (1998) and Senge *et al.* (2004). However, one of the very significant challenges associated with work intensification is the lack of time available for thinking about and reflecting on those changes. Senge *et al.*, in particular, comment on the need to provide those experiencing change with an opportunity to step back from their relatively local concerns in order to adopt a more holistic perspective. Developing an understanding of the historical evolution of universities and associated change in traditions could be a very useful part of that holistic perspective. But it would take time and attention away from the very object of their sense of loss – personally directed scholarly work. Blaming is faster and easier.

Allen Collinson's (2004) interviewees, on the other hand, have not invested in the same anticipated academic career as have many of the respondents discussed by Ylijoki (2005) and Anderson *et al.* (2002). As a consequence, there is little sense that they are either grieving or blaming. The same can be said of the responses of the younger and/or more junior academics to Anderson *et al.*'s (2002) survey. For example, those authors note that the respondents on the lowest/first level of academic appointment 'were least likely to regard job satisfaction to have decreased, and similarly they were least likely to say it was a change for the worse' (p. 97). These academics appear to accept that their identities will always be 'under construction' in contexts that are characterised by indeterminacy, partiality and complexity. Implicit in this statement is an acknowledgement that universities are changing, and will continue to change, sometimes in unexpected ways.

Thus, this discussion suggests that the particular set of traits, beliefs and allegiances adopted by academics are themselves constrained by a range of external as well as internal factors, irrespective of how those factors are understood. Given this suggestion, there are two questions I want to explore here. Both relate to the notion of academic identity as a set of claims by individual academics about themselves. First, what is being claimed and of what value to today's academics is this claim? Second, what new options might academics claim?

Exploring identity claims

As noted above, both Ylijoki (2005) and Anderson *et al.* (2002) share claims about academic work that are, in large part, a call for recognition of loss. Although that loss is articulated in terms of personal autonomy and/or academic freedom, there is a strong implication that it involves a deeper sense of loss of respect within universities as organisation, and a loss of prestige within the broader public. I suggest this because, in most cases, respondents appear to acknowledge that specific aspects of the context that supported the claimed version of academic identity have changed in ways that are unlikely to be reversed. The common factor in all such discussions is the acknowledgment of work intensification – there is more to be done and no additional time for that work.

There are three issues that I wish to raise in relation to this. The first issue involves the basis of these claims. On the one hand, traditional notions of academic identity (and values) are heavily reliant on Enlightenment theory and ideals, and are thus significantly aligned with the philosophical (and therefore identity) work of Descartes, and those who built on it (Gray 2002). Yet cutting-edge disciplinary work is increasingly unlikely to endorse that same theory or its ideals. A more critical reading of the three cited discussions would suggest that the claimed notions of academic identity have themselves become a dogma – outwardly focused (in this case on a former 'golden era', and the patronage that it delivered) and expressed in terms of concerns for stability and tradition. And associated with the sense of loss that accompanies this dogma is a tendency to blame the loss on academic managers and managerialism. The irony here, as observed by Ralston Saul (2001: 99), is that '[m]oralism has found a natural friend in managerialism. Both are top down, judgemental and exclusive.' Is it the case that academics tend not to bring their disciplinary insights and critical capacities to bear on their own situation with the same rigour that they use in their disciplines?

Another reading of individual behaviour is provided by John Gray (2002), who argues that rationality and reason account for little of our actual behaviour:

> Our conscious selves arise from processes in which conscious awareness plays only a small part. We resist this fact because it seems to deprive us of control of our lives. We think of our actions as end-results of our thoughts. Yet much the greater part of everyone's life goes on without thinking.
>
> (p. 70)

Ralston Saul (2001: 276) puts it differently: 'If you try to squeeze reality or individualism [or identity] inside reason, they simply won't function.' Perhaps academics are simply demonstrating that they are human. When invited to reflect on their situation, they share ideas that have been affirmed in conversation with like-minded individuals. That is, common-sense judgements which, when accompanied by moralism, become taken-for-granted dogma.

The second issue involves personal experiences. Earlier this year I was appointed to my first substantive academic leadership position. My initial approach, in an unfamiliar institution, involved seeking to understand how those whom I was expected to lead viewed their own work contexts. I met individually with a number of academics, each responsible for coordinating different degree programmes. I invited them, amongst other matters, to share with me what was working particularly well, and what was causing them frustration. Consistent with the earlier stories, the universal frustration was lack of time. At a later whole-of-faculty discussion, those present were asked to identify 'things we should start doing, or do more of', and 'things we should do less of, or stop doing'. The list of 'start and do more' was impressive in its ambition, and potential value. On the other hand, the collective wisdom could identity very few 'things to do less or stop'. And this was in spite of quite clear invitations from the leadership group to identify aspects of their work to reduce. In the months following this, I have brought forward specific proposals to change current work arrangements in order to reduce the workloads of those with whom I met earlier. In ways consistent with the whole-of-faculty discussion, those who had previously complained of the burden those arrangements imposed are now amongst the strongest defenders of those same arrangements.

The irony here lies with the accusation that loss of time, and therefore autonomy and academic freedom, is to be blamed on academic managers and managerialism. Although I am not suggesting that the policies and procedures adopted by most universities are blameless, my experience is that collegial practices associated with 'the golden era' provide no panacea in terms of responding to the complex environment in which universities now operate (Barnett 2000). Like their peers in so many other salaried professions, academics tend to cling to those roles and practices which have been a source of personal meaning and professional satisfaction, regardless of the cost. Academics' capacity for debate may interfere with their potential to imagine differently effective practices, as suggested by Peter Senge and his collaborators (2004). These authors indicate that the first move in any significant organisational learning requires the collective suspension of debate and/or judgement about what should happen. The reason for this is that those reactions are likely to be governed by established habits of action – 'we invariably end up reinforcing pre-established mental models . . . [and therefore] remain secure in the cocoon of our own world view, isolated from the larger world' (p. 11). What they call for, as the first move, is that those involved develop a capacity to open themselves to their preconceptions and traditional ways of making sense, and the identities associated with these.

The third issue involves the reliance by academics on their role in developing disciplinary knowledge as a basis for their identity claims. This reliance is reflected in the almost universal reference to a loss of time – to think, to read, to write – in the literature on academic work. Whereas there is a sense here that 'the good academic life' ought to involve such opportunities, the reason given for these opportunities invariably centres on these as opportunities for research, that is, creating personally and professionally and morally significant knowledge. There is a deep sense that academics feel they have lost the opportunity to personally decide what questions or topics they will research. This curtails their right to exercise their professional autonomy in the pursuit of *pure* research.

The shift in focus for academic identity from teaching to research, with the resulting focus on knowledge creation, has led to pressure to capitalise that knowledge, as discussed by Clarke and Rollo (2001), and Gibbons (2000). Thus, rather than contributing to the growth of pure disciplinary knowledge – to science – academics are being asked to contribute to innovation – to research that develops knowledge-rich applications. This pressure is evident in the preference of governments to support research that articulates directly with industry and economic benefits. Thus, in most Western nations, university-based research is being called upon to contribute to national economic well-being, through engaging with the marketplace. The very pressures for, and nature of, project-based research can be attributed, in no small part, to the success of some academics in knowledge creation. Yet 'research productivity', however it is measured, tends to be characteristic of the work of a small minority of the academic workforce.

Alternative identity options

What new identities might be claimed? There are two lines of thinking I want to explore briefly. The first involves options associated with the postmodern notions of identity, and the second involves options more closely aligned with disciplines and pedagogies. Before discussing these I want to note the risk posed to universities and the new generations of academics if the 'senior generation' is unable to successfully complete their grieving. That risk is associated with the importance of occupational socialisation as noted in Allen Collinson's (2004) report, whereby senior academics often act as role models and mentors for those new to the academy. The risk is that the mythology associated with the 'golden era' and its assurances, most strongly associated with long-term academics, may impede the process in which junior academics engage with current challenges and opportunities.

Universities have been characterised as sites of 'supercomplexity' (Barnett 2000). If this is the case, then academics are well positioned to learn to live with complexity. Rather than some unitary notion of identity, this acknowledgement and engagement invites a postmodernist perspective of identity. As indicated in the earlier discussion, postmodern notions of identity allow for a range of subject positions, each with their own traits, beliefs, and allegiances, and each context-sensitive. Rather than identity as a claim that de-contextualises and unites the academic workforce (against the forces of corporatism and managerialism), it might be more productive to see academic identities as context-specific assemblages that draw on a shared but open repertoire of traits, beliefs, and allegiances – a creative commons for identity assemblage. This commons might include traits such as rigour, scepticism, inquisitiveness, integrity, creativity, imagination, and discipline, associated with more traditional notions of academic work, with additions such as networking, laterality, hybridity, flexibility, multi-tasking and media capability more representative of 'supercomplexity'. There are numerous positive aspects and opportunities within the current context of universities, as suggested by the number of people aspiring to join the academic workforce. And this assemblage would provide opportunities to identify continuities between the beliefs and allegiances of the longed-for 'golden era' and the current era of supercomplexity. The tension between collegial-focused management and performance-focused management might invite a reinterpretation of collegiality in ways that welcome context-sensitive debate, discussion and dissent.

A second option for reworking academic identity involves a refocusing on the centrality of learning to academic identity. Learning may provide a unifying commitment for academic identities, even those under construction in the 'creative commons' discussed above. Learning is central to research, and to teaching, and to service. Indeed, discussions of knowledge capitalisation point to the need for creating and sharing knowledge through teaching and learning (Clarke and Rollo 2001). But learning itself needs to be understood as always contextualised – learning is always 'of something'. Historically, the disciplines emerged as relatively distinct domains of knowledge and ways of knowing. Embedded within each are particular ways of learning. Thus, and in keeping with some aspects of the previous discussion, there are options to develop academic identities as learning-focused identities, with disciplinary-specific traits, beliefs, and allegiances. This is different from the discussion of academic identities presented in the three studies discussed earlier, where research was a central focus for identities. In particular it would acknowledge the central role of teaching to academic work, and the need for academics to both understand student learning and undertake their own learning through research.

Nostalgia for a golden era of academic identity, like any other object of grieving, will not provide a basis for renewal. On the other hand, the first option discussed above offers a focus for successful grieving, and therefore for 'moving on' for those who are grieving. The second option offers the potential to include aspects of the role that are central to academic work. Both stand in some tension with the pictures of academic identity presented in the three studies discussed earlier. They paint a picture of academic identities fixated on a largely imagined past. This is a problematic fixation for those it represents, and for universities in the current era. As a journalist might write: it is dangerous to go into the future while looking in the rear-view mirror. Or as Curtis White (2004: 2) states more eloquently: 'We cannot create in a fresh and lively way while looking at our world from a stale (even if familiar and comforting) perspective.'

Chapter 3

Have students got a voice?

Denise Batchelor

> It is primarily through his voice that a person makes known his inwardness, for he puts into it what he is.
>
> (Hegel 1978: 181)

Introduction

'Yes', 'It depends' and 'No' are all possible responses to the question 'Have students got a voice?' At first sight the question might seem surprising, even rhetorical: asking whether students have a voice implies that a loss has occurred, and yet on the face of it the validity of this loss is difficult to sustain. The plethora of student response data and student satisfaction surveys appears to undermine any argument for loss of voice. The sheer quantitative evidence of quality evaluation techniques suggests a contrary conclusion: far from being lost, the student voice is pre-eminently present and evident. How then might it legitimately be claimed that, despite all these checks and mechanisms, the student voice has been lost?

The answer depends firstly on the definition of voice. What does having a voice mean? What kind of voices do students currently have, and are there other dimensions to the meaning of having a voice that are under-developed?

Secondly, the answer depends on the value assigned to these different interpretations of having a voice. Students gain the voices they are allowed or invited to have; they lose those that are less valued.

Thirdly, if the answer to the question 'Have students got a voice?' is negative, are there consequences to this loss, and are there ways in which these lost voices might be recovered? Certain conditions may be necessary for strengthening and recovering the student voice, such as active listening, silence and space. In the time-poor climate of contemporary higher education, realizing these conditions involves students and teachers in taking risks.

Three currents therefore percolate the question 'Have students got a voice?'

The very posing of the question raises the possibility that voice might be lost. The tone of its asking, whether inquiring, evaluating or challenging, potentially:

1   probes the meaning of voice;
2   suggests the possibility that some voices are valued whilst others are vulnerable;
3   issues an invitation for the retrieval of voice.

This chapter will build upon the three impulses of inquiry, evaluation and challenge inherent in its title, and examine the nature of the loss of voice that the question suggests.

Having a voice

Rée (2000: 16) draws a parallel between voices and faces:

> individual voices have a rather special significance in human life. We respond to them as we do to faces: as immediate embodiments of personal character and sensitive indicators of fluctuating mood.

Rée's insight, together with Hegel's understanding, in the epigraph to this chapter, of the peculiar revelation of identity signalled through voice, hints at the uniqueness of an individual self. The voice as the instrument for communicating that uniqueness itself also shares a special distinctiveness. Asking whether students have a voice probes whether they are enabled to develop a voice that expresses who and what they are, and reveals their identity in Hegel's sense of communicating inwardness and Rée's sense of embodying personal character.

Having and expressing a voice are to do with creativity and self-expression, the profession of self and the injection of what one is into the outside world. The progressive showing of the person is communicated through having a voice. The expression of voice is diverse, like different singers' and instrumentalists' readings of a work: Ferrier's interpretation of a Mahler song differs from Baker's, Perahia's rendering of a Bach variation differs from Brendel's, and yet all are valid voices.

Losing one's voice is partly about lacking some or all of the capacities for creativity, interpretation, self-profession and self-projection. But loss of voice is also to do with students lacking opportunities and conditions such as active listening, silence and space to discover these capacities in themselves, and to express them in their own way.

'Having' a voice also suggests possession. Another way of thinking about having a voice is as a state of gradual self-possession, of ownership and control of self attained through growing self-knowledge. Conversely, loss of voice suggests dispossession. Having a voice as a student is to do with progressive self-formation and self-construction, shaping one's own individual identity and not accepting ready-made paradigms of studenthood: if students are offered a detailed topography of who they are and what they know, their ontology is not of their own making.

Processes of self-realization and self-possession entail gradual self-recognition and self-affirmation. Taylor (1999: 88) explains that according to the expressivist view, what we really are is not known in advance of its expression:

> Rational self-awareness is rational awareness of a self which has been expressed in life and thus made determinate. The fullness of self-awareness is reached when this expression is recognized as adequate to the self. If it is not, if it is seen as truncated or distorted and requiring further change, then the self-awareness is not complete, however lucid the perception of inadequacy . . . The truncated being can only go on to a fuller expression in order then to recognize what he really is.

Here, recovery and development of voice would mean moving through progressive stages of incomplete self-awareness until a stage of completeness is recognized and achieved. At each juncture, the student would lay claim to a voice of increasing complexity, expressing more dimensions of himself and thus gradually achieving his being. Each step is accompanied by new realizations but also by a potentially disorientating loss of certainty and an altered sense of self. Conversely, loss and dispossession of voice mean lacking opportunities to develop a voice through experiment, experiences of uncertainty and changing understandings of identity.

Having a voice is retrospective as well as prospective, and entails looking backwards as well as forwards to achieve self-understanding and self-acceptance. Students entering higher education, especially those classified as non-traditional students, sometimes express the wish to 'move on', to lose their previous identities and change. They hope for some form of transformation through higher education.

However, the process of moving forward almost invariably means revisiting and accepting past self-perspectives in order to form a new self-image. For example, classroom situations or assessment issues can reactivate memories of past difficulties or failures: the student who never liked teachers or the student who was afraid of taking examinations will be reminded of those past experiences as he goes about his studies in the present. To achieve a reconciliation between past and present student identities, looking backwards as well as forwards is necessary to move towards a different self-perspective.

Distorted voice

Voice cannot express identity faithfully, in Hegel's sense that a person puts into his voice what he is, if that voice is distorted. Then, the self it seeks to express is incomplete or impaired. If the voice is distorted, this means the self or identity is hidden or lost by the very voice that endeavours to express it. Weil (1990), considering the influence that society exerts on the individual through language, concludes that, although language is precious because it allows us to express ourselves, it can also prevent us from expressing ourselves. A significant aspect of recovering the student voice entails changing the available vocabularies that suppress and distort voice, to enable identity to be revealed and the self to flourish.

As they progress through their higher education, students uncover different levels and intonations of voice in themselves, but some of the vocabularies of studenthood on offer overpower that developing and sometimes tentative voice. In particular, the condition of studenthood is colonized by impersonal commercial languages of consumerism and commodification: students are invited to internalize these vocabularies and the values they privilege, to the detriment of alternative ways of being a student. For example, students may be construed as paying customers whose satisfaction or dissatisfaction drives and influences the presentation and delivery of the educational products offered for their consumption.

Students are trapped in a paradox: endlessly canvassed and consulted through course quality evaluation questionnaires, it is as if theirs are the voices everyone longs to hear. But the restricted scope of the commercial language of evaluation can have the effect of silencing them. If the questions do not engage them, the paper discourse becomes stilted and anaesthetized. If openness is encouraged, but the definition of openness is limited, students are confined to articulating their ideas through a language that is not their own. Clarity of expression is lost. They are limited to using a blandly uniform 'academic Esperanto,' lacking the range of idioms and dialects that communicate individual diversity, and not owned.

Entrepreneurial voice

The approach of consumerism saps and weakens the student voice although it is designed to strengthen and empower it. Marginson (1997: 122) suggests that modelling higher education as a market in self-investment leads to a formulation of self-managing individuality as 'homo economicus', a competitive economic subject motivated by exploiting his individual utility. The student is an investor in the self, a 'self-entrepreneur'. Such a language of speculation is overtly affirmed in the Dearing Report:

> we expect students of all ages will be increasingly discriminating investors in higher education, looking for quality, convenience, and relevance to their needs at a cost they consider affordable and justified by the probable return on their investment of time and money.
>
> (para. 1.21)

Part of the bargain to be struck between the student and society is commercial. The predominant idea of a student here is of a venture capitalist, seeking to invest his resources for maximum personal benefit. Dearing's reference to preparing students to be entrepreneurs tacitly assumes this to be a positive aim. However, some of the consequences may be negative. Sennett (1998: 26–7) is concerned at the personal fragmentation caused by the tensions and incompatibilities between an ontological voice and an entrepreneurial voice once individuals join the workforce. He argues that behaviour leading to success and survival at work produces different effects in private life. The modern workplace is marked by weaknesses of loyalty and commitment:

> How can long-term purposes be pursued in a short-term society? How can durable social relations be sustained? How can a human being develop a narrative of identity and life history in a society composed of episodes and fragments? The conditions of the new economy feed instead on experience which drifts in time, from place to place, from job to job . . . short-term capitalism threatens to corrode . . . those qualities of character which bind human beings to one another and furnishes each with a sense of sustainable self.

There is a loss of personal identity, a weakening of personhood in a context dominated by entrepreneurial values. A voice largely omitted in higher education policy is the personal voice of students: there is silence on the complex nature of the self and its alternative interpretations. Students are encouraged to think of themselves in certain ways, and not in others. Loss, absence and concealment of certain understandings of student voice then become the price of some contemporary interpretations of being a student in higher education. The suppression of certain modes of student voice threatens to erase from students' horizons additional meanings their academic identity might have, and silences embryonic voices in students themselves that seek to express alternative understandings of who they are, who they might become and what they know.

Reciprocal voice

Having a voice is achieved not only in isolation, but through different combinations of solitary and collaborative procedures. The student both discovers and creates new aspects of his voice through engagement with other students and with staff.

Constructing a voice is a reciprocal activity between teachers and students. Allowing space for the development of the teacher's voice creates space for the student voice to develop. Self-enquiry in teachers leads to a more complex and nuanced voice in students. For the teacher, observing what helps his/her students to find their voices is also a guide in the formation of his/her own voice. As they begin a semester of seminars, tutors are faced by many unknowns about their students' learning styles, and consequently about the voice they might develop in interaction with them. Teachers' voices, like those of their students, are not fixed but fluid.

Pedagogically, teachers have a wide range of learning and teaching strategies to choose from. However, it is important not to determine too rigidly or too soon which methods to use. Teaching techniques and learning styles that are effective with students in one group can prove unproductive for those in another, even with students taking the same unit of the same course. For example, on an accounting and finance degree where two different seminar groups follow on from a main lecture on Statements of Standard Accounting Practice, one group may respond best to a tutor-led group discussion to clarify theoretical aspects of the material. Another group will prefer to break down into smaller groups to consolidate their understanding of the theory through interpreting case studies. Tutors' sensitivity in varying their repertoire of strategies, and attuning their own voice in response to differences in their students, will in turn free them to have a voice.

Valued voice

Loss implies a value judgement. In considering loss of the student voice, value judgements affect decisions not only about which students should be present in higher education, but also which voices are most worth their while developing when they are there. The loss implied by the question 'Have students got a voice?' is therefore not so much about the absence of the voices of particular groups in the constitution of the student body, although matters of access and exclusion, including self-elimination, are certainly significant. It is more to do with the impairment, suppression, decline or even disappearance of certain modes of student voice.

The concept of student voice may be anatomized into three constituent elements: an epistemological voice, or a voice for knowing; a practical voice, or a voice for doing; and an ontological voice, or a voice for being and becoming. In contemporary higher education, developing an ontological voice, a voice for being or becoming, is deemed less important than developing epistemological or practical voices, and is less validated, yet it is fundamental to realizing those other voices. A voice for being and becoming is a vulnerable voice, whose progress can be inhibited or arrested depending on how dispensable it is deemed to be, by students themselves as well as by others.

Paradoxically a voice for being and becoming, the voice of self-realization, is to be found at the heart of higher education recruitment literature. 'Become what you want to be' and 'Become who you want to be' are two invitations currently being extended to potential students by post-1992 universities. The openness and directness of these challenges extend invitations full of hope and possibility: individuals are in control of their own self-definitions and personal transformations of identity. However, such a raising of hopes, if unsupported, creates unexpected vulnerability. The challenge is how to recover and sustain ontological voice in a context which sometimes appears indifferent to these values, although its language endorses them.

At first sight the institutional language which defines the idea of a student, permeated as it is by references to self-realization, would seem to endorse both Hegel's and Rée's perspectives on voice as revealing and communicating an individual's authentic identity. A perusal of registry guidelines and course submission documents adumbrates the kind of student perceived as typifying a successful graduate from a course. The term 'self' recurs as a common denominator throughout this literature, in phrases such as 'self-reliance', 'self-awareness', 'self-direction', 'self-motivation', self-management' and 'self-empowerment'. All of these phrases are used in a positive sense, to signal approval for a nexus of qualities seen as desirable and achievable, and which lie at the core of a student's being and becoming. They constitute at one and the same time a rational project for the self-managed self, and the criteria for the successful self. However there is a risk that states such as self-actualization or self-knowledge, and the complex work of developing a voice capable of progressively registering and expressing these processes and dispositions, cease to be recognized for the lifelong undertakings they are.

Lifelong learning has a sense of learning *for* life, as well as learning throughout life. It has ontological as well as vocational dimensions. Having a voice is not a project for the short term. Newman (1920: 92–3) expresses learning for life as the formation of a disposition of mind:

> A habit of mind is formed which lasts through life, of which the attributes are, freedom, equitableness, calmness, moderation, and wisdom . . . This then I would assign as the special fruit of the education furnished at a University.

Progressive self-realization and self-knowledge, which inform the process of becoming and the formation of an ontological voice, are diminished by being restricted to the status of quickly achievable orientations directed towards successful activity in the world. This is not to argue that activity in the world is unimportant, only that a dimension of meaning relating to a student's being as opposed to his doing is lost if this activity, and the definitions of success it privileges, is overemphasized. The fuller significance of the language is impoverished.

A further erosion of meaning is risked from the effect of repetition if the same litany of self-related qualities recurs frequently throughout an institution's literature. This deadening of meaning through repetition is a serious loss. It is dangerous if the 'brutalization of language' (Marcuse 1972: 259) within institutions creates what Marcuse (ibid.) terms a 'psychological habituation' to a fallacy – here, the mistaken idea that developing complex qualities is easy, painless or instantaneous. Instantaneity of expression is not the same as instantaneity of acquisition. Acquiring the semblance of complex qualities is fundamentally different from living out the values those qualities are founded on, and actualizing them in a committed way. Barnett (2000) suggests some qualities of the self that may arise from scholarly activity: compassion, humility, generosity and courage. Virtues such as these are at the core of a person's being as well as his doing. Striving for them involves a long and difficult struggle, fractured by failures. Aristotle (1998: 38) observes that it is possible to fail in many ways when aiming at virtue:

> to miss the mark is easy, to hit it difficult.

Managers might object that it is naïve in the current competitive higher education market, where funding is conditional on student numbers, to demur that institutional marketing language is at odds with the reality it promises. Surely, to some extent, rival institutions are compelled to imply that students can 'have it all' with them? Everyone will make the necessary reservations. But one cost of the hyperbole is that deeper strata of meaning are being lost as the vocabulary of the self is stretched to breaking-point. A vocabulary which values self-realization can signify the reverse, devaluation, if its implications are not fully explored. It enervates rather than empowers the expression of an ontological voice.

Students appear to have it all through successful assessment for the self-related qualities promised, but at the same time they may lack these qualities, because there is scant time to understand what the qualities mean and the demands they make, let alone to acquire them and shape a voice that expresses them. The institutionally assigned rhetoric of the self misleads by suggesting that complex virtues can be developed within a finite timespan, in a particular context, and are accessible to measurement and assessment in the same way as mastery of Financial Accounting theory might be gauged, or of Business Law.

Vulnerable voice

Ontological and epistemological voices are closely interrelated. Both modes of voice relate to two questions that all students ask in their own way, questions that form part of the hinterland to the question 'Have students got a voice?' Although they are old questions, they are always new for each student, and part of the process of recovering the student voice entails restraint in supplying answers too soon. The first is the question Montaigne had engraved around the ceiling of the tower in Bordeaux where he retired to record the workings of his own mind in his *Essais*: 'What do I know?' The second is the question underlying all matters of identity: 'Who am I?'

Taken together, these two separate questions, 'What do I know?' and 'Who am I?', represent the possibility for a fusion of personal and academic identities, of ontological and epistemological student voices. In the process of striving to answer them a student is uncovering a voice into which he puts what he is, in Hegel's sense that voice reveals a person's inner nature, and a voice that embodies his special identity, in Rée's sense that voices, like faces, have a unique significance.

Opportunities for students to integrate their voices for being and knowing, and progressively realize a growing wholeness of voice, are sometimes absent in current constructions of student identity. Inequality and unevenness in the value placed on ontological and epistemological voices make the student voice vulnerable in the sense that it is a fractured voice.

Becoming who and what you want to be is a complex and demanding endeavour. Its challenges and struggles should not be hidden or diluted. Otherwise the exacting aspects of self-actualization may be interpreted as aberrations, signs of failure rather than indicators of progression. For example, students in a competitive higher education culture where there is an expectation of successful performance may achieve high assessment grades. Yet on the way to that external success, and as significant factors contributing to it, students may experience periods of internal doubt and self-questioning that dislocate their previous ideas of their personal and academic identities.

Such a sense of displacement can range from a feeling of temporary loss of perspective to one of deeper disorientation and loss of balance, leading students to question who they are and what they know. Students need spaces where they can express the vulnerable aspects of the experience of forming their academic and personal identities, and finding an integrated voice

A voice for being is always in the process of becoming rather than completion. In this sense it is a vulnerable voice. The concept of vulnerability, with its connotations of weakness and defencelessness, appears at first sight to offer an insecure premise from which to work out an answer to the question 'Have students got a voice?' It could be objected that vulnerability is the condition from which the student voice needs to be recovered, rather than being a factor in its recovery. However there is a positive side to vulnerability. It can also mean an opening up, rather than a closing down, of possibilities for having a voice.

Vulnerability offers the possibility of openness and receptiveness. Vulnerability lacks defensiveness and is unprotected. For students to have a voice, this undefendedness can be helpful, not harmful. Undefendedness need not signify only infirmity and exposure. It can also mean the courage to be open to new experience.

One reason vulnerable epistemological and ontological voices can be dismissed by policy-makers, managers, teachers or students in higher education is that their vulnerability can be judged to be a final state of weakness and failure. The positive formative potential of their openness and undefendedness, their vulnerability *for*, is discounted.

A condition *of* vulnerability, a state *of*, suggests finiteness and limitation, a state in which further progress is not possible. 'Of' is a containing preposition, defining boundaries. A condition *for*, on the other hand, indicates openness to the possibilities of movement and development. 'For' implies something to be done, to be achieved, a goal to be reached, a process to be activated. It denotes movement, action, growth, change and possibility, but not an eventual outcome. Recovering the student voice is partly about moving from a closed state *of* vulnerability to a more open condition of vulnerability *for*.

Vulnerability in the sense of openness and receptivity is a necessary condition for the self-formative process which lies at the root of having a voice. Bourdieu and Passeron (1979: 55) place self-creation at the very core of the condition of being a student:

> a student's creativity can only ever be a self-creation . . . to study is not to create something but to create oneself.

Bourdieu's proposal hints at a harmony and unity between knowing and being – epistemological and ontological voices – and an academic identity that is an authentic self-expression. It is a statement full of hope. The person who is a student need not force himself into the identikit model of a student that is portrayed in some higher education institution publicity material or induction programmes. He can discover his own individual way of being a student.

Recovering voice

How might an ontological voice, a voice for being and becoming, be fostered? What opportunities can be created to strengthen a voice that is vulnerable, creative and self-interpretative, that develops in strength and confidence partly through experiences of disorientation and uncertainty, and that moves backwards and forwards along the spectrum between retrospection and prospection to capture and express a present identity? What openings could usefully be offered to students from a wide range of national and cultural backgrounds to find their own voices? All of these students will have their own concepts of selfhood, and place different emphases on the value of individual and group identity.

I suggest that three factors are important in strengthening the chances for students to have a voice: active listening, silence and space.

Active listening

Having a voice partly depends on someone hearing that voice with understanding, and coaching it forth. There is a sense in which you are who listens to you. Active listening is a complex activity that involves the listener in an act of constructing the speaker's voice and interpreting his/her meaning in such a way that the listener does not distort the speaker's communication.

The very phrase 'active listening' summons up an opposite, passive listening. Passive listening carries connotations of a spongeous absorption of what the speaker communicates, a porous listener somehow impervious to and unchanged by what s/he hears. The activity and energy are all on the speaker's side. Active listening is not about activism. 'Active' is a misnomer if it implies energetic exertions such as over-rapid intervention, the rush to give advice, to interpret and solve problems, the impulse to speak for the speaker, and give him/her a voice by substituting the listener's own. Such activism results in avoiding listening, however benevolently intended by the listener, or gratefully received by the student who wants a directive approach.

The active element in listening paradoxically entails the exercise of restraint. This amounts to far more than passive waiting. It involves an inner activity by the listener that is the opposite of directive activism targeted at the student. It requires the listener's readiness to hold back, to be silent, and to develop the capacity to be open to new possibilities of meaning in what s/he hears, to be prepared to be surprised and changed. The listener's openness then in turn frees the speaker to use the silence to explore *his/her* own current meaning structure.

The clearing of the ground in the listener's mind so as not to prejudge, the disciplined withholding of preconceptions, makes the listener vulnerable. It makes demands on her/him. Vulnerability in the listener is a key quality for recovering vulnerable student voices. The listener is consciously exercising restraint on any tendency to label the student. Such labelling provides protection against reflection and a refuge against students, especially their ability to change. Conversely, the listener's chosen vulnerability, in the sense of her/his openness to being surprised and changed by what s/he hears, allows her/him to hear nuances of meaning from students that s/he might otherwise miss.

The quality of listening is therefore one sense in which the student voice in a mass higher education system is a new sound to be discovered, not a recollected or expected voice to be recovered. As well as the content of the student's communication, the newness may lie in the listener's understanding of what is communicated in a fresh way.

Listening actively to the student experience in order to understand it entails listening to what its constituent elements mean to the speaker, not what they might mean to the listener if s/he were in the student's place, or are intended to mean by the institution to a generic student. The active listener is probing beneath the words used to the unique meanings with which the speaker has invested those words.

When students feel that their own meaning has been heard, it has a remarkably freeing, releasing effect on them (Rogers 1983). Moments of being listened to and understood in this active, creative way may occur infrequently in a student's educational experience, but their impact is powerful and long-lasting. They are epiphanies of private transformation and illumination. They are often connected with change in students' self-image, the realization that they have a choice about the structures of meaning they hold about themselves, and the horizons they have set to their own potential and identity. They have come into their own, they have their own voices, into which they put what they are and which reveal their special identities.

Silence

Silence appears to be a barrier to students having a voice. It strikes at the heart of the educational transaction when defined as a dialogic exchange. But silence poses a double paradox: it simultaneously signifies the absence of voice, yet it is a necessary condition for recovering and hearing that voice.

As a dimension of active listening, silence is less a negative withholding than a positive invitation, a waiting on the development of complex and nuanced modes of voice. The resolution between absence and presence of the student voice depends on the listener's ability to discriminate between different kinds of voice: the absence of one form of articulation creates the silence in which another, perhaps previously silenced voice might be heard.

In an article for trainee student accountants, Naylor (1997: 75) stresses that learning how to listen properly to clients is good for business. He identifies the ability to focus on silence as a precondition of becoming a good listener:

To begin, focus on silence. Silence is the framework for all sound. Listen to the depth and texture of it – to the layers within silence. The deeper you go, the more sensitive your ability to listen will become.

Silence like this is focused and receptive. An active listening silence is usually an essential condition for enabling students who have retreated into silence to have a voice. However, for academics as teachers and personal tutors, being silent may feel alien, uncomfortable or even like failure. In contrast to Naylor's focus on silence to enhance good listening, silence can unsettle listeners. Lago and Shipton (1995: 36) cite being unable to cope with silence as a common pitfall in communicating for personal tutors:

> The tutor often needs to extend his or her existing silence threshold – i.e., ability to comfortably sustain silence – for during such periods the student is often working particularly productively.

Similarly, teachers' silence may be interpreted as a sign of inability to engage with the growing activism of the learning and teaching process. New teachers under observation as part of their professional development are assessed on the number of students they interact with, and how many students in the group speak. The way in which a silent student may be participating is difficult to register on the scale of measurement available.

Students have many silences. These may be silences of withdrawal, inarticulacy or conscious election. At the extreme is the silence of those who withdraw from their courses. There are silences in the classroom, whether a literal absence of sound, or the metaphorical silence of an inauthentic or mechanical response. What is at stake in these silences is not only the loss of the potential communication but also the risk of broaching the silence. Students take a risk when they speak in terms of the accuracy of the hearing they might receive; listeners risk their preconceptions being disrupted by what they might hear.

In students' silences, a distinction can be drawn between enforced and self-enforced silences. Enforced silence occurs when others will not allow students a hearing; self-enforced silence results from students not taking the opportunities given for allowing them a hearing. The quality of students' silence therefore has different dimensions. It may be the muteness caused by a lack of responsive listeners or the silence of elective refusal, a feeling of institutional and personal impotence or a genuinely chosen negative stance. The common result is that they do not have a voice.

Although students may become silent through believing they do not count, their silence does not always result from lack of self-esteem. The quality of the silence and attention communicated by listeners can be active, indifferent or selective, and will affect students who are considering speaking in different ways. But even when the audience *is* receptive, some students choose silence.

Their self-imposed silence poses challenges for tutors and other students, who may both believe that students do not have the right to remain silent, but share a common responsibility to speak. This is a difficult area. Imposing speech can be as counterproductive as enforcing silence. Valuing silence as a dimension of active listening is at the core of moving students towards having a voice.

Space

What possibilities does space, whether external or internal, offer students to recover their voices? How might the spaces students inhabit encourage them to have a voice, in the sense both of capacity and performance? Space does not automatically guarantee the emergence of voice. Voice is recovered only when certain kinds of spaces are nurtured.

Physical space, and curricular space to a certain degree, are external spaces that are granted to students: in this sense they are outside students' control. However the idea of space can be extended to include the inner intellectual and experiential space that is configured by students themselves.

For students who believe higher education will mean some form of transformation, its spaces are potentially metamorphic. No matter how cramped their physical conditions or crammed their study programmes, students always create *their* space for their raw dream of what higher education might mean for them as individuals, how it will change things for them. This space is the site of their internal utopia, an ontological space. Its voice expresses a rich seam of student experience, and is as powerful, if differently coded, on the most vocational professional course as on an undergraduate humanities programme. It is a resilient voice.

Opportunities for expressing and hearing this voice may occur in the personal tutoring space. In some higher education institutions, there is a practice of assigning students to a lecturer who acts as their personal tutor. Sometimes this arrangement is made only for first-year undergraduates, or for students who are new to the institution through being direct entrants to the second or third years of undergraduate programmes. Supervisors may also double as personal tutors for postgraduates.

There are many understandings of the personal tutoring role, and in several institutions it has been replaced by alternative systems for student support. Here, I am interpreting personal tutoring as a relationship between tutors and students that is pastoral as well as academic, and within which students, if they choose to, can talk about their personal experience of studenthood as well as the progress of their academic work. The personal tutoring relationship has the potential to create a space for students to express a voice for being and becoming as well as a voice for knowing, a voice which affirms who they are as well as what they know.

In personal tutor meetings, the possibility of listening to students' meaning is very great. Meetings offer space to students and lecturers genuinely to talk and listen to each other on an individual basis. They can be between the personal tutor and one tutee, or a small group of students. The situation is less formal than in a teaching context – although informality is daunting for some students – and makes it possible for role definitions to be relaxed: for example, the tutor can show more of her/himself as a person.

There is also the opportunity through conversation to discover more about a student's learning style. In a new university, where student–staff ratios can be 25:1 in seminar groups, it is difficult in the space of a weekly two-hour seminar to form a sufficiently detailed picture of each student. Dyslexic students, those with hearing difficulties who attend classes with a scribe, and students with visual impairments who need enlarged print materials may find it helpful to be able to discuss with their personal tutors what assists them in learning. Students who are silent in class, whether through shyness, fear of failure, cultural inhibitions or some shock in their private lives, can be drawn out in personal tutor meetings, and their voices strengthened. Additionally, the voices of those judged to be 'good' or 'model' students should not be neglected. It is understandable when time is short for personal tutors to focus on the exceptions, students with difficulties, but this can lead to the loss of other student voices who equally want a hearing.

However, although a personal tutoring system seems to offer ontological space for students to have a voice for being and becoming, there is a temptation for students and tutors to fill the space before its possibilities are recognized. In a packed semester timetable, an empty space is like a puzzling anomaly, yet its very lack of shape and definition offers those inside it the chance to structure it in their own way. It is preferable to resist developing prescriptive personal tutoring models that precisely define the parameters and use of the space.

Space for self-discovery should not be filled up by ready-made interpretations of what students are like and what they need, however eager students are to know what the right voice is for success. If students are given a ready-formed voice rather than the space to construct a voice of their own, they are protected from the challenges of constructing their own voices. Space is both a risk and an opportunity for students to have a voice.

Conclusion

Have students got a voice? The mode of student voice I have argued for runs counter to certain dominant concerns in contemporary higher education policy, which are to do with enhancing graduate employability and marketability. An ontological voice, a voice for being and becoming, a fragile and vulnerable voice that can be recovered only when it is heard with openness and understanding – do students want or need such a voice, which could even be construed as a handicap, when they have to concentrate on practical employment prospects, successful performance and tangible results? What use is it?

Not only is an ontological voice as important as an epistemological or practical voice, it is fundamental to enabling those other voices to be realized. A student voice that eventually becomes strong, confident, secure and authoritative may begin on a much more tentative note. Barnett (2000: 167) observes:

> It is not knowledge that will carry them [graduates] forward but their capacity to embrace multiple and conflicting frameworks and to offer

their own positive interventions in that milieu. What counts is not their knowledge but their mode of being.

It is questionable whether the priorities of the marketplace are constructive for persons, or strengthen ontological voice. They can as easily lead to acute vulnerability. Sennett (1998) suggests that an entrepreneurial culture leads to a sense of personal fragmentation. The flexible enterprise culture for which students are being prepared, with its priorities of short-termism and success, can lead to a corrosion of character. It also exposes individuals to the constant risk of failure without nurturing in them any inner qualities of resilience and self-dependence that might enable them to survive such pressures. Far from being an irrelevance, a creative fusion of ontological, epistemological and practical voices is the voice most likely to enable graduates to sustain the stresses of the marketplace.

What is increasingly advocated in contemporary higher education is a completed voice, external rather than internal, and public rather than private in its orientation. Yet this apparently complete voice has elements of incompleteness about it. The emphasis on an active voice has led to the diminution of a more contemplative voice.

Hughes (2005) suggests that being contemplative does not mean having beautiful contemplative experiences while floating above the mess of life. It is to do with an attitude of openness to experience rather than an approach of moulding experience to fit into existing preconceptions. A contemplative voice is exploratory, uncertain, not always in control, and suffers periods of obscurity in thought that seem like failure. It can be an apparently unproductive voice without an immediately clear result, whereas the student voice today is required to be demonstrably productive rather than speculative, matured and developed rather than maturing and developing. Yet a fluid voice does not replace the voice of skills, but supplements it. Having a strong ontological voice forms the foundation for a successful public, performing and achieving voice.

Chapter 4

Identities of academic developers
Critical friends in the academy?

Gunnar Handal

Introduction

The intention of this chapter is to explore the identities of a group of people hold-ing significant positions in academic institutions – academic developers. I will describe briefly what type of positions academic developers hold, which functions they carry out and what academic development means, at least in the context of this chapter. Based on research, I will argue that the academic developers them-selves hold quite different views of their functions and mission. Drawing on a socio-cultural understanding of identity formation, I will argue that this reflects a situation in which faculty developers as a group lack a unifying professional iden-tity. By analysing some central conditions for their work, I will discuss how this may be understood and explained. Whether this is a satisfactory situation or not, for the professional group as well as for the university, will also be discussed. I will then argue that the metaphor of 'the critical friend' is a potential professional identity for the academic developer and explain why this might be a particularly potent identity within the academy. Finally I will discuss if and how a develop-ment towards a shared professional identity of this kind may be realised.

Academic development

Academic development is a growing profession. The number of people engaged as academic developers is increasing (Gosling 2001). It is becoming 'normal' for a university to have some sort of unit or positions engaged in this type of activ-ity. The term 'academic development' may, however, be ambiguous. In this con-text, it refers to activities in an academic institution to improve the quality of its education. It is particularly related to activities that involve the academic faculty in their educational functions (course planning, teaching, assessment, supervision, tutoring and so on). It also involves working at the institutional level with structures and functions such as rule systems for recruitment and promotion of faculty, and the development of quality systems for the institution's education and strategies for supporting educational development projects. Academic developers consequently are people who are employed in positions with the main function of assisting the faculty and the institution in such developmental activities.

The academic developer, therefore, is a person in the academy who is actively and purposefully engaged in contributing to change – change of aspects of the academic culture and the practice of academics within it. Such changes are intended to influence the practice of educational activities within the institution, but they may also influence the identities of the members of the academic culture – as teachers. Consequently, the academic developer may – in the long run – contribute to influencing the identities of the academics. Seen in this perspective, the academic developers may have a significant and influential role in higher education that goes beyond changes in educational practice and into changes in culture and identities. Research shows that academic development activities have for instance resulted in conceptual changes among academic staff (Ho 2000) and to changes in thinking and practice concerning significant aspects of teaching and the role of the academic teachers (Gibbs and Coffey 2004; Lycke and Handal 2005). It is more difficult to demonstrate effects in terms of changes in culture and identities of academics as a result of academic development activities, and more and better research is needed in this respect (Lycke 1999; Trowler and Bamber 2005). Experiential evidence from my own extended practice in this field of work, however, indicates that such changes are definitely related to teachers participating in academic development activities. If this is so, it also becomes interesting to look more closely at the professional identity/identities of this professional group.

What does an academic developer do?

Academic developers work in different ways. The type of activity that most immediately meets the eye of a typical academic teacher is probably the course or workshop that one has been invited to and even participated in. These activities come in a broad range from the odd half-day workshop to extensive programmes for pedagogical qualifications of academic teachers up to diploma or master's degree level. Other activities are related to consultation work with departments, faculties or groups of teachers who plan for or are engaged in development of different aspects of their programmes (course structure, integration of new forms of teaching/learning experiences, assessment forms and so forth.) A third type of activity concerns services connected to systematic follow-up of course evaluations. Finally, at the institutional level, academic developers may be called upon to participate in development of quality systems for teaching, to serve on committees responsible for an institution's educational activities or to carry out and report on surveys related to critical aspects of such activities (amount and reasons for student non-completion in particular programmes, need for and provision of research supervision for master's and doctoral students and so on).

In some university settings academic developers work alone, even in positions where only part of their job is set off for such activities, but more often they work in units of different size, often rather small, sometimes in more comprehensive centres that also include technical services for teaching, ICT services to teachers or student advisory functions (Gosling 2001). The picture that emerges is consequently a rather heterogeneous one. I will return to this shortly.

Orientations and identities of academic developers

Given this background, it is not surprising that people who work as academic developers in higher education have different ways of referring to themselves and of describing their tasks, their functions and their identities (Fraser 1999, 2001; Land 2000, 2001). Some would call themselves 'staff developers', others 'faculty developers', 'educational developers' or 'organisational developers' and others again – as I do here – 'academic developers' (Brew 2002). Likewise, some might refer to themselves as 'developers', some as 'consultants', some as 'researchers and teachers' and others again as 'change agents'. In other words, this is by no means a unified and coherent professional group, if indeed it should at all be referred to as a profession in a strict meaning of the term (Handal 2000). The way they see themselves individually or as a group, on the one side, reflects their practice of academic development and, on the other side, influences it. In turn, their self-definition may also affect their professional identities.

A recent comprehensive and theoretically well grounded effort of a classification of conceptions of academic development is the one by Land (2000) in which he lists 12 *orientations* to academic development practice. They range from 'managerial', 'entrepreneurial' and 'researcher' to less immediately positive ones like 'political strategist' or 'vigilant opportunist' (Land 2001: 8). These orientations have come out of interviews with people in the UK working in positions as some sort of academic developer. They are not characteristics of individuals but identifiable and different *conceptions* that each individual professional may hold in different situations. In interpreting these results, Land also suggests that these conceptions mirror two important distinctions in faculty development practices. One is their tendency towards 'emancipatory' or 'domesticating' purposes (ibid., p. 4). The other is between practices related to individual academics and those related to the academic institution or system.

A perspective on identity formation

In trying to understand why academic developers conceive their roles so differently or, in other words, demonstrate quite different identities, we need some frame of reference for looking at professional identity formation. The theoretical framework I draw on here is based on socio-cultural theory. More specifically I will use some concepts developed by Etienne Wenger (1998), one of which is the 'community of practice'. He uses this concept to describe an organised group that works together in certain ways. It has to demonstrate in its practice *mutual engagement*, a *negotiated joint purpose* and a *shared repertoire of resources and practice*. In order to be considered a community of practice, an academic development unit should work according to common ideas about its practice and towards a common purpose and should share knowledge, ideas and a repertoire of practice as well as a set of resources for its work. Many academic development units would match these requirements, but – as we have seen – probably to different degrees. However, there are reasons to believe that the communality in intentions, knowledge and practices will be greater within than between such units.

Reasons for greater communality may be found in the way communities of practice are established according to Wenger. He describes two complementary processes. Firstly, there is a process of *participation*, which refers to purposive interaction among members in a group or community and which in turn leads to negotiations of ideas, meanings and practices and results in shared experiences. Participation involves social interaction among the members of the community of practice in work situations. Secondly, there is a process of *reification* in which the members of the faculty development unit together develop rules, material structures and symbols. These reifications represent what has been developed through joint participation in the practice of the community and they can even be handed over to new members of the community. Both these processes will operate more effectively within a unit working together in an institutional setting of a particular university than across separated units.

Particularly interesting in the present context is the connection that Wenger makes between communities of practice and *identity*. Wenger says: 'Building an identity consists of negotiating the meanings of our experiences of membership in social communities' (ibid. p. 145). We build our identities by participating in social communities where we negotiate with others' meaning in what we do. We define ourselves in relation to the (different) communities we participate in by identifying with them or by distancing ourselves from them. And we enter into negotiations with the other members of our communities of practice about our common practices and the ways we understand them. In this way, we form our identity in interaction with a community of practice through a process of influencing and being influenced, or rather through a process of negotiation as Wenger would prefer to say.

The academic developer's relation to different 'communities of practice'

Academic developers have (at least) *two* sets of communities to relate to in their professional functions: the community of practice of the academic development unit and the wider community of practice of the academy.

On the one hand the academic developer belongs to a small, *internal*, but often significant community of practice: that of the academic development unit. Participation in this professional community involves negotiation among academic development colleagues. This participation defines idealistic as well as realistic ways of understanding the aims and processes of academic development practice and is *reified* in statements of purpose, strategies and divisions of labour, internal organisation and what counts as symbols of success or failure. This is probably the community of practice that is most influential in contributing to the identity formation of its practitioners.

On the other hand academic developers work in close interaction with the academic community at large and with smaller disciplinary communities within it. *Participation* in and negotiation of their roles and activities in such communities also contribute to forming their identities. Rules (for ordering their services), organisational placements (in academic departments or in the administrative structure) and symbols (titles of positions) are *reifications* that these communities offer to the identity formation of the academic developer. Seen in this perspective, you become what you do and you do what is expected of you, or rather what the others let you do, in the academic community you work with. Thus the identity of the academic developer may be seen as developed also in interaction with the academic community at large or with the particular disciplinary subculture with which s/he works most regularly (like a particular faculty or department). We may refer to this as the academic developer's *external* community of practice.

With this as a background, we may look at characteristics of the institutional contexts where the primary, internal community of practice – the unit of academic development – is based, and where the process of identity formation (and reformation) as an academic developer is most influential. As we have seen these communities vary in *size*, in their *type of organisation and organisational placement* and in their *briefs*, and they are inhabited by members with quite diverse *educational and professional backgrounds* and belonging to *different professional organisations*. This means that the internal community of practice with which each academic developer interacts may be quite diverse and that – across units – the variation is quite substantial. I will look at two of these factors in more concrete terms.

Educational and professional backgrounds of academic developers

People who belong to a community of practice do not form their identities *solely* in negotiation with this community. They bring their 'luggage' from other communities to which they have historically belonged. Most of the people who work in academic development have not been educated particularly for this job through a professional programme designed particularly for such a role. They come with a number of *educational backgrounds* as physicists, historians, medical doctors or economists; they are people who have become so fascinated by the *teaching* of their discipline that they have changed their career paths to become developers of the teaching of their discipline rather than researchers and teachers within it. Some have been trained as personnel consultants, some as psychologists, some as schoolteachers and some as educationalists. Few academic developers have gone directly from a master's or PhD in education into academic development; rather they come with experiences from other jobs outside or inside institutions of higher education. This means that they have been through processes of identity formation in other communities of practice before entering the field of academic development. When entering academic development they bring their *former* professional identities with them into negotiations of their new identities as academic developers. These individual *latent* identities may interact with their actual new identity formation as academic developers – and in unpredictable ways. Depending on the educational and professional backgrounds of the people in academic development, one might expect that the understandings, meanings, values and orientations in these communities of practice will vary considerably, as may the identities of those who work within them.

Organisation and placement of academic development units

Academic developers do not negotiate their identities solely in *social* relations and in relation to the practices they engage in, but also in relation to the structural, material and organisational surroundings that they (and their unit) are part of. The placing and institutional form of the academic development unit will consequently constitute part of these formative conditions. If the unit is placed as part of the administrative structure of the institution, identified as an 'office' with positions holding management/administrative titles, this will probably influence its orientation to its work. The academic developers might in such cases see themselves in a technical or administrative support position. If, on the other hand, the faculty developers are placed as a unit within an ordinary university department, and hold academic positions, this might influence their orientation to their work differently. They might consider themselves more as colleagues of the academic staff. The practice of the unit would probably also be different as would the professional identities of those who work there.

Placing the unit in *the line of management* where it is given the mandate to implement the policy of the leadership of the institution may create a particular orientation of its work and its employees. Alternatively, placing the unit in a position where other faculties and departments may come and ask for consultation and help in *their* implementation of management policy establishes a different orientation of the faculty developers as well as of the people asking for their services. In the latter case, the academic developer is not seen as an instrument of the management in implementation of its policy but rather as assistance for the department or faculty in finding their ways to implement management policy. Such organisational differences will most likely also influence the culture of the unit and the identities of those who work there.

An international professional group

Despite the variation in titles, organisations, mandates and educational back-grounds discussed above, it is not difficult to identify academic developers as an international professional group – although loosely coupled. A large number of universities all over the world now seem to have some sort of staff and even 'units' working within this field. There are national informal networks or associations in many countries and an international umbrella for 17 of them in the International Consortium for Educational Development, with biannual conferences and a scholarly journal. Journals for the field also exist nationally with a varying scope, frequency of publication and level of scholarly ambition. This should also be considered a framework for professional identity formation. However, its strength varies. In some countries (Australia, the UK and the USA) they take the form of well established associations (HERDSA, SEDA and POD respectively) equipped with national journals and conferences (which also serve an international audience). In other countries, the individual academic developer (or unit) has much less professional support in these forms. It seems obvious that such differences have consequences for the collective professional identity formation of the academic developer.

The academic developer in the broader academic context

Academic developers in many cases operate as outsiders in disciplinary contexts and cultures where they are not fully at home and where their identities often are unknown and even contested. Consequently, they are rather *vulnerable.*

One way of meeting this challenge that is chosen in some universities is to staff the faculty development unit with people with different disciplinary backgrounds and allocate them for work with faculties with corresponding disciplinary orientations. This has the advantage for the academic developer of finding a more immediately legitimate place among the teachers s/he works with and being able to 'speak their language' (more or less literally). The disadvantage is that even this process of matching disciplinary background with disciplinary culture only works to a limited extent. Background knowledge of history gives limited legitimacy for consulting with faculty members who teach modern languages, although they may have a common connection to the faculty of humanities. In practice, this often leads to an organisation where most of the faculty developers are widely deployed within the university, often with only part-time functions as developers and lacking continuous contact with a professional collegial group of their own. This may also influence their identity which may be more dominated by the disciplinary communities of practice that they work with and less by their colleague developers.

Alternatively, faculty developers may be located together in a unit staffed with people who may be able to work generically with different disciplines. This solution provides the academic developers with a community of practice populated with people of their 'own kind', which might provide better opportunities for professional discussion and help in their work and form part of a continuous process of further professional development. In many cases, it may be an advantage to be an outsider to a disciplinary culture as you may see things differently from what is culturally taken for granted by the faculty. It also gives the faculty developer the legitimate possibility to ask 'silly' but still authentic questions – questions about things that are taken for granted locally but that may still be challenged for developmental purposes. This provides the faculty developer with a potential for analysing and interpreting the educational culture and practice of a department in ways that may be new and consequently challenging for the department. However, it also creates a certain risk of rejection if the challenge is too strong or the department feels too insecure or threatened.

Some academic developers prefer to *seek secure arenas* where their identity is known, accepted and not challenged and where they can pass as members – although somewhat peripheral – of the departmental community of practice. Others are *excitement/tension seekers* who love the challenge of being among – and in confrontation with – representatives of different cultures. These differences are probably partly due to differences in personality but may also reflect differences in the personal feeling of self-security that comes with experience.

Two orientations – and the way they are different

The identity of academic developers in relation to their academic colleagues in different parts of the university is discussed by Ashford *et al.* (2004). The metaphors used there to characterise the academic developer as a professional are thought-provoking. Two quite different orientations for academic developers appear (here slightly adapted/adjusted):

Orientation A: *Change agent*, guide, expert
Orientation B: *Midwife*, interpreter, collaborator

These positions differ concerning the *degree of direction* and *mission* involved in the developer's practice.

The *change agent* orientation (A above) implies that the developer sees her/himself as someone who wants to contribute to *change* in some particular *direction*. There is a directional aim for his/her activities. There is something particular in terms of the outcome of the process that the change agent wants to achieve and which it is not entirely up to the 'client' to decide about. This aim may, for instance, be some change in understanding and/or practice in a particular direction, although not always very specifically described. S/he would at least *not* be satisfied with *any* change, for instance a change in the direction opposite to the one s/he had in mind. The change agent or 'guide' (see above) definitely has such a direction in mind. The 'expert' will also be looked upon to give direction, based on knowledge and understanding of the situation where choices have to be made.

The *midwife* orientation (B above), on the other hand, implies another identity.

The developer sees her/himself as *assisting* in a process of other people's development towards what they themselves want to do or become. S/he will provide facilities and support (material, social, intellectual, emotional) for such development, but will not in the same way point out the direction of the development or the outcome of it. The midwife metaphor is illuminating in this respect, as not many midwives would try to make a mother give birth to someone else's baby than her own. This orientation may also imply that the developer acts as someone who manages meaning across contexts, who tries to interpret a situation (for instance teaching) in a different 'language', using terminology from a (more) theoretical position(s), or who tries to explain to faculty what is *actually* meant by the 'edict' that is issued by central management, without changing the message.

These orientations are here formulated as extremes on a dimension, but in practice with a number of viable alternative positions in between. However, they may serve as a means of clarifying substantially different orientations that may influence or be a result of the academic developer's identity. Which one is the most effective is difficult to decide. The change agent position will provide possibilities for implementing a direction of change within an institution that is considered critical for the quality of its teaching. It may, however, be more difficult to implement as it may be experienced as alien (or even contrary) to the ideas of the grassroots. The midwife position will give more disparate results when it comes to direction of the changes but may be more effective in its implementation because it corresponds to the ideas of those who will be implementing it. The optimum combination is probably to work according to the midwife position but challenge the faculty to consider making 'its' development contribute, at least to some extent, in the direction that the change agent would like to see happening. This is a delicate balance to achieve.

The academic developer in the role of the court jester

Another metaphor (Ashford *et al.* 2004) that is more or less independent of the two positions discussed above, pictures the academic developer as the Fool or the *court jester* at the ancient royal courts. The jester may influence those in power by offering controversial – yet often wise – ideas in a form that is simultaneously convincing and playful, thereby permitting the Fool to get away with it. This jesting role, however, represents an inferior and ridiculed position. The Fool is in a position to teach, to point out the folly of others – to speak truth to power as it were – but also runs the risk of rejection, humiliation or even punishment for overstepping the cultural mark, and always within the tacit mutual recognition of the Fool's ultimately inferior status. There are many positive connotations to this metaphor: the Fool is often the wise guy who points out important things, who knows how to influence and motivate people and change the course of events. Conversely, it catches the role of inferiority and ridicule that academic developers sometimes experience. Neither should we forget that the metaphor also implies the use of indirect and subtle ways to achieve desired results. There is a clear idea on the part of the Fool about which results are important to achieve and there is a definite element of hiding the real message so that the receiver is not aware of what is really happening. This element of *deception*, possibly *manipulation*, is one that is difficult to combine with the ethos of the academy and the value of open argumentative discourse, and should consequently be avoided.

Academic teacher – academic developer; a complementary role-relationship

The metaphors discussed above illustrate that, when forming their *own* identity, the academic developers also define the role of the other – those whom they work with, 'develop', 'change' or 'collaborate with'. It is like in any other complementary role-relationship: the two positions define each other. Consequently academic developers will, in many cases, by the way they practice their roles, 'enforce' their identity on the faculty they work with. Depending on the reaction to this, the academic developer may see the faculty as reluctant or congenial to the developer's ideas.

Vice versa the faculty may see the academic developer either as an *intruder* or as a *contributor*. Seen in any of these roles they may try to force a role upon her/ him according to *their* conceptions, needs and interests. This may be experienced so massively by the academic developer that it is difficult not to be influenced by it and end up in a role that one may really not appreciate. Repeated experiences of this kind may also influence the identity of the person who encounters them.

A possibly fruitful role for the academic developer in an academic institution

In trying to adjust to contexts that vary in terms of disciplinary content, degree of acceptance, rejection or indifference to (assistance in) educational development, how can academic developers avoid becoming like 'a chameleon on a tartan rug'? How can they 'talk to crowds and keep [their] virtue, or walk with kings nor lose the common touch', as Kipling put it? Probably by developing a reasonably clear identity that is in keeping with the role they can manage to cut out for themselves in their institution. This means that in an academic institution they must act academically. In the next section, I will develop this further. I will here change my perspective to a more normative one: What is potentially the most fruitful role for the academic developer?

The critical friend

The role – or identity – that I would like to pursue further here is that of the *critical friend*. It has proven difficult to actually find the origins of this concept. It seems to be used by different authors without a uniform reference (Simons 1987; Tiller 1990; Handal 1999). However, it may be connected to two lines of thought: one is the idea of individual 'practical theories' (Polanyi 1958, 1966; Handal and Lauvås 1987; Johannessen 1988) or 'cultural codes' (Arfwedsson 1983) of groups. Such theories or codes function as bases for individual or collective practice and are more or less open to reflection and to change. The tutor or consultant who is assisting a practitioner in this process may work precisely as a friend who through assisted reflection tries to help someone identifying problems and possibilities in daily practice. The other line of thought is the idea of being critical (Carr and Kemmis 1986) and of posing questions that challenge someone's thinking and practice, possibly also from perspectives outside those that the practitioners themselves feel familiar with.

At first glance the concept may seem to contain a contradiction, the one between friendship and criticism. Friends are people who are close to us, who support us and provide confirmation. They often disregard our weak spots or excuse them, rather than confront us with them. Criticism is generally conveyed by someone who represents contrasting or alternative points of view or other interests and who may even be hostile to us. But, given more than a cursory thought, it is clear that a real friend is someone on whom we can rely and who will even hold a critical mirror before us when necessary.

Criticism as an academic virtue

Criticism has always enjoyed a strong position in the academic world, both in rhetoric and in practice. A common element of scientific work is the critical approach to accepted methods, results, interpretations and explanations. Without criticism of existing knowledge, we would experience almost no scientific progress. Thus, criticism of scientific processes and products is an accepted and highly valued academic activity. It finds its practical forms in seminar discussions among students at all levels, in referee activities for journals and conferences and in the ritualised discourse in defence of a doctoral thesis. New members of the academy are socialised into it via these central elements of academic culture, by first acting as observers of it and later personally taking an active part.

At times, such criticism can be merciless – particularly between competing or antagonistic groups or between different schools of researchers. More often, however, it is not. Good criticism is generally relevant, argumentative, well documented and something we learn from. The examples mentioned above, of situations where criticism is practised, indicate that there are times when criticism is very positive. The critic – by providing a thorough analysis – points out which aspects of a work contribute to a positive as well as a negative evaluation. In other words, we operate with a concept of criticism that is by no means *solely* negative.

Some scholars who have worked with evaluations have chosen to refer to such criticism with the French term 'critique'. This term evokes connotations of the type of criticism that is carried out in various forms of *art*. In such instances, a 'connoisseur' in the field comments on the positive and negative aspects of an artistic work (a painting, book, play, film and so on) based on his/her qualified judgement – usually in a public forum.

Learning to live in an academic culture entails, among other things, tackling the roles of giving and receiving criticism in ways that are accepted by this culture. To a varying degree, we all become masters of this trade, and those who are really proficient in the art of critique receive high cultural esteem. For all of us, critical appreciation is a central element in our academic identity.

I bring up the concept of criticism or critique in this context, because academics – as *researchers* – are used to and positively inclined towards the idea, and are used to working with 'critical friends' who read and discuss their papers and articles, support and correct their work and celebrate the successful acceptance of their products.

The same is not as obvious when it comes to academics as *teachers*. There is no similar tradition for the academic teacher to be surrounded by critical friends, and the role of being one is not well developed. Still, I think this is a fruitful identity for the academic developer precisely because there is a well-known and valued parallel in the world of research which may function as a model. *Acting as a critical friend is acting academically* and is consequently a role for the academic developer which is in line with the university culture.

A critical friendship involves:

- a relationship of confidence and trust;
- a belief in the professional competence of the critical friend;
- willingness in the critical friend to form and express judgement;
- expectation of personal integrity of the critical friend;
- empathy.

Consequently this is the type of relationship that academic developers might strive to establish with their colleague teachers in the university. It takes time to build and it requires positive experiences on both sides to legitimise it. It demands a combination of honesty and tact and is first and foremost based on theoretical and experiential knowledge of teaching and learning in higher education. The critical friend has to have something to contribute in terms of analyses, perspectives and advice, but it must be in keeping with the goals and intentions that the teacher (or department) has in mind.

Different forms of critique with more or less direction

Where is the identity of the critical friend placed in relation to the two orientations described above – the change agent and the midwife? It is evidently closer to the second than to the first of these. The starting point is the way the academic teachers see the world of teaching practice and their place in it. The critical friend as midwife tries to assist the practitioner in understanding teaching in a richer and more varied perspective (by means of theory about the phenomenon). In this way, the critical friend follows up the ideas of articulation of and reflection on practical theories of those involved in order to establish potential ground for further development. But it even involves a touch of the critical friend as the change agent. The academic developer also brings to the academic community of practice ideas for development that s/he thinks might be fruitful to pursue.

When being invited to a department or group of teachers for 'consultation' about some aspect of educational practice they are concerned with, the academic developer might first try to clarify the intentions of the 'client'. What do they want to do, and why? The relevant type of critique in this phase is *endo-paradigmatic*, which means that it operates *within* the collective practical theories or code of the community of practice of the client and does not challenge its boundaries. In practice the faculty developer might say: 'If I understand you correctly, this is what you want to achieve and this is what you suggest doing – and this is why. In that case I would suggest that you . . . and keep in mind . . . in order to make it work optimally.'

Alternatively, or at the next stage, the client would be invited to reflect on some of the intentions underlying the existing or envisaged practice, but from different – even challenging – perspectives. It might take this form: 'The way you plan your teaching/programme implies a . . . way of understanding learning. An alternative understanding might be . . . . What do you think about that? What would be the consequences of this alternative for your teaching/programme?' In this case the academic developer would be exerting an *exo-paradigmatic* type of critique that challenges and goes beyond the client's paradigm of teaching and learning. Even in this last case, the critique is presented in solidarity with the client with the intention of serving the client to move in his/her own direction, but in a direction that may have changed in a way that is informed by the perspectives of the academic developer.

Conclusion

This chapter has shown that academic developers have a wide range of identities and that there are good reasons for this: they work in different organisational settings, with different mandates, with very varied career backgrounds and with a relatively weak professional organisational support. This has consequences for their *participation* in communities of practice and for the *reification* of their knowledge, values and practices; elements that are critical for their identity formation. This also has consequences for their practice as academic developers and ultimately therefore for the identity formation of academic teachers as *teachers*. This might seem like a situation which is difficult to change. And it is, particularly in a short-term perspective and on an international scale. However, I have argued that a fruitful identity for academic developers to strive for is that of the critical friend. The primary reason for this is that it corresponds with roles that are deeply embedded in the academic culture when it comes to research and correspondingly might be more readily accepted and implemented than some of the other metaphors of identity that have been discussed.

In order to make professional development happen along this line, it is first of all important to identify a professional identity that corresponds to the ethos of the academy – as argued above. Further, it must build on classical mechanisms for professional development like providing professional education programmes for academic developers, strengthening their professional organisations, conducting research not only on educational aspects of higher education but also on academic development in itself and expanding the professional literature (journals, monographs and textbooks). Increasing the possibilities for academic developers to engage in research may turn out to be particularly influential in shaping identities in keeping with the ideas suggested above, although this has not been discussed in this chapter. These are all mechanisms that have proven helpful in the development of other professional groups and the identity formation of their members.

Chapter 5

Beyond administration and management

Changing professional identities in UK higher education

Celia Whitchurch

Introduction

Despite an ongoing process of professionalisation, the roles and identities of administrators and managers in UK higher education are neither clearly conceptualised nor understood. Over time, a relatively homogeneous group of staff in the pre-1992 sector, which modelled its collective identity on a tradition of public service, has expanded and diversified. Roles have become increasingly fluid, and career pathways are no longer linear or pre-determined. The identities and voices of this group of staff, therefore, remain susceptible to uncertain and even contradictory constructions.

Conventional descriptors of professional identity, such as affiliations to knowledge, institutional or system structures, fail to capture the dynamics of day-to-day working and professional relationships in contemporary higher education institutions. Nor do broad-brush terms such as 'management' and 'administration' offer sufficient clarity. Moreover, the polarisation of work between academic activity and a separate, supporting infrastructure is becoming outmoded. New understandings are required, therefore, for a range of professional identities and voices that increasingly cross academic and organisational boundaries. This chapter considers these changes, drawing in part on interviews with 35 senior and middle-level administrators and managers in higher education institutions in the UK.

Contexts

As a starting point, the definition of 'managers and administrators' given in a publication by the UK Higher Education Staff Development Agency (HESDA 2001) is used. This distinguishes them from contiguous groups such as clerical and technical staff; teaching and learning, library and information science professionals; and academic managers such as pro-vice-chancellors. Professional administrators and managers may be either specialists, such as those in finance and human resources, or generalists, such as those in student services or departmental management. However, as will be seen, there is increasing fluidity between functions and identities as the composition of professional staff in universities diversifies. Nevertheless, when references are made to 'professional' staff in this chapter, this refers to administrators and managers, to differentiate between them and academic managers, such as deans or pro-vice-chancellors. It is not, however, intended to imply that other categories of staff in universities are not also professionals in their own right.

In UK higher education, professional administration and management had its origins in a tradition of public administration, exemplified in government service. This was strongest in the pre-1992 universities, in which 'the Administration' was seen as a discrete entity, separate from the academic community that it 'served'. The identities of professional staff were based on that of the disinterested civil servant, who vocalised the legal and regulatory aspects of policy and its implementation, providing continuity and upholding standards. The academic administrator's role as 'guardian of the regulations' (Barnett 2000: 133) has its origins in this tradition. Thus, academic administrators were regarded as a repository of information, providing the collective memory of an institution, which was passed on from one generation to the next. They were a source of continuity, compensating for the limited terms of office of rotating academic managers such as deans and pro-vice-chancellors (McNay 2005).

In the academic administration model, relationships tended to be structured and hierarchical, so that staff replicated the work patterns and approaches they learnt from those senior to them, rather than creating new spaces. To quote one head of administration:

> There was a sort of perception that you served your time and you knew your time would come and all the rest of it.

National salary scales for administrators and managers, related to those of academic staff, reinforced the idea of a professional cadre of staff who might build a career across institutions. Attached to the Administration would be expert functions such as finance, estates, and human resources, but there would be little permeability between them. Strains of the civil service model still exist; particularly in what is sometimes referred to as academic administration (Barnett 1993), that is, registry and secretariat functions.

The post-1992 (former polytechnic) sector had a stronger ethos of 'management', whereby institutions were staffed by permanent directorates, rather than rotating academic managers as in the pre-1992 sector. According to one head of institution, this created 'a bit of a gap' between administrative staff undertaking clerical, process-oriented roles, and managers operating at the directorate level. It was not easy, in this context, to combine the role of administrator and manager, or to move from one to the other. By contrast, in the pre-1992 sector, administrative staff at all levels were likely to be involved in giving regulatory and policy advice to academic colleagues. Because of these different cultures, there was little interchange of professional staff between pre- and post-1992 institutions before the sectors merged but, as cross-sector movements began to take place after 1992, the system became more heterogeneous. What began as a relatively cohesive cadre of professional administrators in the pre-1992 sector (Bosworth 1986), therefore, has become a coalescence of overlapping professional groups across the system (Allen and Newcomb 1999; Whitchurch, 2006a), which is subject to constant reconfiguration.

Sourcing the identities of professional administrators and managers

In order to describe distinctions between administration and management in a theoretical frame, the identities and voices they offer can be modelled in terms of 'soft' and 'hard' characteristics, as shown in Figure 5.1. Building on Becher and Trowler (2001: 36), and Trow (1993), 'soft' attributes represent people-oriented, conciliatory approaches, aimed at achieving either a personal service, such as welfare advice to students (soft administration), or a consensual policy framework for decision-making (soft management). The softer approaches of each modulate the more purposeful quasi-legal upholding of regulatory processes, standards and values (hard administration), and the pursuit of an institution's unique selling proposition in the market (hard management).

'Soft' administration

Soft administration traditionally encompasses staff in supportive roles; typically protecting others from potential hazards. In a student services environment, this would include one-to-one advice, designed to ensure that individual students who come into a one-stop shop obtain the academic and pastoral attention that they require. Similarly, in a school office, a business manager might provide a personal briefing to the head of school on the budgetary and management information required for a management meeting, so that the head is not ambushed in a debate about the filling of a post. This kind of work is resource-intensive, geared towards meeting the particular requirements of a particular client at a specific time and location. Information has to be conveyed in such a way that can be understood by, and be of benefit to, the receiver. It therefore demands an ability to comprehend and empathise with the needs of another, and its voice can be characterised by the term 'generosity'.

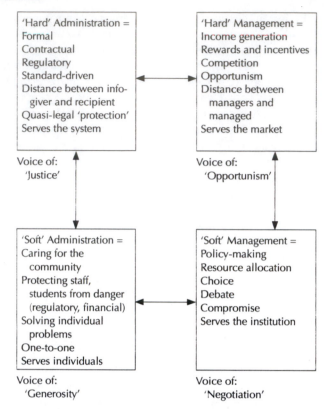

'Hard' Administration =
Formal
Contractual
Regulatory
Standard-driven
Distance between info-
    giver and recipient
Quasi-legal 'protection'
Serves the system

'Hard' Management =
Income generation
Rewards and incentives
Competition
Opportunism
Distance between
    managers and
    managed
Serves the market

Voice of:
    'Justice'

Voice of:
    'Opportunism'

'Soft' Administration =
Caring for the
    community
Protecting staff,
    students from danger
    (regulatory, financial)
Solving individual
    problems
One-to-one
Serves individuals

'Soft' Management =
Policy-making
Resource allocation
Choice
Debate
Compromise
Serves the institution

Voice of:
    'Generosity'

Voice of:
    'Negotiation'

Figure 5.1 'Soft' and 'hard' characteristics of administration and management.

'Hard' administration

The idea of 'hard' administration is drawn from ideas of public service account-ability, even-handedness and justice, and is expressed in rules and boundaries that regulate activity and ensure fair play. It also involves an increasing burden of le-gal and statutory requirements (such as health and safety, financial and academic audit, data protection and freedom of information). It emphasises the application of procedure, rather than bespoke or individual solutions. It is system-oriented and is designed to maintain security of provision and to avoid disaster, such as breaches of legal requirements or financial accountabilities. It remains a critical thread in the lives of professional administrators and managers, not least because of the reputational damage that can be caused by adverse publicity attracted by breakdowns in good practice. As external accountabilities have grown, this func-tion has become more high profile in meeting, for instance, the requirements of the quality assessment agencies for teaching and research, and an increasingly litigious environment, in relation to both staff and students. It therefore speaks a language characterised by the application of 'justice'.

'Soft' management

'Soft' management brings understandings of issues such as institutional potential and reputation into the frame when hard decisions are being made, for instance, around market positioning and the diversification of income streams. Thus, the financial risks and advantages of expansion into a new campus serving part-time, non-traditional students are weighed against the qualitative impact on the shape of academic programmes, modes of delivery and the university's overall teaching and research profile. A 'soft' management view would consider the future of small-scale subject areas in the context of synergies between disciplines, rather than purely in terms of cost benefit analysis, and look for options around the possible re-alignment of programmes.

Internally, 'soft' management is characterised by negotiation in the distribution of resources, using external market pressures as one, but not the sole, element in decision-making. In tight circumstances it would focus on capacity building, playing to institutional strengths and adjusting activities to achieve optimal solutions of benefit to a majority of people. Finally, 'soft' management promotes institutional research and development, so that traditional roles in anticipating and solving problems develop into broader scenario-building capabilities, as the institution's mission is contextualised and reappraised against its environment. It therefore speaks a language characterised by 'negotiation'.

'Hard' management

'Hard' management represents the business aspects of operating in a market environment, with the aim of generating commercial income. It is driven primarily by considerations of financial profit and loss, and also by ambitions to build new markets. If it becomes dominant in an institution, it is likely, also, to create an ethos of internal competition, usually through reward and incentive systems, such as the return of overheads to principal research investigators, or the pricing of services between internal 'customers'. Thus, internal competition between individuals or departments is used to point up performance levels, for instance, in terms of research income or overseas student fees, and a win–lose culture may inform strategic direction, putting pressure on staff not simply to operate at maximum effectiveness, but also to demonstrate their value via competitive benchmarking. Its language is, therefore, characterised by 'opportunism', geared towards seeking and recognising gaps in provision, and how new needs might be recognised and met.

Legacies of administration

The civil service tradition, informed by an ethos of public service, underpinned those aspects of administration associated with ensuring consistency, fairness and appropriate standards, and for providing disinterested judgement in the application of policy and procedure. The voice of 'service' that the administrator provided was, therefore, not unique or distinctive to the individual, and could be substituted by the voice of another person trained in the same administrative cadre. Arising out of this, there is a sense in which the public administration ethos offered a kind of non-identity, described by Self as:

> the anonymous and cloistered role of the high official, which derives from an environment that is deliberately protected from personal po-litical involvement, as well as being somewhat removed from direct operational tasks.
>
> (Self 1972: 180)

Moodie and Eustace (1974) applied this to a university setting:

> They [administrators] formulate issues and arguments, they count, they inform and they render all necessary services to their master, but they have to act in accordance with decisions which they have no formal power to determine.
>
> (Moodie and Eustace 1974: 157)

This comment also has the implicit suggestion of subservience, thus a suppressed identity and voice. In the words of one respondent:

> Administrators were expected to be seen and not heard, not to speak at a committee, except perhaps the Registrar, and then only when asked to give an opinion, you know, 'Registrar, can you remind us of the Regula-tions' or something, that kind of thing.
>
> (Head of administration)

In this situation, the only way an administrator could offer information or articulate an opinion would be to act as 'ventriloquist', enabling academic colleagues to speak with authority on matters for which the administrator provided the missing text, for instance, admissions figures, financial information, or intelligence about activities of competitor institutions. Individuals, therefore, adopted a generic identity that depended for its existence on a common system. In Hall's terms, they were characterised more by 'sameness' than 'difference' (Hall 2000: 16). This kind of inheritance contributes to the 'invisibility' described by Szekeres (2004, 2006), the 'liminality' described by Gornall (1999) and Conway (2000), and the lack of recognition or status offered to administrative staff, described by McInnis (1998).

The anonymity of official personae created rituals described by one head of institution as being like those of a 'medieval court', with associated forms of address according to one's place in the social system. The various constituencies of the university colluded in this, notwithstanding any private understandings about the value of professional staff. This led to a kind of muted communication or dialogue, whereby the 'silence' around what was not articulated publicly was filled by tacit, private understandings as to who was the source of information, even if that person did not act as spokesperson. As one head of administration put it:

> I think that senior academics . . . recognise full well the value that they get from support services . . . *whether they would admit that* always is another matter. [author's italics]

Thus, academic and professional managers deferred to the formal enactment of roles, at the same time as obliquely acknowledging the other's power and authority:

> There are quite a number of occasions where you are introduced by somebody and they say that you're the person who really runs the University.
>
> (Head of administration)

Rhetoric around ideas of 'service' also masked any agency on the part of professional administrators and managers:

> What I hope we do is provide a service. It may be a service the university *doesn't know* it needs, but it does and we provide it as best we can.
>
> (Head of administration)

This comment demonstrates the kind of underplayed confidence of the traditional civil servant, whereby all parties are aware of underlying dependencies in the relationship, but enact these within a formal ritual of advice given and received. In this scenario, the voices in the dialogue become oblique, and their expression indirect. This 'muteness' can be used to create an element of inscrutability, as described by another head of administration:

> There is that thing about actually finding out from people what it is they think without giving a lot away.

Thus, whereas in some circumstances silence may be interpreted as implying invisibility or insignificance, in others it may also infer control, and be used as a tool in situations requiring negotiating or political skills, depending on the degree of agency adopted by an individual.

Administration meets management

The 1980s saw the beginnings of a journey towards management that represented a significant culture shift, particularly for professional staff with a background in academic administration (Whitchurch 2004, 2005). Major changes had occurred in the working environment, whereby reductions in government funding meant that institutions were obliged to become more market oriented, so that:

Any time after about 1980, you really couldn't be a strong academic institution if you weren't either stinking rich or . . . sufficiently well-managed to . . . stay the right side of the line.

(Head of administration)

Many UK universities responded by establishing devolved budgetary and planning arrangements, superimposing distributed management arrangements and executive decision-making on hierarchical committee and administrative structures. This process has been documented by Clark (1995, 1998, 2004), who refers to a 'central steering core', or senior management team, with professional managers out-posted to faculties and schools to stimulate activity in the 'academic heartlands'.

Under these arrangements, posts in schools and faculties that had come within the purview of the academic administration, and had had titles such as 'assistant registrar', were converted into 'business manager' posts, with responsibility for budgeting and resource allocation. At this point, people who had originated as academic administrators came face-to-face with 'management'. Staff in such posts often had dual lines of accountability, for instance, with a direct line management relationship with a professional colleague in the university centre, and a dotted line relationship with an academic manager, such as a dean. For others, the reverse might apply. They were, therefore, likely to be influenced by the needs of the academic locale in which they were located, as well as being expected to express a corporate, institutional view.

The multi-vocality that could arise from such dual lines of responsibility is illustrated by a business manager in an academic department, who had strong loyalty to colleagues there. At one point, however, there had been a lack of congruence between her approach and that of the head of department in producing a business plan for presentation to the central management team. The manager described the necessity of appearing to face two ways, in order to distance herself from a plan with which she felt uncomfortable:

I had to see [a member of the university's senior management team] afterwards and say that this . . . didn't have my input in the way I would have wanted it, because I don't see how it's sustainable; so I felt really awful saying, you know, 'this is me . . . I don't want to have to defend it because I can't.'

This brings into focus the tensions for someone who had line management responsibilities to a head of department, but did not want their competence to be questioned by the central management team, and felt that their professional credibility might be at stake in both locales. The use of the words 'this is me' illustrates that, while the individual had allegiances to the department, she had another voice that was asserted when she wished to distance herself from a document that might have reflected badly on her. She was, therefore, trying to locate herself in two places at once. This meant using different voices to express different aspects of her identity (as a team player in her department, and as a corporate player at the centre).

Notwithstanding these kinds of tensions, staff who made the journey from 'administration' towards 'management' found themselves having a closer involvement in executive decision-making, in the choices to be made around resource allocation, and in the implementation of change strategies. They also assumed more developmental roles, such as assessing opportunities by which the university might extend its range of activity, for instance, through franchise operations. This meant taking a view about future possibilities, as well as the means of achieving them. Yet, at the same time, there is evidence of discomfort on the part of both academics and professionals about openly acknowledging this movement towards 'management'. Although it might be understood implicitly that references to 'administration' involve a spectrum of activity, including 'management', this is not necessarily articulated publicly. Thus, one manager reflected that:

> It's . . . safer to call it administration, but we all know we mean management.

Again, this suggests a dual identity, one for public consumption as an 'administrator', and another for private consumption as a 'manager', and also a dissonance arising from the way that these concepts are articulated and understood across the university community. Similarly, at national level, there has been a reluctance to move away from the term 'administration' in the titles of the two professional bodies representing professional managers and administrators, that is the Association of Heads of University Administration, and the Association of University Administrators, possibly because of lingering sensitivities deriving from a public administration ethos, about where final responsibility lies for 'managing' the university. This is in contrast, for instance, to the situation in Australia, where the national association is titled the Association of Tertiary Education *Managers*. Such sensitivity may also derive from a literature that polarises management and academic agendas (for instance, Parker and Jary 1995; Prichard and Willmott 1997; Deem 1998), and from which the term 'managerial(ism)' has emerged, with pejorative overtones of excessive power and control on the part of managers. The result has been a confusing of the two terms, whereby 'managerial' has become interchangeable with 'management', with the implication that the meanings of the two words have become synonymous.

Although career professionals undoubtedly regard themselves as managers (Whitchurch 2005), it would seem that their hesitancy about using the term 'management' derives not only from the perceived legitimacy or otherwise of the term 'management' in universities, but also from the perceived legitimacy of administrators and managers having a distinctive voice and identity that is separate from, as well as derived from, academic identities. These uncertainties are reflected in the statement that:

> good university management means recognising and distinguishing what
> is best left relatively 'unmanaged' from what must be firmly managed.
>
> (Holmes 1998: 110)

One possible interpretation of this comment is that functional areas such as finance and estates must be firmly managed, whereas other areas such as academic policy development may evolve in a more oblique fashion. However, as academic activity becomes entwined with contributory functions such as study skills, outreach, or the construction of sophisticated research facilities, it is increasingly difficult to place clear boundaries around 'management' and 'academic' activity.

As these distinctions blur, professional staff find themselves occupying space that gives them greater discretion in the way that they contribute to complex institutional agendas, particularly in relation to extended projects that have accrued around, for instance, student support and welfare, and business partnership (Whitchurch 2006b). In these kinds of areas they are constructing and managing their own working territories and managing collaboratively with colleagues, as well as continuing to undertake operational and line management in conventional office settings. There would appear, therefore, to be a challenge for a new generation of professionals to find identities and voices that both are distinctive to them as individuals and can be regarded as legitimate in the university.

Service meets partnership

Concurrent with these developments, there are indications that those continuing to operate in service-oriented roles, in 'academic administration' mode, which in the past offered stable understandings about responsibilities and boundaries, are finding themselves increasingly exposed. On the one hand, this approach could make for synergy if joint working between head of department and administrator was symbiotic:

> Like Sir Humphrey [in the UK television series *Yes Minister*] . . . taking a
> burden of work off the head of department's shoulders.
>
> (Departmental administrator)

On the other hand, it could also create hazards, for instance, if the head of department decided to distance herself from a policy that the administrator was responsible for implementing, after the policy had been agreed. The administrator could then become positioned as an outsider, and find herself in a vulnerable space:

> You do feel, not 'naked' . . ., but you are 'open to the elements' kind of
> thing.

Not only is there potential for harmony to become disharmony, but any harmony that is achieved is likely to be provisional. Within this model, therefore, individuals could be caught between an identity that is dependent on that of academic colleagues and one that places them outside the structural frame in which they thought they were located.

As administration moved towards management, the idea of service began to mutate into an ethos of 'partnership', in which professional staff assumed greater agency and responsibility. One head of administration described this more discretionary kind of relationship between professional staff and their academic colleagues as a:

> notion of partnership, that we're working in this together; . . . you know, 'I am perfectly happy for you to get all the kudos for that, but I'm not necessarily going to hide completely behind'.

In partnership working, professional staff not only become more visible, but also more accountable, for instance, for the success or otherwise of projects which they are responsible for designing and delivering. This means that they not only take or share responsibility, but also are exposed directly to the effects of success or failure, for instance, the impact that this may have on their career and professional life chances.

A recruitment manager exemplified the repositioning of someone who, as an admissions officer, would traditionally have been in a position of 'service' to a faculty dean. She referred to this inheritance as 'this façade, that we pretend exists'. However, while the faculty dean technically retained line management responsibility for the admissions process, the professional manager had, in practice, been given delegated authority to take executive action in circumstances for which she had built up case law through practice and precedent:

> Unless there's a really serious problem, the dean wouldn't be directly involved . . . but it does give a useful framework at times so, for instance, if a department and I have a major disagreement over a student, then the dean can act as the arbiter.
>
> (Recruitment manager)

The relationship had moved, therefore, from a hierarchical to a triangular one (Figure 5.2). This shift of relationship represents, for the professional manager, a move from simply being the provider of technical advice about, for instance,

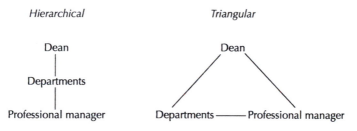

Figure 5.2 From a hierarchical to a triangular relationship.

A-level scores and meeting target numbers, to having a recognised place in a coalition of management, in a flatter, more collaborative structure. As a member of this coalition, she was contributing to judgements about meeting student intake targets, the impact of broader entry qualifications, and the effect that any decision would have on the teaching process. In Barnett's terms, therefore, she was part of the 'conversation' between the academic community and the institution (Barnett 1993). Thus, communication had become two-way, and the professional manager an active player in dialogue and debate, having a legitimate and independent voice, rather than being solely a conduit for information. These shifts of positioning are reflected in the evolution of a discourse of 'partnership' from one of 'service'.

Overlapping territories

Partnership working involves both a sharing of common territories, where academic and management decisions coalesce, and also the creation of new, often composite territories, where professional managers might bring together the contributions of others, and also make an independent contribution. One senior manager described her relationship with academic colleagues in terms of equivalence, but difference:

> I hope they would see me . . . as working in partnership . . . especially once we've worked together for a little while and they begin to appreciate the sort of things that my involvement can bring . . . and certainly I don't feel that I'm providing a service.
>
> (Senior manager)

Feeling that she was working in partnership enabled this person to define her own space, at the same time as 'educating' colleagues about what she was able to offer, for instance, the ability to take a holistic view of how a planning document might be written. Thus, she was continuously 'negotiating new meanings' (Wenger 1998: 226) with her colleagues.

Likewise, a finance officer describes how she moved in and out of her specialist function:

> operating on the outside of finance, to[wards] the university, and operating inside finance, having a very effective team.
>
> (Finance officer)

She described this mutuality as 'a bond and a relationship' that she had developed with colleagues in the senior management team, effectively creating something at the interface that went beyond service, consisting of the building of a shared field of practice. Although, in this case, common territory was facilitated by the existence of a head of institution who was 'financially cute' (literally crossing into the finance officer's territory), the finance officer was also proactive in crossing boundaries to understand and acknowledge academic mindsets, whilst placing academic agendas in a practical context:

> You need to have a community of scholars; . . . But I can . . . understand the arguments for . . . leading edge research, blue skies thinking, creating new ideas . . . which actually service the economy in the longer run.
>
> (Finance officer)

Similarly, a human resources officer shows appreciation of the way that meanings are constructed in the university, and how these can exist across internal subcultures, whereby people 'name and frame' (Bernstein 2000) the same activity in different ways:

> I do management development with them, what I would call management development. They wouldn't call it that, so what they'd say and what I'd say are two very different things.

Furthermore, she had picked up a discomfort among academic colleagues when she was speaking in the language of her own professional background:

> That's our jargon and that's our language . . . you can see they are fidgeting.

This recognises that a number of professional languages were being spoken, and that it was necessary to find a language that would 'meet [colleagues] half way, because they [too] have a language of their own, that has been developed culturally'. An awareness of these different languages in the university, therefore, is the first step in acquiring the facility to interpret and translate them. This facility then provides the opportunity for professional staff to sojourn amongst different speakers, to listen to and to draw out meanings from a number of voices.

The impact of the post-1992 institutions in furthering crossover between management and academic territories is illustrated by a head of administration who had worked in both sectors. After her move to a post-1992 institution, she had been criticised by her head of institution for not involving herself in academic decision-making:

> When I first came here I was . . . sort of honed in the kind of old university culture; I refrained from offering any comment on academic matters; . . . because, you know, you wouldn't have expected to be consulted in the old system . . . [The vice-chancellor], when he had my first appraisal with me, . . . was actually quite critical of me for not doing this.
>
> (Head of administration)

Thus, although some commentators have suggested that there has been a polarisation of agendas between academic staff and professional managers (for instance, Halsey 1992), there is also evidence that these groups cross into each other's territories (Middlehurst 2004; Whitchurch 2004), with professional administrators and managers undertaking functions that in the past might have been undertaken solely by academic staff. These can include, for instance, giving recruitment talks in schools; attending recruitment fairs overseas; negotiating research grants and contracts; writing bids to external bodies for the funding of academic programmes; and compiling documents for the Quality Assurance Agency or Research Assessment Exercise.

Conversely, there is also movement in the other direction between the traditional roles of academic and professional managers, whereby academic managers were responsible for policy and strategy, and professional managers were responsible for the delivery of these. Thus, in some institutions academic managers, such as pro-vice-chancellors, are being given portfolios for administrative areas such as resources, creating 'fuzzy space' between the pro-vice-chancellor, the head of administration and/or the head of the functional area. In some cases, pro-vice-chancellors are also being given line management responsibility for staff in their functional area. This further blurs relationships, for instance, between a pro-vice-chancellor (resources), a director of finance, and staff in the finance office. This reconfiguration of professional space means that identities and voices associated with particular roles are being disturbed, and are being re-made by individuals, according to their particular circumstances and positionings, creating a dynamic that cannot be understood simply by referring to organisation charts or job descriptions.

Re-articulating professional space

Although the model in Figure 5.1 is one way of describing the range of characteristics associated with higher education administration and management as they have evolved over time, the increasing fluidity of professional space in the contemporary university makes this framework begin to seem restrictive. Neither the terms 'administration' and 'management' nor other generic descriptors now used, such as 'professional services' (Lambert 2003: 94), take full account of the permeability that has developed between institutions and their external environment (Bauman 2000), or of the multi-functional projects that have emerged across the university (Whitchurch 2006b).

The difficulty of finding an appropriate terminology was reflected by a head of administration, who spoke of the existence of 'something other' than administration or management, although they could not 'quite put into words what that "something other" is.' In order to articulate that 'something other', new ways of considering professional identities and voices are needed. For instance, beyond the frames of administration and management, new roles have emerged, in which professional administrators and managers increasingly work with 'Mode 2' knowledge, which is:

transdisciplinary rather than mono- or multi-disciplinary . . . carried out in non-hierarchical, heterogeneously organised forms which are essentially transient . . . [and] not institutionalised primarily within university structures.

(Gibbons *et al.* 1994: vii)

Thus, the planning officer who develops a connecting narrative for the university plan provides a new 'layer' of text, interpreting one aspect in the light of another, for instance, a new build or refurbishment in the context of academic directions and ambitions. In this way s/he is creating contextual knowledge, which contributes to both acceptance and delivery of the plan.

The following examples of individuals who extended their identities beyond roles that originated within academic administration illustrate the kind of diversification that has taken place.

The niche builder

The ability to develop applied forms of 'Mode 2' knowledge is represented by a group of professional managers who have dedicated themselves to building composite, niche knowledges within their institution, in areas such as quality, widening participation, or external relations. They are exemplified by a manager with responsibility for pan-institutional information and data management, which in the past would have been a function restricted to student records in a registry environment. She believed that she had been appointed to the post because she had familiarity with all aspects of what she termed the local 'business environment', and was also able to contextualise her technical knowledge with the needs of, for instance, finance, human resources and payroll.

Thus, she was able to ensure that the component parts of the total activity worked together ('the interlocking interfaces and then the combination system'), by communicating between representatives of different functions, within and outside the institution, and 'articulat[ing] a technical problem to people who aren't technical', thus performing an act of translation. Through her contacts, in both the commercial and university sectors, she was able to build intelligence about the future that could be invested in her local niche. Despite being well placed – through contacts with suppliers – to move into the commercial sector, she had a strong affiliation to her institution and to the higher education system:

It would take an amazing offer to get me out of here . . . I mean I do have loyalty to the university . . . there's lots of people around, it's dynamic . . . you see students, they're in the library doing things, you actually see what we are all working for . . . I enjoy that.

(Information and data manager)

Thus, the ability to apply generic knowledge to local circumstances, creating bespoke, contextualised knowledge, and to act as interpreter and translator within and between constituencies, become key elements in the developing roles and identities of professional managers.

The professional manager

The concept of the *professional manager*, as distinguished from the 'professional administrator', emerges as the pre- and post-1992 sectors merge over time. A student services manager whose role would, in the past, have been contained within academic administration indicated that she was deliberately building her identity in this way. She had distanced herself from the 'administrative' label, because she saw this as representing 'the soft welfare underbelly' of the institution, and felt that she would gain more credibility in career terms by establishing new business processes and being recognised as a change agent.

She had, therefore, consciously tried to build a transferable identity that would enable her to move within the sector. Such a move could allow her to cross into academic territory, for instance to a pro-vice-chancellorship. Progress towards a new identity involved developing generic skills and attributes as a manager, rather than focusing further on her knowledge base in student services. She acknowledged, with some regret, that in order to do this she had relinquished the 'luxury' of policy-making. Because her work necessitated arguing for resources, she had been obliged to adopt a voice that was more political, reflecting the fact that, in her current locale, managers were expected to enter the debate and to 'take a position' so that 'people know where you stand' on specific issues, such as whether or not additional students should be admitted to generate income, despite the pressure that this would put on facilities. The various repositionings that this person had gone through in identity terms meant that she was 'not really sure what kind of professional [she was] any more', hence the reorientation as a *professional manager*.

The pathfinder

In a world of increasing uncertainty and unknowability (Barnett 2000), anticipating and determining the future direction of institutions has become increasingly risk-laden. Past success is unlikely to be an indicator for the future:

> unwillingness to go by precedents and suspicion against accumulated experience . . . are now seen as the precepts of effectiveness and productivity. You are as good as your successes; but you are only as good as your *last* successful project.
>
> (Bauman 2005: 44)

The blurring of boundaries within and outside the university, and the increased significance of professional networks, means that the accumulation of experience takes place simultaneously as well as sequentially; indeed, learning from the past could be regarded as a hindrance. Another group of professionals act as pathfinders in mapping institutional cultures and assets amid this swirling environment. In doing this, they are open-minded in their continuous interrogation of the projects with which they are involved, recontextualising local activity, and drawing upon contiguous knowledge territories:

> Things work best when you have a working knowledge of other areas . . . it's important to know about funding arrangements for students, because if you're going out to recruit, that's often the question you're going to be asked.
>
> (Recruitment manager)

Pathfinders also create new knowledge fields, particularly, as one partnership manager suggested, where universities find themselves in 'virgin territory', without the knowledge or experience to navigate it. This person had constructed a package encompassing research, enterprise and regional partnership activity. The uncharted nature of much of this terrain had enabled her to stake out new territory for her institution. Thus, the role involved 'a whole new brief in terms of how research fits with the wider third leg academic enterprise kind of agenda.' Delivering the overarching project involved lateral links, for instance with academic directors of research and external partners such as the local Regional Development Agency, and she was at the centre of a communication web. She had adopted an exchange approach, characteristic of Senge's 'learning organisation' (Senge 1990), in developing understandings between the three areas:

> I educate them [external partners] about research, as they educate me about . . . our engagements with business, the community and other social entities, the regeneration agenda . . . and all of that stuff.

In terms of career development, she saw merit in working in an area that was continually reshaping itself:

> I'm quite happy to be in this department [the business development office], because it's the one area of the university which is growing . . . that is serving a timely need and agenda. I'm happy to have lost all of that *administrative function of supporting research students* . . . it's just not good for your career development. [author's emphasis]

By relinquishing processing functions associated with registry work in favour of roles involving innovation and development, she was able to pick up intelligence that would enable her to adjust her identity to meet changing conditions:

> I see myself moving into the business development kind of area a lot more; which gives me the opportunity to re-package myself for new jobs outside the sector.

Thus, *pathfinders*, as well as contributing to their institution's developing identity, were also reconstructing their own identities.

New becomings

As they establish and chart new professional space, the identities and voices of professional administrators and managers display a palette of shades beyond the monochrome profiles associated with the 'generalist administrator' or the 'professional specialist'. The partnership manager described the diagnostic and reflective role played by this new kind of professional, who is increasingly integrated within the community of the university, and who contributes to its collective wisdom or knowledge base:

> Ideally you want a leavening of the old hands, and new staff coming in with fresh ideas and so forth; but you need that kind of leavening of institutional wisdom that, you know, carries on and helps oil the wheels in its own way.
>
> (Partnership manager)

The idea of 'leavening' (defined in the *Oxford English Dictionary* as 'pervasive transforming influence' or 'fermentation') implies an incubatory function, helping activity to germinate, and also involving an investment for the long term, from which there might not be an immediate outcome:

> We're not ploughing the ground, we're not sowing the seeds, we're not watering the ground, we're kind of gathering up stones first . . . Something like that.
>
> (Partnership manager)

Such professionals place as much emphasis on the cultures of their institutions as on their structures, looking beneath the surface of institutional life for root causes, acting as interpreters between different constituencies, and forming a bridge between them:

> [For academic staff] It's often just about, you know, bureaucracy and administrative interference and this, that and the other, when I'm not sure they're actually saying that, they're saying something else. They're kind of saying that 'I'm busy and I'm stressed and I just can't cope with it any more' . . . That's something I've argued when I dare, to various people within the university. There's something about . . . a cultural malaise, and some rigorous cultural self-analysis needs to go on with a view to, you know, trying to change things, so that academics feel more empowered to do more different things.
>
> (Partnership manager)

Here the manager is giving voice to a key problem for universities, whereby academic and management agendas are seen as competing narratives inducing a 'cultural malaise'. When she talks of change, it is in terms of creating a more facilitative and sympathetic culture, rather than the imposition of regulatory constraints, showing sensitivity to suppressed voices in the university, of individuals who are unable to articulate the stresses that are affecting them. She takes it upon herself not only to interpret what they are saying, but also to transmit this message to those who may not want to hear it, bringing into view something that could otherwise remain hidden. At the same time, this manager is acting as a catalyst, seeking to minimise cultural inhibitors that may be blocking the development of academic activity.

By acquiring a deep understanding of the university as community, as well as of its changing environment, administrators and managers contribute to the 're-contextualising' (van Oers 1998) of the university against what can be competing imperatives, such as public and private income streams, globalisation and regional partnership, mass higher education and research selectivity, and a requirement to contribute to the nation's economic and social welfare, as well as enhancing its stock of knowledge and cultural capital. These imperatives demand the ability to undertake predictive roles, and to weigh up future possibilities against existing institutional potentials. In carrying out this function, administrators and managers cannot rely on structural or policy frameworks they have inherited from the past and are, therefore, reconceptualising them.

Thus, in Henkel's terms, the professional identity of administrators and managers might be said to have shifted from something that comprises essential elements (an 'essence') to something built by individuals over time (a 'project') (Henkel 2000: 13–14). Rather than acting solely in accordance with pre-determined frames, such as job descriptions or institutional precedents, this group of staff display a capability also to be protagonists, with increasingly active and interpretive voices. They are, thus, participating in the construction of their own professional selves, demonstrating agency as well as 'acknowledging the impact of social and structural constraints' (Woodward 2002: 30). These identity movements represent a process of continual 'becoming' for professional administrators and managers, in which:

What we are at present matters less than what we are becoming.

(Kemerling 2001)

Conclusion

Beneath the broad mantle of 'administration' and 'management' lie a range of multi-layered identities and voices. These have extended over time, in terms of both the breadth of knowledge carried by professional administrators and managers, and the depth of their involvement in connecting core academic functions to the mixed economies against which contemporary institutions operate. More specifically, these identities and voices display a facility to apply and interpret knowledge in increasingly sophisticated ways, translating between internal and external constituencies, and contributing to organisational research and development. Not only has the collective identity of professional administrators and managers diversified, but individuals also show themselves capable of adopting a range of voices and identities over time, and across the various projects with which they become involved, re-inventing themselves professionally as the need arises.

Thus, the binary division between academic and other professionals in the university (or 'diarchy' (McMaster 2005)) is being replaced by a mosaic community, in which administrators and managers, along with other professionals, are interleaved. Moreover, this is not a static picture: an ongoing professional fluidity, generated as universities grapple with conditions of increasing risk and uncertainty, means that it is perhaps more of a kaleidoscope than a mosaic. In constructing and renewing their identities, professional administrators and managers become part of the dynamic that 'allows the institution to go on changing itself and adapting effectively to a changing society' (Clark 2004: 174).

However, this chapter suggests that identities are more complex than is implied in Clark's description of administrators and managers as 'bureaucrats' (Clark 2004: 86), which belies their increasingly multi-dimensional profile as members of the university community:

> Increasingly, they [professional managers] participate in institutions' basic academic work, and like faculty, they have important expertise about the academy to contribute in shared governance.
>
> (Rhoades 2005: 5)

Similarly, in another chapter of this book, Taylor promotes the idea of a 'creative commons' that reflects universities as sites of 'supercomplexity' (Barnett 2000). He suggests that, rather than academic identities being constructed solely in opposition to 'the forces of corporatism and managerialism', they should become more 'context-sensitive', incorporating traits such as 'networking, laterality, hybridity, flexibility, multi-tasking and media capab[ility]'. In counterpoint, this chapter suggests that this process, including that of exploring 'alternative identity options', is already under way for professional administrators and managers.

Acknowledgement

The author acknowledges the support of King's College London and the UK Leadership Foundation for Higher Education in relation to the projects on which this chapter draws.

Part II

Responses

In any analysis of a swiftly changing profession, there are challenges in reading the past from which one has come; and even the recent past. There may, indeed, as Robert Burgess here intimates, be temptations to create a 'myth of a golden age'. Such a myth may characteristically take one of two forms. On the one hand, there may be a sense that, in the past, there was a unity to university life. At least within a single institution (a particular university), its members could have a sense of themselves as members of that particular institution, with its traditions, its ethos, its collective memory and its hopes of itself. On the other hand, there may be a sense that, at least, say as an administrator or academic, one knew intuitively what the role entailed. Its duties and its boundaries were well enough understood, not only by its incumbents but also by the whole academy. Everyone knew their place and, under those circumstances, it was easy enough for the whole institution to tick over quite nicely.

This section can be read certainly as a way of engaging with and taking forward the issues identified in Part I but it can also been seen as tacitly addressing the issues in the above paragraph. Are contemporary academic identities known in any assured sense? Do they have boundaries to them? To what extent are they regimented and to what extent is there room for improvisation? Are there common elements to academic identities in the contemporary university – or are they increasingly discrete, so adding to the fissiparous nature of academic life? Can we even talk of an 'academic community' any more or has such an idea now dissolved as academic identities (vibrantly plural) proliferate? Has it always been thus, or is this a new situation?

The answers to these questions furnished by the following chapters can be read in different ways but one set of readings takes the following form: academic identities have long been complex (both across each other and internally, within each role) but they are changing and widening and becoming fuzzy. Academic identity, as Gerard Delanty here suggests, is an arena wherein Zygmunt Bauman's thesis as to the 'liquid' character of contemporary life is vividly displayed. Whether in Victor Borden's depiction of professional managers, or Ray Land's examination of academic developers or in the separate analyses of academic identity in the chapters by Laura Miller, by Lynn McAlpine and her colleagues or by Gerard

Delanty: in all of these chapters, we surely glimpse strivings amidst openness, and efforts by individuals within communities to make something of themselves.

Of course, in such a situation of flux and openness, there is little in the way of security. Even the language we use is 'troublesome'. The terms 'university' or 'academic' in this context may usher in unwittingly sentiments with which individuals may be reluctant to associate these days. Such terms may not be part of the identity that some individuals are trying to construct for themselves; and even not part of the discourse of the sub-groupings with which they would align themselves and in which their own identities are affirmed. That the language of identity is hazy is only another way of saying that the identities here are themselves fluid.

But with fluidity can still come direction and force. There are here *some* signs of direction. For example, in Victor Borden's chapter there is surely a sense of a continuing professionalisation of the role of professional managers and administrators, even as (in the USA) their sub-groupings grow. If such a movement springs from internal desires for professional positioning and validity, Ray Land, Robert Burgess, Laura Miller, and Gerard Delanty, too, in their separate ways here, observe an intensity of expectations being placed *upon* those in universities. So, while the chapters here testify in significant ways to the themes of identity construction amidst 'ambiguity', 'indeterminacy' and 'liminality', there are intimations here of subtle and not-so-subtle framings of academic identity.

And yet, despite such framings of academic identity – brought about both by national policy movements and the evolution of institutional missions – opportunities open for individuals to play their part in the framing of their own identities. It may be the case, as Ray Land urges, that individuals have to live with not just multiple but self-contradictory identities, but this very multi-dimensionality in which universities move offers new spaces for identity self-construction. That, at least, is part of the argument of the chapters by Gerard Delanty and Lynn McAlpine and her colleagues.

But, then, if that is the case, if there are new spaces, new opportunities, to develop one's identity *creatively*, how might that be achieved? To what extent might one ally oneself with existing groupings or might one branch out to form new groupings in which one's identity might flourish and be affirmed? That latter possibility is surely latent in the chapter by Lynn McAlpine and her colleagues, in their depiction of 'Activity Systems', as those in universities seek 'to find some meaningful role and purpose in relation to [their identities] in the polycontextuality of the lived experience'.

A further conundrum then arises. If there are new opportunities for the creative construction of self-identity, if individuals have several identities, to what extent is any of those identities taken on? Laura Miller tellingly uses the term 'performance', a term that is nicely ambiguous in this context. Are the performances entered into with commitment, and sincerely acted out, or are they simply enacted as performances, with little of the person invested in them? The persona in the committee room is simply taken on for strategic purposes but is not a significant part of the individual's identity; or, rather, this identity is held in a rather shallow way. On the other hand, picking up a point from Ray Land, an identity may be taken on completely (we may even want to speak of the person's 'integrity') but the identity may be one of resistance to the perceived environment. And then, of course, issues arise as to the subtlety with which that identity is played out: is the letter to the *Times Higher Education Supplement* simply dashed off in seconds or is a longer game being played out?

Here, we are returned to one of our opening questions: is there any unity to this proliferation of identities on campus? If the basis for any past unity has dissolved, might a new basis for unity be found? Might the idea of 'academic community' be given new meaning? Embedded in these chapters is just such an idea. How, though, might it gain a purchase?

In the chapter by Robert Burgess, we glimpse new urgencies in a university working as a community, in gathering together all its capabilities in addressing collectively the challenges that face it. In the chapter by Lynn McAlpine and her colleagues, we also glimpse a sense that, even as identities multiply, different groups across the university are increasingly having to work with each other. The university's internal networks overlap and intersect. The near-invisible identities of some groupings – such as those in libraries, information technology, marketing and estates management – are, in the process, becoming more visible. Additionally, we may observe that universities are being encouraged to develop their own missions (in the interests of 'diversity'). Accordingly, each university will want to ensure that its impact is more than the sum of its parts; and so, again, there will be motivations in the direction of an inner institutional unity.

What this reflection opens out is that not only should we acknowledge an individual's multiple – and *horizontal* – identities but we should also embrace the prospect of multiple *vertical* academic identities. A member of a research centre, a department, a faculty and now, afresh, a member of the university in its new corporate identity: yet new challenges open for identity on campus. And their working through has yet to unfold.

Chapter 6

The myth of a golden age?

Reflections from a vice-chancellor

Robert G. Burgess

Universities are a product of the social and historical context in which they are located. In the last forty years they have undergone a major transformation. The numbers of students entering universities to study at undergraduate and postgraduate levels have increased. The volume of research conducted in universities has undergone considerable development and teaching has received much more attention, with the result that it has greater importance in the overall profile of the higher education sector. In addition, there is a range of activities now in place as part of the routine work of universities that even in the recent past would have been regarded as relatively rare or somewhat obscure. They include: consultancy work, the commercialization of intellectual property, the development of spin-out companies, entrepreneurial activities and systematic fundraising from corporate donors as well as from alumni. Alongside these 'new' activities there have also been major national changes in the higher education sector, which has witnessed an increase in accountability through the development of institutional audits of teaching and learning by the Quality Assurance Agency and the audit of research through the Research Assessment Exercise conducted by the Higher Education Funding Councils. As a consequence, the position of both academic and administrative staff in higher education has undergone considerable change. But what patterns have existed in the higher education system?

As the Robbins report (Robbins 1963) indicated, in 1900 only 20,000 students were studying in full-time higher education, but by the time the report was published in 1963 118,000 students were in the sector. Despite this improvement in participation it still represented only 5 per cent of the age group, but by 2006 43 per cent of the age group participated in higher education. This has been neatly summarized in a paper by Ken Roberts that was reported in the *Times Higher Education Supplement* (THES 2006a), in which the key features associated with the 'typical' student in the 1960s are compared and contrasted with the key features of university students at the beginning of the twenty-first century (Table 6.1).

Table 6.1 The typical student: 1963 v. 2006

1963 – The way we were . . .	*2006 – How times change . . .*
Elite	Ordinary
Only 5% of young people attend university	More than 40% of young people attend university
A wide choice of graduate jobs	Two in five chance of starting in non-graduate job
Male	Female
From fee-paying or selective schools	From a non-selective secondary school
Likely to achieve a 2.2	Likely to achieve a 2.1
Solvent	In debt
No term-time job	Term-time job
Goes out on campus	Goes out in town

Source: Ken Roberts paper, as summarized in THES (2006a).

As the Roberts summary reveals, there have been some major changes in the pattern of student recruitment into the higher education system and the profile of the 'typical' student. By 1996/97, the Dearing Committee (1997) was able to report that 1.6 million students were studying in higher education. Indeed, we can point to a greater proportion of students from lower social class groups attending university – a situation that has been promoted through widening participation policies being operationalized as higher education institutions have organized events in schools, visits to universities and week-long summer schools in subject areas. All this additional work has been developed to proactively promote higher education but it will be some years before we know whether it will deliver students from under-represented groups in higher education.

Among changes in the composition of the student body, already, we can highlight shifts in the gender composition of the student body as in 1962–63 only 26 per cent of students were women, whereas in 1979–80 women accounted for 37 per cent of students, and by the time the Dearing report was published they constituted 51 per cent of the student body (Dearing 1997). However, if we consider race and ethnicity as a further variable, we find that students from a range of ethnic groups participate in higher education but Bangladeshi students are under-represented in relation to their proportion in the population (Burgess 1999). In this respect, the data points to various ways in which opportunities have increased for a range of students over the last 40 years, and also suggests by implication ways in which universities and the working conditions within them will have changed.[1] It is to some of these changes that we now turn.

---

1 For a detailed discussion of trends in higher education in the ten year period 1995–96 to 2004–05 see UUK/SCOP (2006) – a trend report now in its sixth year. In particular, the report indicates the increase in enrolments over the decade by 44 per cent for postgraduates and 30 per cent for undergraduates with women students being in the majority at all levels and postgraduate education being dependent upon international student recruitment.

Was there ever a golden age?

Commentators in the first part of this volume point to a loss that has been experienced by those who work within universities. In particular, they highlight the loss of time to engage in academic work, whether that is scholarship or research. They also highlight a loss of freedom and autonomy and point to a situation in which academics face a range of further duties when nothing has been removed from their workloads. Among the issues that have been identified is the loss of collegiality and collegial decision-making; it is argued that collegiality has been replaced by managerialism and corporatism, and collegial decision-making has been replaced by executive decision-making. It is also argued by some academics that there has been a reduction in contact with students and a separation of management from academic roles. But what evidence exists to support these statements? Is there evidence to suggest that there was ever a golden age in universities when there were opportunities to do research, engage in high levels of contact with students and participate fully in the decision-making processes? Or is the golden age a myth? In short, did it ever exist?

Meeting managers

As Celia Whitchurch has indicated, the term 'management' is very loosely defined. In her chapter, she highlights how there is a separation between administrators who manage and what she calls 'professional academic managers'. This is a very artificial sub-division of higher education staff. Indeed, Middlehurst (2004) suggests that the pattern of academic management and leadership has undergone considerable change. No longer is the management of higher education confined to vice-chancellors but it has been broadened out to include a senior management team. These teams are sometimes composed entirely of academics and may include pro-vice-chancellors with portfolios of responsibility including learning and teaching, resources, external relations, international activities and research. Meanwhile, in some institutions, deans are also taken into the senior management team in order to transmit policies throughout their faculties. Finally, a partnership model can be developed, to which Whitchurch also refers. This is a model whereby senior management teams are composed of leading academic and administrative staff within the institution. They might be composed of all the pro-vice-chancellors and balanced by senior administrative staff, including the registrar, the academic registrar, the director of finance and the director of marketing.

Such a group brings together academic and administrative leaders who can develop a university-wide view of major initiatives and major policies, and who can engage in the interpretation of policies for the purpose of implementation. Universities are large, complex organizations where leadership is essential. Senior management teams bring together academic managers with specialists in fields such as finance, estate management and academic development, who together can lead the strategic development of the institution. They engage in strategic decision-making on behalf of their institutions, developing and providing ways to implement national policies in a local context. However, it is essential that such groups are clear about the academic value system and the purpose of a university to engage in the advancement of knowledge and the transmission of teaching.

It can be argued that it is the core purpose of a university to deliver high quality research and high quality teaching, with research directly informing teaching. It is, in turn, argued that the key task of academics is to communicate their subject and the results of their research activities to their students. In Henkel's study of academic identities, several of her informants reported that they had derived their own academic identity by being taught by a member of staff who was able to convey the excitement of doing research and developing their subject (Henkel 2000). However, the academic research leader may be engaged in not only fundamental but also applied research, consultancy and the commercialization of research, which call for a different skill set and make new demands and intellectual challenges.

The role of research

One of the hallmarks of a university, in comparison with other educational institutions, is that the staff engage in the development of the subjects in which they are located. As several commentators have indicated in the first part of this volume, identification with a discipline is often seen as the way in which an academic identity is established (cf. Henkel 2000). But research can take many forms.

Research activity may be fundamental and it is often supported by the research councils, or it may be supported by charitable bodies and trusts. It is this kind of research activity that allows the principal investigator and his/her research associates to engage in work of a fundamental kind that contributes to the knowledge of the subject and results in subject boundaries being extended and developed. This research has the power to transform, to develop new interpretations and to result in new areas of academic endeavour to be developed. Research can also be conducted in relation to development activity. In this respect, research may be conducted for an industrial enterprise where research application is the main purpose of an investigation. In medicine, research may be conducted on behalf of pharmaceutical companies through clinical trials and the development of new drugs. Meanwhile, in the social sciences, research and development activity may take the form of evaluations of particular spheres of activity. For example, the implementation in the school system of records of achievement gave rise to a whole range of evaluative work during the 1990s (Pole 1992) – an initiative which, in turn, has led on to the introduction of personal development plans in higher education.

Another aspect of research activity relates to work with postgraduate students, which has been relatively under-developed in the UK until the last decade. Postgraduate research now forms an important aspect of the research base and shows an increase in the numbers that participate. At the time of the Robbins report (Robbins 1963), 7,475 students were registered for postgraduate research degrees whereas in 2004–05 58,080 full-time students and 53,910 part-time students were studying for a research degree (HESA 2006). In this respect, postgraduate research students have increased the research base in universities; especially in the physical and life sciences, medicine and engineering, where they constitute part of the broader research team. Meanwhile, in the social sciences and the humanities they are working as independent researchers who are, again, being inducted into the disciplines in which they are located and, in turn, develop a systematic training in their discipline[2].

In the last fifteen years, we have witnessed in the humanities and the social sciences the introduction of recognized programmes for doctoral candidates that provide a systematic coverage of methodology. These courses are compulsory and ensure that graduate students are socialized into their disciplines in such a way that they are conversant with a full range of conceptual and methodological tools (Burgess 1994a,b). There are also further opportunities to work on the borders of individual disciplines where multidisciplinarity and interdisciplinarity occur – a situation whereby those in universities bring to bear different bodies of knowledge on tackling 'real world' problems that will not arrive with disciplinary labels attached to them. Indeed, alongside individual research programmes sponsored by the research councils there are also research programmes that bring together the work of different councils. For example, the programme on 'Technology Enhanced Learning' led by the Economic and Social Research Council (ESRC) relies on funds provided by the Engineering and Physical Sciences Research Council (EPSRC), includes assessors drawn from the scientific and user communities as well as the social sciences, and is intended to promote work that is drawn from different subject areas. But how does all this work get communicated? How is it translated into teaching and the provision of courses?

The provision of courses

The university sector has seen an explosion in the range of courses provided at undergraduate and postgraduate levels. At the undergraduate level alone, the Universities and Colleges Admissions Service currently advertises 50,300 programmes (UCAS, personal communication). In addition, universities have also undergone considerable expansion at the postgraduate level. Indeed, just as higher education expansion at the undergraduate level took place in the 1980s so in the 1990s the development of university-wide graduate schools resulted in an increase in the number of students reading for postgraduate degrees, especially taught courses. Again, if we return to the time of the Robbins report, the number of home full-time postgraduates studying in higher education institutions in the UK totalled 2,030 (Robbins 1963: 103). To put this in context, these students would not even constitute the total number of postgraduates studying in the University of Leicester in 2005–06, where 8,710 were registered.

Many taught course programmes developed at master's level are being studied

---

2   See UUK/SCOP (2006) for a discussion of postgraduate student recruitment that demonstrates how UK higher education is dependent on international students for expansion in this area.

for vocational purposes or are vocational in their orientation and have a link to the research base as students engage in independent study by writing a dissertation alongside a series of taught courses. For example, master's programmes concerned with management in all its forms as well as those programmes in specialist fields such as law, psychology, criminology and human resources are frequently offered by universities. Large numbers of social science programmes have a vocational orientation and this is also happening in the natural and life sciences. It is this style of work that has also led to the proliferation of new programmes at doctoral level. While research degrees continue through PhD registrations so, in turn, new doctoral routes have been developed. In particular, professional doctorates are commonly available in the UK in education, clinical psychology and engineering. But this has been a relatively slow development in the UK; ten years ago it was reported that in Australia as many as 16 different professional doctorates were on offer at 29 Australian universities, as shown in Table 6.2.

Such a range of degrees raises questions about what constitutes 'the doctoral level' and how this can be delivered through a variety of different programmes. In turn, it also illustrates how the higher education community can respond to the vocational demands of part-time students who do not wish to register for the conventional doctorate (provided by the PhD) but instead want to engage in advanced study for a vocational purpose by following courses and writing a dissertation on an intellectual problem that directly arises out of their work experience.

These developments at doctoral level, together with the provision of taught master's courses with a vocational purpose, result in a shift in the way in which universities are developing postgraduate opportunities. These new developments

Table 6.2 Types of Australian professional doctorates (1996)

Field	Award	Number
Education	EdD	22
	DTeach	1
	DScEd	1
Business	DBA	9
	DOrgDyn	1
	DPA	1
Psychology	DPsych	4
	DClinPsych	1
	DHealthPsych	1
Health sciences	DPH	2
	DHSM	1
	DNurs	1
Design	DEnvDesign	1
Architecture	DArch	1
Law	SJD	8
Humanities	DCA	2

Source: Sharman and Sekhon (1996).

result in new workers, new work and, in some cases, new subject areas being developed (cf. Abrams 1981). For example, in the arts and humanities significant master's programmes are available in conventional subject fields such as English and history but also in specialist interdisciplinary programmes such as museum studies, Victorian studies and the English country house. Such programmes can make links between fundamental and applied research, promote interdisciplinarity and engage the vocational interests of some students. At both undergraduate and postgraduate levels, new combinations of subjects are brought together and new subject areas are opened up, leading to greater specialization among students. Many of these developments result in new challenges in the teaching programme and new demands on the teacher in higher education.

Teaching

The Robbins report subscribed to the idea that there was no sharp division between research and teaching. Indeed, it commented

> There is no borderline between teaching and research; they are complementary and overlapping activities. A teacher who is advancing his general knowledge of his subject is both improving himself as a teacher and laying foundations for his research. The researcher often finds that his personal work provides him with fresh and apt illustration which helps him to set a subject in a new light when he turns to prepare a lecture.
>
> (Robbins 1963: 182)

The Robbins report continued by discussing ways in which research could be communicated through teaching programmes and through lectures and classes. It also pointed to ways in which teaching as well as research should count towards promotion, especially at the ranks of senior lecturer and professor. Indeed, it was recognized that professors were leaders in the teaching of their subject as well as in their research areas. All of this suggests that the core academic values of a university were seen to be embodied in high quality research and high quality teaching. But what kind of infrastructure has been available to support those engaged in these activities? It is only in recent years that we have witnessed the systematic introduction of staff development on any scale in higher education and, alongside this, the development of subject centres for innovative work in the curriculum and the establishment of a Fellowship scheme to recognize excellence in teaching.

A further development has been the creation of Centres of Excellence in Teaching and Learning. The development of these Centres came about through a direct recommendation in the White Paper on the future of higher education (HMSO 2003) and resulted in a competition for centres of teaching excellence that would be comparable in scale and scope to designated centres of academic research. The scale of funding, both for recurrent and capital activity, was similar to that provided for research centres. Seventy-four of these Centres of Excellence have received £315 million in funding – the largest investment of government funding for teaching quality enhancement in higher education. All of these initiatives have provided an opportunity for those engaged in their development to conduct pedagogic research as well as fundamental research in their disciplines. In this respect, new opportunities are being opened up for individuals to gain promotion through work on teaching and learning in their disciplinary fields, as well as enhancing the student learning experience. Research and scholarship in pedagogy has therefore started to gain wider recognition within the academy rather than being taken for granted.

Accountability to students

One area which has shown rapid development over the last forty years has been the participation of students in the governance of higher education. Students are represented at all levels of an institution, engaging in departmental staff/student committees as well as in major policy committees of the university. The president and vice-president of a students' union can be found on the university council, the senate, and major committees concerned with policy and strategy, learning and teaching, research, the estate and finance. In this respect, the student body can comment on all the activities in which an institution engages. Alongside participation in the development of academic policy, students have also been actively engaged in the evaluation of teaching and the curriculum. At the end of each module it is usual for the course teacher to evaluate the work that has been done and for the evaluations to be made available publicly. More recently, the Higher Education Funding Council for England has developed a National Student Survey, the largest independent survey ever conducted among students in England and Northern Ireland. The survey took place in 2005 and again in 2006 and has looked at teaching quality in individual subject areas and also the infrastructure available in terms of libraries, computer services and so on. Subsequently, this has led to evaluations that can be drawn on by potential students considering entry to the higher education sector. This provides greater transparency whereby potential students can learn more about the programmes on offer and the views of current students on the quality of provision.

Some changes in higher education

We have identified some changes that have occurred in the higher education sector over the last forty years. In turn, the expansion of student numbers at undergraduate and postgraduate levels, and the development of new postgraduate courses at master's and doctoral levels, have resulted in huge changes in universities. However, on close inspection there have also been other opportunities. Among areas that have been opened up and developed are pure and applied research, and course development at postgraduate as well as undergraduate level. There have also been major changes in the composition of the student body and the social origins of students who participate in higher education. Alongside these new developments it is essential that, in managing the higher education sector, academic values are maintained so as to provide a high quality experience for the student. As Barnett (1992) suggests, peer review is absolutely fundamental to the way in which a university operates. In this respect, peer review is essential in research and teaching and in the recruitment and promotion of staff. This is strongly supported by Kogan, Moses and El-Khawas (1994) who comment that academics

> share conditions, status and functions. A shared belief in such values is the need to demonstrate the evidence and logic behind statements, or an altruistic concern for one's students.
>
> (Kogan *et al.* 1994: 29)

If these values are held by those in the higher education community, it will mean that partnerships will be built between different members of staff, no matter whether they are acting in an academic or an administrative capacity. In this respect, rather than the university community being split by tensions arising out of different value systems among staff, the latter will be united in shaping not only their own discipline and their own institution but also the higher education sector and the way it responds to requests made by government and other external bodies themselves seeking to influence the higher education community. But we might ask: what kind of identity does a vice-chancellor need to develop at a time of major change for universities?

Developing the vice-chancellor's role

The transformation of the higher education community has prompted questions about the key attributes required of vice-chancellors (THES 2006b). Among the requirements that are associated with the role are a range of generic skills that include:

- leadership;
- the ability to engage in teamwork;
- decision-making skills;
- people management;
- finance and business skills;
- communication skills;
- knowledge of recent legislation in employment, health and safety, discrimination and so on;
- planning for capital developments.

It could be argued that all these qualities are required by anyone who is engaged in leading and managing a large organisation. However, in higher education, the development of an academic identity based on leadership in a disciplinary field is seen as an essential attribute that shapes the way in which a vice-chancellor takes decisions or approaches financial planning and estates management. All these areas need to be systematically developed by vice-chancellors to move their organizations forward. Key strategies need to be developed, not just in research and teaching but also in a range of other areas. In these circumstances, vice-chancellors need to be able to link together seemingly disparate areas and communicate them effectively to colleagues who will have to adapt to the changing world of higher education. But such a range of demands made upon an organization requires a team of people supporting the vice-chancellor with its collective expertise. As a result, universities now require experts in finance, marketing, public relations, industrial development, human resources and fundraising, to name but a few areas. Yet at the very heart of the university is the vice-chancellor working with academic and administrative colleagues. It is this group working together in a collaborative way that will shape the university by establishing and developing an institution that provides research, teaching and expertise to fulfil the requirements of contemporary society in the twenty-first century.

Acknowledgement

I am indebted to Jo Wood for her assistance with background research for this chapter, together with her constructive comments, and help in presenting this material for publication.

Chapter 7

Scenes in a university

Performing academic identities in shifting contexts

Laura Miller

Introduction

In *The University in Ruins*, Bill Readings portrayed a university environment in which market-led 'discourses of excellence' had replaced the traditional relationship between scholarship and society so that institutional purposes were 'up for grabs' (1996: 2). Over ten years on, this volume describes the voices and identities that have emerged in the new structures that have replaced the traditional university. This chapter uses the notion of performance to highlight the way that academics and students evaluate themselves and each other and orient to their perceived roles. The emphasis on performance destabilises the idea that identities are fixed and unchangeable, instead describing them as dialogic and emerging through interactions. This chapter paints (and then discusses) some imaginary scenes in the modern university, following a brief reprise of the factors that have influenced them. Its aim is to explore the ways in which lecturers, researchers and students struggle to know their purpose in the modern university and to ask how positive engagement between emerging identities is possible in contemporary academic contexts.

Academic contexts: what's changed?

In previous university administrations, collegiality influenced decisions about research and teaching. Sometimes elitist, such collegiality seemed often to be based on tribal loyalties which meant that university departments resembled 'closed-shops' (Becher 1989) with strict hierarchies shaping institutions and dividing disciplines (Neuman 2001). Each subject was structured by pre-determined ideas about what paradigms were favoured and which were out of bounds (Martin 1998). Although such forms of administration provided certainty about the kinds of academic identity that were preferred, they were arguably limiting and exclusive. In theory, government targets for increasing participation should enable more flexibility in the development of academic identities and voices, as Peter Taylor suggests in the first half of this book. He challenges the idea that there was a golden era in higher education, pointing out that the dissatisfaction expressed by today's academics is often a mark of their failure to adapt to the shifting discursive terrain of the modern university.

Some of the realities of contemporary university life, however, are difficult to adapt to. Managerial, bureaucratic and market-driven structures have been superimposed onto disciplinary practices, changing the climate of university departments. Increasingly, for example, the opportunity to seek support from one's peers is undermined by the introduction of part-time or fixed-term research and teaching contracts. As a result, many academics have little contact with their department, or feel that their interactions and involvements with peers are limited or undermined (Abbas and McLean 2001). Some fear that there has been a corrosion of academic integrity in a context that favours the 'thin morality' of competitive individualism over a 'thick morality' that connects learning to citizenship and the 'common good' (Apple 2001). In this context, a heteroglossic student voice has emerged, which Denise Batchelor here attributes to competing agendas (to 'learn' and to 'consume'). To recapture the heart of academia, Gunnar Handal (in this volume) suggests that different 'communities of practice' might engage with one another in meaningful dialogue across the various agendas, with academic developers called on to facilitate such engagement. These conversations, he argues, are necessary if academia is to thrive.

But, even if academic developers can facilitate such discussions, the fear is that – in an age of top-up-fees and increasing competition – true ratiocination is not possible. Increasingly beset by financial concerns, students may sue establishments that fail them, which is why Oxford University is asking new undergraduates to sign a contract in which they agree to 'work hard.'[1] The voices and identities described earlier in this book reflect the fact that universities and students are obliged to orient to the concerns of putative employers.[2] With the government's target of 50 per cent participation, and the idea that degrees should produce a skilled workforce, higher education institutions face a new kind of 'university challenge'.[3] Whereas, once, competition between institutions was based on an

---

1 BBC 'Students Get "Work Hard" Contract' from http://news.bbc.co.uk/1/hi/education/4665390.stm, accessed on 23 March 2006.

2 The implications of this trend are frequently debated in the media. For example: Donald McCleod, 'Floud defends rise in new subjects' in *The Guardian*, Thursday 21 February 2002. Downloaded from http://education.guardian.co.uk/administration/story/0,,653375,00.html on 22 March 2006.

3 This term refers to the long-running television quiz – shown on BBC2 – in which the brightest students from competing universities are tested on general and academic knowledge.

undefined notion of intellectual merit, the current system views success in terms of the ability to attract high student numbers and funding. Students know that their completion of degree courses doesn't guarantee success: in employment terms, some graduates are more equal than others (Connor *et al.* 1996). The argument that such inequalities are a reflection of *value* or *worth* ignores some of the ideological and structural factors in play: Universities UK point out that non-traditional graduates face discrimination by employers (Harvey *et al.* 2002). It appears that we are trapped between two processes (of commodification and litigation), which Celia Whitchurch describes in her account of the adversarial management style that has replaced the 'soft' forms of administration that once governed the university. So how do these factors shape the nature of interactions and identities in university contexts? In an attempt to answer that question the following scenes and discussions provide snapshots of the kinds of performance that are manifest in the modern university.

Scene 1: orientations

'This is the English department,' the guide tells a group of new students as they take a campus tour, 'but since you already speak the language, we don't need to go in.' The comment amuses the crowd and a passing English lecturer, but the latter is also left wondering whether the joke is on her.

In everyday terms, the word 'academic' refers to an idea that is so out-of-date or pointless that it is considered moot. A general antipathy towards scholarship pervades popular culture (characterisations of out-of-touch scholars inhabiting ivory towers proliferate). Such anti-intellectual tendencies may explain our tolerance of the increasingly utilitarian approach to academia that has come to dominate following the 'colonisation of the life-world' of the university by market forces (Habermas 1984). The new, functional, approach to the university is illustrated by the scene above, which is a fiction but a possibly compelling one for its plausibility. The effect of this cultural wariness towards scholarship is apparent in university lecture theatres and meeting rooms; the tension between being *too academic* and not being *academic enough* finds expression in the discourses of students, researchers, lecturers and managers, as discussed in previous chapters.

Students have long been described as instrumental in their approach to learning (e.g. Considine 1994; Delucchi 2000; Gumport 2000; Riesman 1998). This is viewed as both a good and a bad thing. On the one hand, it fits in with the broader socio-economic context in which success is judged through performance and rewarded accordingly; on the other, it encourages a cut-and-paste style of learning that fails to engage with ideas at a deeper level. If thoughts are relevant only when they are considered useful, then important meanings are lost. More reflexive ideas may not necessarily get the trains to run on time, but they provide the kind of intellectual space that makes civilisation possible. Arendt (1978) alluded to this point when she described those thought processes that make us 'fully awake and alive' so that 'you will see that you have nothing in your grasp but perplexities, and the best we can do with them is share them with each other.'

Ideas of the sort that Arendt describes are not abstractions but are important in socio-economic, cultural and political contexts. Habermas (1984) elaborated on this point when he described the 'institutional public sphere' (a terrain of morality and ethical conduct, determining justice and law, belief and ideology, and, not least, politics) in which such complexities can be discussed. Institutional practices, he argued, can create 'ideal speech situations' that nurture 'communicative competence' (not just in the sense of presentational skills) that make true democratic engagement possible. Today's universities – increasingly beset with managerial and economic concerns – are far removed from the kind of public sphere that Habermas envisaged. As earlier chapters suggest, there is often a lack of real engagement between students and lecturers (such conversations as there are being tainted by discourses of obligation and entitlement). Frustration taints exchanges between academics and managers (framed, as they are, by a mutual distrust). Jargon pervades, blocking the pathways through labyrinthine ideas and it becomes inevitable that we (the researchers, the lecturers, the students and the managers) feel as if the university has failed us – or that we have failed it. But all is not lost.

Today's entrance lobbies, seminar rooms and lecture theatres are filled with a multitude of voices, disturbing the calm of dreaming spires and challenging the bureaucratic efficiency of the administrative university. Corridors are lined with bulletin boards and posters that give silent but visible voice to the ongoing battles for the soul of academia, while revealing an engagement with broader socio-cultural concerns. They are signposts to hidden voices; our ability to understand them and respond requires analytical skills – the same ones that are needed to decode a fast-changing world and the ongoing controversies that polarise it. The cultural commonplace about academic ideas being pointless because little is at stake in them is challenged by the reality of university life, in which – as we shall see – academics and students alike are grappling with very tangible problems. They are relevant because *so much* is at stake in them.

Scene 2: the seminar room discussion

Student 1: Your argument is rubbish – you have no idea what you're talking about.

Student 2: What are you doing? I thought we were supposed to be debating?

Student 1: I am . . . What do YOU think I'm doing?

Student 2: You're being abusive.

Student 1: No I'm not.

Student 2 Yes you are.

Student 1: No I'm not.

Student 2: Are.

Student 1: Not.

> *Student 2:* [Sighs] This isn't an argument, either. You're just contradicting me.
>
> *Student 1:* No I'm not.
>
> *Student 2:* Yes you are: An argument is a series of statements leading to a definite proposition.
>
> *Student 1:* No it's not.
>
> *Student 2:* It's an intellectual process, not an automatic gainsaying of anything the other person says.
>
> *Student 1:* Not necessarily.
>
> (with apologies to Monty Python)

The aphorism that we teach our students not what to think but *how* to think highlights an important principle that guides university teaching. Knowledge is understood to be partial and contingent; each discipline invites particular approaches and none is without contention; dialogue between perspectives is often emotionally charged. This doesn't mean that academics advocate an intellectual free-for-all in which any idea goes (although the anti-relativist backlash expressed in sections of contemporary popular culture suggests otherwise). It reflects an aim – across all disciplines and subjects – to encourage critical reflection on the forms of knowledge and methodological approaches that are available to us. In this way, academic study provides us with a tool for building knowledgeable and reflexive forms of identity. If the move towards interdisciplinarity were simply an extension of this logic there would be fewer problems with it, but the enforced merging of several disciplines (for administrative and bureaucratic purposes, rather than solid intellectual ones) results in a range of confusions about what to teach and how. Often, lecturers are required to teach subjects they know little about: Moran (2001) describes such inderdisciplinarity as 'the most seriously underthought . . . concept in the modern academy.'

For a student attending a university lecture in this context, the lack of coherence that emerges from such *ad hoc* disciplinary mergers distances the student from any real understanding or engagement. The debates students hear often reflect power struggles (around the boundaries of disciplines and epistemologies, exposing the ideologies that keep them in play) and are abstruse. It is understandable that at times they do not engage or do so through seemingly empty performances: their response does not necessarily reflect a lack of academic literacy, although we extend remedial classes to those whom we perceive to be in need of them. The trend towards providing academic literacy classes fails to address the idea that students may be resisting academic identities for strategic reasons (Benwell and Stokoe 2002). In part, their hesitant utterances can be understood to be a 'face saving' device (Goffman 1967) that responds to the normative constraints governing interactions: their silence (observed by Batchelor in this volume) is often part of an ironic detachment whereby they show their peers that they are not trying too hard. Withdrawn or reticent students provide their lecturer with an incentive to develop new forms of engagement that orient to students' own concerns. If a lecturer is successful in interpreting student silence as an attempt to find new levels and means of engagement, the educational enterprise is redeemed and the building of academic identities is made possible.

The 'face saving' described earlier might also be a result of the increasingly obscure (over-modularised) degree structure: students may not want to admit to being terminally confused and silence is better than embarrassment. Whereas lecturers are often aware of the epistemological boundaries that are being crossed and the conventions whereby they can be maintained (or eliminated), students are not. And even when lecturers know how to explore the complexities for themselves, they still need to learn how to communicate them to students (and write about them for each other). Meanwhile, the forms of argumentation that are required from students in one university classroom are often very different to those expected in other contexts, meaning that students are often unsure what academic identity they are being asked to achieve at any given time. There is a case, then, for providing a more knowledgeable engagement with the disciplines (Gozzer 1982; Sinaceur 1977), outlining their epistemological and ideological controversies while explaining their relevance to the subjects being studied. Once students have learnt about the disciplines they are being asked to move across, they can do so in an informed way, resulting in more enlightened dialogue (Messmer 1978).

This level of engagement is beneficial for a number of reasons. Each academic discipline has its own language and culture. The ability to translate across them enables academics and graduates to communicate knowledge in ways that make it more accessible to others. This is important for a number of different reasons, not least because it satisfies employers' demands for graduates with transferable skills (such as the ability to speak about ideas and communicate with others). More importantly, however, it allows for the kind of dialogue across disciplines that Habermas envisaged in his description of the public sphere. It generates a form of communicative competence that allows those involved in academia to make articulate contributions to public life through their areas of expertise and gives them the ability to work with other forms of knowledge. One of the ways of nurturing such communicative competence is to apply the theories and disciplines being taught to the social and cultural contexts in which we live. As we shall see in the following sections, no discipline exists in isolation and much of the knowledge that emerges through scholarship has direct implications for society. Academics have long been seen to have an important role as 'public intellectuals' (Graff 2003): our teaching and research in all areas relates to social issues and we are increasingly invited to provide scholarly insights about the cultural and ethical dilemmas that relate to our disciplines to the media.

Scene 3: intellectuals in the public gaze

> Do you have a professor who just can't stop talking about President Bush, about the war in Iraq, about the Republican party, or any other ideological issue that has nothing to do with the class subject matter? If you help . . . expose the professor, we'll pay you for your work.
>
> (Glaister 2006)

The above text is published on a website dedicated to exposing politically motivated academics (specifically those who oppose G.W. Bush's administration in the US, although the campaign claims to target partisan scholars, whatever their orientation) (*The Guardian* 2006). Meanwhile, in the UK, a lecturer was suspended on full pay at Leeds University following student complaints about his racist attitudes.[4] These two cases highlight a contemporary trend in higher education, whereby controversies are to be neutralised rather than confronted. In the past, however, academics took it upon themselves to engage in rigorous debate over contentious issues, hoping to resolve them through rational means.[5] Academic scholarship once relied upon open dialogue and the ability to engage in reasoned debate. The actions of the Nobel-Prize-winning nuclear physicist Joseph Rotblat highlight this point. A Polish immigrant to the UK, Rotblat developed communicative links between scientists on either side of the Iron Curtain at a time when politicians and diplomats could not talk, averting an escalation of the nuclear crisis.[6]

Contemporary academics are at the forefront of other technological and theoretical developments that have social and moral implications (as is the case with cloning).[7] Despite this, institutional attempts to neutralise debates (of whatever kind) rather than discuss them are commonplace in universities that favour market concerns over notions of academic freedom and integrity. As George Bernard Shaw famously stated, 'the way to get at the merits of a case is not to listen to the fool who imagines himself impartial, but to get it argued with reckless bias for and against.' Do current events provide us with apocryphal tales about the stifling of such argumentation in an academic climate in which intellect is subservient to economic and political concerns? If so, what can be done to avoid turning out morally neutral performances of our academic identities?

Laurence Stenhouse (1979) claimed that academic learning is not 'a static accomplishment like riding a bicycle or keeping a ledger; it is, like all arts of high ambition, a strategy to be adopted in the face of an impossible task.' Above all, he argued against the application of the universal standards that have since become commonplace within universities. He alluded to the difference between attaining objectives (such as have been developed in QAA grades and RAE scores) and educating (or guiding towards knowledge and understanding through research).

---

4 http://www.timesonline.co.uk/article/0,,2-2100915,00.html (accessed on 27 March 2006) highlights the case.

5 A notable example is the debate about the methods and arguments of eugenicist scholars (such as Murray and Hernstein, authors of *The Bell Curve* (1994), which links IQ and 'race').

6 On 9 July 1955, Rotblat and ten other scientists, including Albert Einstein, Bertrand Russell, Frederic Joliot-Curie and the 1962 Nobel peace laureate, Linus Pauling, issued a manifesto in London declaring that researchers must take responsibility for their creations, such as the atomic bomb. His CV, as presented on the Nobel Prize website, details some of the ways in which he linked intellectual endeavours to public concerns; it can be found at the following url: http://nobelprize.org/peace/laureates/1995/rotblat-cv.html (accessed on 27 March 2006).

7 For this reason, academics attempt to regulate themselves, exploring the social and cultural implications of their research – as is the case in the development of bioethics (see url: http://ethics.acusd.edu/applied/bioethics/index.asp, accessed on 27 March 2006).

Implicit in Stenhouse's work was a concern about the evacuation of principles, social commitments and even emotions from university teaching and research.

Scene 4: All the world's a stage . . .

The idea that education provides a form of 'cultural capital' for students (Bourdieu 1993) has long inspired academics to think about what they teach and how learning influences the kinds of graduate identities that emerge. For some, there is a fear (discussed earlier) that the academic landscape has been shorn of morality (except via disciplinary and ethics committees) and inculcated with market values. If this is true, then we can expect to see lecturers and students becoming less emotionally and intellectually invested in the subjects discussed in the university classroom to the extent that lectures are simply a matter of disseminating value-free and user-friendly information. As earlier chapters describe, such a view is one that many in the academic community would resist.

If our role as educators is to contribute to the well-being of society, then it makes sense to ask: in what society would we like to live and how can our work shape it? The demands of the modern university – while exhausting – invite fairly straightforward kinds of performance. Lectures can be delivered via PowerPoint presentations and notes can be distributed on the intranet; publications (of varying quality) can be produced in accordance with the demands of the department. Students and managers may be happier with academics who work in this way. Lecturers, however proficient at providing bridge-notes on quantum physics or postmodern theory, are often aware that the implications of that knowledge are under-appreciated or misappropriated. For example, the co-option of sociological and psychological concepts is prevalent in marketing contexts (Brown 1993), but scholars are concerned about the cynical misuse of such ideas (as, for example, when psychological theories are distilled for the masses to sell lifestyle magazines, through inculcating a sense of bourgeois anxiety in the reader). Meanwhile, we may turn out competent researchers by academic standards, but to do so in a value-neutral way might be a problem in today's 'risk society' (Beck 1992).

Many of today's lecturers are deeply concerned about the emptiness of their profession and the desiccated forms of identity that universities create when academic knowledge is subsumed by market forces (as earlier chapters describe). The importance of ideas and their meaning to students (and society) is compromised by an institutional discourse of excellence that reflects neo-liberal rather than pedagogic agendas. Although it makes sense to engage in a form of face saving (that is, the production of valueless performances) to preserve our fragile educational identities, we do so at a cost. The detachment that is felt across the academy is perhaps a thread that unites this volume. Our quest, as members of the modern university, is to revitalise education and research – not just so that it is relevant to industry and potential employers, but so that it serves society as a whole. That includes our students – especially if we hope that they will have a positive impact on future generations. It is easy to see in a value-free market-driven university context why many feel that such an aim is futile.

Concluding comments

The problem of disengagement has been described and explained in this and pre-ceding chapters. Some inspirational approaches have emerged to create the kind of 'rhetorical democracy' (Hauser and Grim 2004) that would provide an antidote to this trend. The ideas discussed in the first section of this book go a long way to providing such practices; the arts of engaged listening and critical learning help us to reframe the problems encountered by academics and students in a meaningful way. The approaches offered in this book advocate a form of action-research-as-teaching-practice (or deep, committed engagement with our role). Depending on time and resources, such engagement is possible on a number of levels. Interdis-ciplinarity can be developed more reflexively, so that students are aware of the social and cultural implications of the subjects they study: medical practice, for example, benefits from an analysis of the discourses that shape it. In a more gen-eral sense, the injunction to be relevant (to industry and employers) can be used to create meaningful involvement with the wider community, while putting the theories that are taught in the classroom into practice. Students can participate in debates about ethical concerns within higher education, such as whether universi-ties should adopt anti-racist speech codes, rather than feeling alienated from the controversies that surround public life.

Perhaps Celia Whitchurch is right to suggest that the fluid, kaleidoscopic iden-tities and interactions that have emerged in the modern university can serve to enable a context-sensitive form of teaching and learning. The fear is that, if they don't, universities could stifle the forms of academic and civic processes that were once part of the educational endeavour. Reflexivity, discussion and, above all, engagement are key to the success of the modern university. If we, as lectur-ers, researchers, managers and students can move beyond the narrow concerns of the bureaucratic structure and connect with the purpose of learning – to improve understandings of and between disciplines – we can, perhaps, prevent the modern university from reaching the ruined state that Readings predicted over ten years ago.

Chapter 8

The question of identity

Negotiating roles and voices in evolving academic systems

Lynn McAlpine, Marian Jazvac-Martek and Allison Gonsalves

Who are we?

Though our research interests intersect and we are all in a faculty of education, we have different personal biographies and roles in the university. Allison, a PhD student, identifies most as a student. She did a master's in genetics before entering the PhD. And her research interest emerges from this – the gendered, raced, classed experience of enculturation into a disciplinary culture. Marian, a PhD candidate, in part identifies as an academic since, while still a student, she has done considerable teaching and academic development. She is interested in how academic identity is shaped during the journey from beginning doctoral student through to new academic. Lynn, a professor, identifies as an academic, academic developer, and to some extent administrator (always within an academic role). Her work is directed at understanding and supporting the learning of both individual lecturers and disciplinary units.

Co-constructing our story

While remaining attentive to our distinct identities, we have sought to create a collective voice. We began by independent reading and response to Part I. We then met to discuss our responses and, from there, generate goals for the chapter:

- We realized we had been using 'identity' and 'voice' in an unexamined fashion, so we set out to define both more explicitly.

- We became more sensitized to the many roles and structures that are invisible in the academy, so we agreed to make the range of roles and structures that intersect in the academy more transparent, more visible, thus better representing the complexities of voice and identity.
- Exploring the intersection of identity, voice, role, and structure affirmed for us our dissatisfaction with communities of practice as an explanatory framework. So, we have explored Activity Systems theory as an analytic tool for more fully unearthing the complexity.
- We assessed how what we have learned impacts on our view of development and developers.

In order to preserve our own identities while speaking collectively, we then wrote independently, each of us focusing on a key idea. Finally, we collectively edited these starting points before co-constructing the remainder of the chapter.

The question of identity (Marian)

Identity and voice can be interpreted from many different perspectives. In Part I, the authors give evidence to this through their own varied use of these terms. We perceive identity as a state of being; it is a dynamic but shifting unity – comprising both the social and personal – that has some coherence. Each individual has a personal identity or self-concept, which encompasses consciousness over time and includes personal biography and the collective influences in one's life. Social identity arises in relation to personal identity when the individual categorizes, classifies or associates in relation to a social grouping and takes on a role and the associated meanings, expectations and standards of that role and its performance within the group (Stets and Burke 2000). Hence, much of what we know about our identities is derived from interactions with others as their verbal and non-verbal communication of appraisal influences our views of self and our roles in relation to other members of the group (Stets and Harrod 2004). This highlights the importance of social groups as they set the context for the creation of roles and interpersonal interactions as well as intrapersonal conversations with the internal voices that underpin identity.

On a tacit level, how one interacts with others through roles is guided by both complementary and competing motives and goals such as self-esteem and continuity, distinctiveness and belonging, and efficacy and meaning (Vignoles *et al.* 2005). Within a social grouping or structure, one's status or position 'infuses interactions with meaning, producing perceptions that facilitate or impede the development and maintenance of positive regard for the self', and accentuates role characterizations (Stets and Harrod 2004: 155). Consequently, one has varying degrees of agency in constructing contexts that allow one's identity and subsequent roles to be verified and reinforced (Stets and Harrod 2004).

On a more explicit level, we consider the expression of identity as occurring through voice and language. Voices help to express identity within social interactions and influence boundaries and negotiations of roles, and maintain the social structures that support multiple roles (Rée 2000). We view voice, like identity, as composed of both a deep inner component and more socially oriented outer components. These outer components of voice are often associated with language in various modalities including spoken language, written text, or physical body language. The inner component of voice can be construed as an important part of one's sense of self and attending to this 'inner voice' can greatly contribute to one's sense of self, and sense of agency and control. Accordingly, there can be multiple voices, some perceptible in the foreground while others are silenced in response to the roles, structures and dialectic in which we experience life and interactions with others.

In this complex composition of identities, roles and voices there is a constant interplay and we agree with the work of postmodern philosophers, such as Lacan, Kristeva, Bosch, Foucault and Butler, who focus on the relationship between an individual's sense of existential fragmentation and the need to assert some level of 'self-unified identity' (Hall 2004: 83). For the postmodern philosophers, as well as for us, identities are always 'under construction' in contexts that are characterized by indeterminacy, partiality and complexity. In our view, such remains the case in the sphere of higher education. Diverse individuals each bring to bear a unique identity, and a multitude of roles and voices to the construction and conservation of knowledge, while experiencing rapidly evolving changes in the academy. Concurrently, each is challenged to continue to construct a personal identity.

In the recent past, with respect to research identities, academics held more autonomy, were free to set their research agendas and determine research priorities, and were trusted to self-regulate (Harris 2005). Today, these same academics are experiencing what Taylor refers to as a 'fundamental pessimism' because they perceive threats to their sense of academic freedom and autonomy. In effect, the stable and legitimizing identities academics held as part of disciplines and institutions are losing their stability and boundedness (Castells 1997); seasoned academics are struggling to manoeuvre and find the appraisals that can help them to continue to build their sense of worth and efficacy.

Handal has pointed out that the identity of academic developers is constructed through participation and negotiation in two communities – the internal one of other developers, and the external one of the wider community of the academy. Developers as a group lack a unifying identity, perhaps because they come from different educational backgrounds, and often have quite different functions and institutional mandates. They are perhaps unique in the academy in being mandated actively to engage in contributing to change, and may be called upon to support institutional efforts for change that they do not support. Thus, it is not surprising that they are embroiled in questioning their identity.

Batchelor questions the existence of the voice and agency of students, and characterizes student voice as distorted and devalued. While she often places voice and identity on an equal footing, we speculate that her focus on voice is due to her perception of students' lack of manifest group identities. In this view, Batchelor doesn't acknowledge the varied collective identities and voices of students (e.g. inexperienced and advanced undergraduates and graduates, continuing education learners, domestic and international, etc.), or their varied experiences. For instance, it is now more difficult for doctoral students to make transitions from student to academic when the stable structures that enabled this progression are fluctuating.

Whitchurch suggests administrators are developing a distinct and legitimate new collective voice in the institution. She believes they exemplify Mode 2 knowledge – transdisciplinarity – and describes their work as carried out in non-hierarchical, heterogeneously organized forms which are transient and not institutionalized primarily within university structures. She proposes that identities rather than being constructed in opposition to corporatism and managerialism should become more context-specific.

Our reading of these chapters made us particularly aware of other identities not accounted for so far. These originate in the many unseen but essential roles, e.g. residence or housing officer, technician, and maintenance personnel, that ensure the mandated teaching, learning and research functions of the academy are accomplished. We have overlooked how their identities have been and continue to be influenced by the complex transformations in the academy in the past decade.

Out of the woodwork: negotiating roles and voice (Allison)

As academics, we tend to focus our efforts for development on the roles that appear most prominent in the academy: the professor, graduate student and undergraduate tend to garner the most attention. However, these voices and identities are not the only roles within the academic community that bear the effects of neo-liberal reform. Even as regards academics, Taylor reminds us that 'there is no such thing as a standard academic career', and indeed academic identities are shaped by the many relationships we encounter – our relationship to our research, our colleagues, supervisors, students and administrators all shape our experiences. For the academic developer, the consequences for the emergence of Mode 2 knowledge, and the shift in academia towards corporatism and managerialism, as discussed previously, bear not only on the academic staff and students with whom developers work directly, but also on the support staff with whom we concurrently construct our experiences.

We suggest an inclusive approach to exploring how the patterns of global change in the academy shape all of our experiences – one that seeks to uncover the structures of the academy that are supported by individuals whose voices are rarely heard in the discourses of our disciplines. Roles that we have identified are varied and often intersect. In addition to lecturers, students, developers and administrators, there are librarians, teaching assistants, academic advisors, principal and vice-principal and their associated offices, deans and associate deans, housing officers, building maintenance staff, cafeteria staff, part-time instructors, graders, departmental secretaries, library technicians, laboratory technologists, research assistants, student counsellors and union representatives.

All these roles occur within structures that we identify as follows: those often overlooked but fundamentally necessary spaces that occupy our academic community and ensure its daily operation. Our definition is broad, and spans definite structures such as buildings, fields and other physical spaces in the university, and the bureaucratic organization of university administration, right down to the often decentralized organization of faculties and the support and maintenance staff that run them. More recently, we see new structures that influence the 'becoming' of identity, and its expression in the university. Giroux (2002) critically examines the influence of corporate cultures on university campuses in the USA. Corporate fast food and coffee chains now occupy student commons, spaces meant to gather students for intellectual purposes. Vending machines dot the walls of virtually every building on most campuses, and even bathroom stalls – formerly a space for graffiti – are prime advertising locations for local and multinational corporations. Buildings are named after corporations. In addition to the corporatization of space, many of our services on campuses, such as security, have been leased out to private interests.

The university, like most other corporate or governmental institutions, operates on a hierarchy of employment. Our learning takes place in an environment where there are many different players executing various roles within the hierarchy. All these players have different roles and voices, some that are legitimized by the dominant discourse in academia and some that are marginalized; legitimacy usually falls near the top end of the hierarchy. Those who occupy roles at the base of the hierarchy bear the immediate consequences of corporatization, yet their voices are rarely recognized and consulted with in our universities. How do we as part of this larger academic community respond to this? For example, the politics of labour in a neo-liberal university becomes more complex with the increased hiring of contingent labour in the form of teaching and support staff. How does this move towards the 'temporary' affect the workload and role and thus the identity and voice of the part-time teacher who takes on more courses and more students with less job security and benefits? And how might we respond as developers?

Thus, for us the most salient of Batchelor's points is that of attending to the silenced voice. We turn to the subject of silences in order to give voice to those roles in university settings that are perpetually silent – building maintenance staff, cafeteria workers, secretarial support staff or campus security staff. The voices of these crucial members of the academy are never heard, yet the impact their roles bear on our academic communities is immense. How are they invisibly contributing to the development of our academic identities as lecturers, students, librarians and researchers? How can we provide a space for such roles, in order to expand the definition of our community to include those whose voices are not privileged in classrooms or academic texts? Although we cannot begin to address these questions here, they lead us to explore the potential of Activity System theory as an analytical tool to account for the ways in which roles and structures within the university are influential in the development of identity and voice.

How might we make sense of this complexity? Living in evolving systems (Lynn)

The field of academic development in the 1960s, 1970s and 1980s was very much rooted in a personal perspective, whether humanist or psychological. In the 1990s, when efforts were made to shift to a socio-cultural perspective, the field (like the writers in Part I) took up Communities of Practice (Lave and Wenger 1991). However, our examination of the complexities of role, structure, identity and voice has affirmed for us the need to question the usefulness of this framework. Like Knight and Trowler (2001), we conclude that Communities of Practice is not a particularly useful analytical tool in describing the dynamism and tensions inherent in the higher education system we experience. In particular, it is insufficient in explaining the relation between structure and personal agency, the dialectical – competing and complementary – experiences of individuals with different roles within multiple embedded overlapping structures. These emerging tensions are referred to, for instance, by Handal and Whitchurch as that of serving both the institution and professors, or by Taylor as of affiliation with both the discipline and the institution.

Thus, like others in our field, we have begun looking to other socio-cultural theories to help us account for the cultural and historical 'luggage' that creates the collectivities we live. For instance, Foucault identifies the ways in which discourse is historically and socially constructed and situated by practices that we develop within the contexts of our different disciplines, which in turn shape collective academic identities. These practices – the language, social behaviours, epistemic beliefs and ideas – are sanctioned by a particular profession, define a particular field of knowledge, and have historical significance (Foucault 1969). Discursive practices are not necessarily explicit; rather, they are naturalized ways of thinking, doing, speaking and writing. Bourdieu (1991) refers to this as the *doxa* or the legitimacy of sanctioned behaviours in (in this case) scientific disciplines. This is an important concept in order to understand the ways in which inequalities of privilege and power persist through generations of academic practice, without conscious recognition; and also to understand how modes of knowledge production become legitimized by an academic community.

Whereas Foucault and Bourdieu provide a critical perspective, we have been seeking a more analytical tool that incorporates personal agency – the recognition of an individual's desire and ability to act pragmatically within structures while maintaining and developing a sense of personal identity. We wish to understand how identity is conceived and developed and how rapid changes can disrupt historical practices. Here, we explore the potential of Activity Systems (Engeström 1987; Engeström *et al.* 1999) emerging from the work of Vygotsky. Our intent is not to reify Activity Systems, but rather to examine its potential to 'open a window' on the construction of our identity.

In our view, Activity Systems theory attends to the recurrent, embedded and historical nature of human activity, the assumption that higher mental processes have their origins in social practices (Blackler 1993). Examining 'practice' as a communicative and interactive process highlights the purposefulness of inter-action and the tools that mediate this (Lambert 2003). Humans create and use tools such as language to coordinate with each other and also to self-regulate; this allows for both repetition of activities but also the creation of qualitatively new events. 'Activity' links mind and society; preserves the coherence of differ-ent actions; and incorporates motivation, contexts of action and mental processes used to enact activities.

Basically, the *individual* directs *action* towards a *purpose* using language and physical *tools* (e.g. computers, documents, phones, pencils). The *activity* occurs in a *community* that shares the *collective purposes and tools* and a *common set of often tacit rules* which enable a *division of labour and power*. For instance, in an undergraduate class, a lecturer and students use *tools*, such as language and black-board, to achieve a *collective purpose*, to complete the course. Both the lecturer and students act within *tacit rules* about, for instance, acceptable behaviour and roles. They understand the *differentiation in labour and power* that is expected. They probably never discuss these rules or their personal conceptions of how the purpose is to be accomplished through their respective roles. In fact, they may avoid doing so as contrasting and competing conceptions of the purpose most likely exist. So, in observing a class, we might hear clearly and powerfully the lecturer's voice as s/he speaks (his/her role expectation) emerging out of his/her identity as an expert in the field. As for the students, we might see some listen-ing and taking notes, others reading for the next class, others napping, and some exchanging notes with desk mates; further, some students may have chosen not to come to class (different student role expectations). We observe no student voice(s) in this class; this may result from students believing that their role is not to have a voice as well as from the lecturer either overlooking creating a space, or choosing not to make a space, for their voices.

The focus on pragmatic action – engaging in historical and embedded practices – acknowledges the strength of social routines that obscure the incoherence, in-consistency and tensions that are likely to be entrenched and resistant to change within the varying structures of a system. 'Ignoring' the tensions around different role expectations makes class routines relatively effortless. Yet the failure to chal-lenge these activities means class roles and structures become ossified. However, since uncertainty is an everyday feature of our experience, there is always the potential for learning new ways of engaging in activities or even creating new activities (Blackler 1993) if we are prepared to give voice to – to make explicit – the inconsistencies of the social routines. Thus, although classes will probably continue to be taught the way they have been for years, an examination of them in which both lecturer and students have a voice may lead to dramatic change – new and different ways of providing spaces for the continued construction of identity.

So far we have examined only one system – a course – and the roles of student and lecturer. Each of these individuals moves among multiple intersecting and/ or nested activity systems which demand and afford different, complementary, but also conflicting roles, purposes, tools, rules and patterns of social interaction (Tuomi-Grohn *et al.* 2003). In these different contexts, individuals maintain and develop their personal identities, while possibly calling forth different voices in relation to their roles. This polycontextuality – movement among different systems – explains the additional level of dialectic experienced by individuals in higher education institutions, that is, the ambiguity, inconsistency, dilemmas and possible discord as one concurrently undertakes different purposes in different activities with different tools and often with individuals who have different roles and come from different structures. Voices representing different facets of one's identity can emerge or be silenced in these different contexts.

The ambiguities of interaction across systems can contribute to the continued construction of identity and voice, but may equally be fossilizing (Engeström 2001). For instance, routines, such as university committee meetings, are unifying mechanisms for the organization; however, truce may exist between committee members since each individual brings from other activity systems (such as department or school) different and competing purposes and tools. And these differences may not be worth reconciling if the purpose of the committee – meeting as required by university timetables – bears little on the other systems that individual committee members invest in more heavily because those are more central to their own identity. Thus, Activity Systems help explain why people act practically with others despite competing purposes and identities, and why rapid changes in the institution disrupt roles, voices and identities.

The reality: identity in a world of multiple systems (all of us)

So far, we have examined the application of Activity Systems to analyse a course and a committee meeting. We now use Activity Systems to analyse the construction of identity and voice for a lecturer, an undergraduate, and one of the invisible roles and silenced voices we referred to earlier, a housing officer. We wish to show how the systems representing a course or meeting are but two of the many systems in which each individual participates – trying to find some meaningful role and purpose in relation to identity in the polycontextuality of the lived experience. We feel comfortable ourselves voicing this complexity for lecturer and student and potentially how it bears on identity construction and voice – and as developers these roles are a primary concern – but can do so for the housing officer only through secondary literature and documentation.

The pre-tenure or tenured lecturer engages in multiple roles in a variety of systems, for instance, lecturer in different courses; reviewer for journals; supervisor for a number of students; consultant on different projects; member of (a) departmental, faculty, university committees, (b) one or more academic societies, (c) research team. Each of these systems has a different purpose and role expectation which may be at odds with the others. The investment that the lecturer makes in each will vary depending on the extent to which the purpose and role are congruent with his/her personal identity goals, and whether they are institutionally mandated or personally chosen. Thus, if a lecturer most highly values his/her research role amongst all roles for the construction of identity, investments will tend to be in ways that support that development. This may mean a lesser investment in the others, an acceptance of the habituated routines; whereas, in research team meetings or as a reviewer of journals, s/he may be more prepared to name and challenge inconsistencies and work towards modifying systems. Another example would be of a lecturer uncomfortable with changes occurring in his/her institution who first engaged actively in a number of university systems (different levels of committee work) to challenge those changes and when not successful chose to withdraw from participation in most institutional systems to protest, and focused instead on external disciplinary ones.

The 'student' also engages in multiple systems, and this is multiplied by the fact that 'students' represent a very heterogeneous group with respect to age, socio-economic status, life experience, culture, religion and sexual orientation. For instance, new undergraduates enter university still constructing their own identities with a multitude of motives and goals. Small numbers of students envisage further education or research careers; many aim for a desired employment after obtaining a degree; and many enter not knowing what they want or where they are headed. As a result, many students – particularly the last group – explore and test various potential facets of identity during their undergraduate years. And the structures of the academy support this. Formally, students pay fees to take courses across an array of disciplines, and are exposed to a variety of conventions for thinking, inquiry and expression of ideas. Informally, outside of classes, they may participate in various student groups, extracurricular activities, sporting and student life events, part-time employment or volunteer work. While each individual can engage in multiple constellations of roles and contexts, they also learn to prioritize certain activity systems as these lend themselves to their personal goals and motivations. For example, if a student comes to realize attending medical school is a personal goal, s/he may privilege systems that bring him/her closer to this goal as well as ones that s/he can contribute to (such as study groups, volunteer work in a hospital) while other systems will become less central (such as sporting events). Cumulatively, such decisions act to strengthen or challenge a student's self-concept and identity.

There are other formal activity systems beyond the course that can play an influential part in development of student identity and voice. Research highlights the crucial role residence life has in the construction of their identities (see for example Light 2001). The same is true of librarians (Leckie 1996). Some of these roles and groups are gaining visibility as they organize via formal associations. For instance, the Association of College and University Housing Officers (ACUHO) is a volunteer association consisting of individuals who oversee and monitor student housing activities on higher education campuses. They perceive their role and primary task as to 'assist and develop meaningful relationships with students' (McCluskey-Titus 2005: 11). They are usually hired on a contractual basis, yet share their lives and living space with students, and are also invested in their complex roles of administrator, role model, informal teacher and counsellor.

As developers, we often overlook – fail to see and hear – the roles and voices of these important individuals and the structure provided by the student housing system and the libraries that support learning. Through recognition of these individuals in other activity systems in which students engage, we acknowledge individuals who may play a profound role in the development of student identity and voice. Further, their roles remind us of the polycontextuality and multivoicedness of the lived experiences of all individuals in the academy.

How might we use this analysis as developers?

This analysis explicitly lays out the complexity of interactions and intersections among multiple roles and structures, and enables us to analyse the dialectic of identity and voice within that dynamic. What has surfaced particularly are the tensions, challenges and distortions that may occur in order to maintain social routines through pragmatic actions. In our examination, we have highlighted what Batchelor refers to as the practical voice rather than the epistemological or ontological ones. How does this help us as developers to understand better the complexities of our own lives and the lives of those we work with in the academy? How does it inform the role, identity and voice of the developer as we move forward into the twenty-first century?

Handal has mentioned the troubled nature of the word 'developer', yet positive challenges lie beyond us in supporting the development, the growth, of the individual – ourselves included. And it is clear from Part I that the notion of development or construction of the self is embedded in the thinking of other authors in this volume as well: in particular, Taylor in relation to the construction of identity in contexts that are characterized by indeterminacy, partiality and complexity; Batchelor in the development of voice created partly through disorientation and uncertainty; and Whitchurch in the importance of development as a personal goal. As she notes: 'what we are at present matters less than what we are becoming'.

The centrality of indeterminacy and uncertainty in all our lives reminds us of Taylor's (1987) model of the learning process in which a key aspect is *experiencing, recognizing and using dis-equilibrium* as a stimulus to learning. Perhaps, as developers, we need to focus on disequilibrium and uncertainty as a starting place in our work.

And what exactly might our work consist of? Centra (1989) characterized development as encompassing four aspects: personal (interpersonal skills, career development, and life planning issues); instructional (course design and implementation); organizational (ways to improve the institutional environment the better to support teaching); and professional (ways to support faculty members so that they fulfil their multiple roles of teaching, research, and service). The traditional focus of developers' work has been working with lecturers around instructional issues – though increasingly driven by organizational concerns. However, Centra's analysis points to a wider role. First, the traditional approach of developers largely ignores the role of researcher, which is key to identity, learning, and belonging for most academics. So, the future for academic development may lie in broadening our work from lecturers to the professionals, since this more effectively encompasses the totality of the academic life. Further, a focus on lecturers ignores the many others whose roles, while invisible to us, influence student learning. Thus, our future may lie in working more closely with others such as librarians – individuals whose mandates are to support teaching and research.

At the same time, since organizational factors remain powerful, there is a dialectic of competing tensions for the developer as we act and move between different but overlapping structures. We are engaged in supporting the construction of identity of students, lecturers and other staff, yet may be required to undertake institutional mandates in discord with our own values and those with whom we work. Further, we are concurrently developing and sustaining our own identities in this often ambiguous and conflicted environment. In the rapidly evolving academy, the challenge for us – one we share with our colleagues across the academy – is to create collective spaces where we may more openly examine the inconsistencies, dilemmas, and possible discord of our experiences in the polycontextuality of our lived academic worlds.

Chapter 9

Academic identities and institutional change

Gerard Delanty

Introduction

A striking feature of the academic environment in the present day is an apparent tension between the institutional context and the personal identities of academics. On the one side, it is widely felt that institutions of higher education are coming increasingly under pressure from market and state forces with the result that individual academics feel that they have little control over the institutions in which they work. On the other side, higher education is an institutional sphere that offers many of those who work within it a considerable degree of autonomy. Academics have a strong sense of their professional identity, which has been traditionally separate from the specific institutional context. It has been widely accepted that academics have as their primary loyalty the scholarly community of which they are a part rather than the specific institution in which they work. This may be a somewhat old-fashioned professorial identity, but there is little doubt that the perception academics have of themselves is often in tension with the institutional context. Whether or not this has increased today or has taken a new form will be explored in this chapter. This tension cannot be understood without a consideration of the changing nature of academic institutions, which can be seen as the site of identity projects.

It does need to be stated that this is the perspective of an academic in a research-led British university. It is clearly the case that a considerable amount of higher education is delivered by institutions other than universities and ones which are not primarily research-based. My reflections in this contribution are primarily concerned with academics who work in the traditional research-based universities and enjoy the privileges of a permanent post.

Identity as positionality

The focus on identity that is the concern of this volume offers an interesting corrective to studies on higher education that deal only with institutional structures. There has been much literature on this in recent years (see Barnett 1999; Delanty 2001; Manicas and Odin 2004; Robins and Webster 2002). The theme of identity, then, suggests a perspective on the subjectivity of the social actor. In this sense, my theme is Bourdieu's notion of the academic habitus, that is, the contextual situation of social action and involving institutional structures, cultural dispositions and value orientations (Bourdieu 1988, 1996). However, against his largely structural reading of the academic and the academic institution as a 'state nobility', the reality is closer to the postmodern scenario described variously by Lyotard (1984) and others. It is in short a good deal more anarchic than in Bourdieu's characterization. Academic identities, I argue, are shaped by the institutional context, but crucially also shape institutions. Agency is one side of the coin whose other face is the institutional organization of roles and rules. Higher education is a striking example of an institution that is best understood in terms of a process rather than a fixed structure and one that is generative of an increasing variety of positions.

It may be a caricature of academic life in an age that has passed to say that academic identities were largely shaped outside the institutions of higher education. The academic, typically recruited from a narrow social stratum, entered the academic world with a preordained identity based on an accredited expertise and a commitment to the pursuit of knowledge, which was generally disciplinary specific. In the twentieth century the doctorate came to be the principle mark of such academic 'voice'. The dominant conceptions of knowledge separated the world of science and scholarship from the world of politics and opinion. In this, the doctorate – an American-led development but based on a German invention – played a key role. With this demarcation of knowledge from belief, identity was for the most part taken care of. The university was supposed to be based on a foundational 'idea', the universality of truth, as in Cardinal Newman's Victorian vision of liberal education (Newman 1996). So when the question was asked 'What is the university?', the traditional response was variously an account of the *idea* of the university. The assumption was that this idea gave a collective identity to the institution of the university and was embodied in the identities of academics. It has been widely commented that this is no longer the case. There is no single legitimizing idea of the university, no grand narrative, but a plurality of ideas and a growing diversity of universities and institutions of higher education. Often called the 'postmodern university', the university has become a battlefield of contending visions of knowledge, since knowledge too has ceased to be self-legislating (see Readings 1996; Smith and Webster 1996). This is the context in which to situate the theme of identities.

Before proceeding further, a few theoretical remarks on identity are required. Identity is not given but constructed in many ways. Although one's identity may appear to be stable and enduring, from a theoretical perspective identity must be viewed as being socially constructed. Viewed in such terms, identity is a project and entails (1) positionality – social actors position themselves in relation to others and in doing so make distinctions between self and other; (2) performativity – social actors perform their identities in different ways, or in other words identities involve action and can be viewed as sets of practices; (3) situation in a context; and (4) mostly discursive construction in narratives and other modes of communication. Two further observations can be made about identity. Identities are frequently overlapping, with a given individual having multiple identities. This multiple nature of identity is one of the major themes in current identity theory. Secondly, identity nowadays is often experienced as in crisis. Nowhere is this more apparent than in academic life. The crisis of identity takes many forms, but one prevalent aspect is the incongruence between self-identity (or personal identities in the sense of the identities of specific individuals) and the collective identity of a group. Institutions such as universities do not easily articulate a collective identity that is capable of acknowledging the numerous identity projects that arise within it. As a result identity is perceived as in crisis. So, in sum, identity is a project that is not fixed but an on-going process of negotiation. Of the various aspects to identity mentioned here, I would like to single out the dimension of positionality as particularly relevant to academic identity. It seems to me that academic identities are very much about taking a position. I shall return to this below.

Institutions as process

Before taking up the theme of identity, I would like in addition to make a few observations about institutions, and higher education institutions in particular. Under the influence of neo-institutionalism, institutions are increasingly seen as rule-systems as opposed to fixed structures (Powell and DiMaggio 1991). As rule-systems, institutions require interpretation by social actors; these actors are not just shaped or determined by the institutions but shape those institutions through their interpretative activity. As in contemporary identity theory, institutions are increasingly seen as fluid, multilinear and more akin to processes in the sense that they are under constant change. Giddens (1984) emphasizes the enabling nature of modern institutions and the reflexive relation between structure and agency. For reasons of space, I cannot enter into a detailed consideration of these approaches to institutions, other than to highlight what strikes me as a pertinent point that is highly relevant to the debate about higher education, namely the idea that institutions of higher education can be theorized in terms of a notion of process. There is enough evidence to make plausible the claim that universities are constantly in motion; change is the permanent condition, with universities constantly responding to external and internal demands. One might take this further and suggest, following Zygmunt Bauman, that universities have become 'liquid' organizations (Bauman 2001). This is true of many institutions, but to varying degrees. Universities are no longer the closed and balanced institutions described by Parsons and Platt (1973) in their major study of the modern American university, which was held to exemplify the relevance of structural functionalism. External pressures

– from the state, the market, the law, research funders – are now translated into internal pressures, as in managerialism, bureaucratization, evaluation and training. In addition, universities – in particular the older universities – are multi-level institutions, with particularly complex systems of governance. Clark Kerr (1963) in a much cited book referred to this complexity as 'the multiversity.'

It is a mistake to see an institution as a closed system of structures. The management of an institution of higher education requires a capacity to appreciate the fact that the institution is a process. Celia Whitchurch, in her contribution to this volume, describes very well how administrative and managerial roles themselves are in flux and are no longer linear or predetermined. This is not just a problem for university managers to adjust to, but it is the context in which all academics work. The context is one of institutions not just responding to change, but having change built into them. This means that the contemporary institution of higher education is not based on stability. When one appreciates this, the job of surviving in the academic world becomes easier. Those who do not make this cognitive adjustment suffer from what is commonly referred to as stress, which is institutional dissonance, or the lack of fit of identity and institution.

The next step in my argument is to link this conception of institutions as being in process with identities. As previously suggested, soft institutions, such as universities, with their fluid and changing boundaries, are clearing grounds for new identities. Identities are not pre-established but are created in specific contexts. Universities, I would like to argue, are one such context in which identities are created. The logic of such institutions – the priority of process over form – is productive of identity building. As a process, academics are constantly positioning themselves and are often being re-positioned. If process rather than stability is the nature of the institutional reality, it thus follows that such identities will be intertwined with the symbolic language and form of the institution. Although higher education has without doubt become a complex territory, it is not what Max Weber believed was the fate of modern institutions – an 'iron cage' of bureaucracy – or what Herbert Marcuse regarded as a 'totally administered world'. Less a monolith than an open system that lacks closure, higher education is in every sense the paradigmatic example of an institution defined in terms of process rather than form or structure.

The connection between identity as positionality and the institutional context in terms of process can be demonstrated in a number of ways, which will be discussed now.

Nostalgia for liberal bourgeois elitism

Do academics have something to complain about? The dominant discourses suggest that academics see their situation in unfavourable terms. The familiar terms of the discourse are workload increase, administrative duties, low pay, and increased managerial control over teaching and research. The narrative is generally couched as nostalgia for the past age of liberal bourgeois elitism.

Whether there was once such a golden age is of course another matter, but I rather doubt it. For women it was a dark age. This is a point that Peter Taylor also makes in his contribution to this volume. A sober look at the current situation suggests a more differentiated picture than the simple narrative that many academics have. The reality today is a world in which more opportunities exist for academics. Importantly, and a source of many academic identities, most academics in permanent research and teaching contracts have a considerable control over their work.

This is particularly true as far as research is concerned. It is arguably the case there is more not less academic freedom. Most academics are relatively free to pursue their research and there are now more career opportunities for women and the less socially advantaged than in the 'golden age'. Academic freedom does not mean unlimited freedom – the freedom to say what one wishes – or the freedom to do nothing. Academics are required to publish and if they fail to do so they rarely perish, since universities rarely if ever terminate permanent contracts on grounds of poor performance.

The institution of academic freedom is an interesting example of how an institutional practice provides a space for identity projects. It is my firm belief that academics with permanent posts have more autonomy than most other professions. The fact that they do not see it like this is in part an effect of their particular kind of self-identity. Most professors see themselves as more like self-employed artisans providing a service to their institution than as servants of a state-funded institution. For many it is more a question of what the institution can do for them than what they are required to do.

Many countries are following the UK example of having a Research Assessment Exercise (RAE). Although vilified as the apex of a system of state control and excessive manageralism, the RAE operates with a definition of research so general that it includes almost everything and, moreover, claims not to censor research but to evaluate it. For many, too, it has boosted academic identities. Teaching is a different matter.

The growing presence of quality assurance measures in higher education teaching has not yet reached a point of determining the actual content of what is taught. Benchmarking is of course in evidence in most areas, but the level of generality cannot be said to amount to a loss of autonomy. In sum, in the core areas of teaching and research most academics still retain considerable autonomy over their work relative to other professions. I would argue that that very autonomy has been the basis of many identity projects.

Dissatisfaction and the academic habitus

The wider society may view academics as privileged, but this is not how most academics perceive themselves. Dissatisfaction would appear to be a constitutive feature of the academic personality. Whether or not academics have something to complain about depends on their positionality. Those excluded from permanent academic posts almost certainly have less favourable circumstances and something to complain about. But positionality, as I have argued, is also about the capacity to articulate one's voice and promote one's identity project.

The academic lives in a world of rising expectations, and where these expectations exceed what can be realized the result will be dissatisfaction. Academic salaries, while guaranteeing a degree of security that many workers do not enjoy, are low relative to what can be earned in the hyper-information economy. For this reason, the lure of academia is simply not attractive for many potential academics. For those whose identity consists of the pursuit of creativity rather than the quest for autonomy, it is possible that the heavily bureaucratized nature of academia is simply unappealing.

The constantly changing world of academia would suggest that the academic habitus today is highly diverse. While many academics work in disciplinary and inter-disciplinary areas, the context of much research and teaching is increasingly post-disciplinarity, where there are no specific disciplines. Disciplines have traditionally been one of the principal guarantors of academic identity.

Multi-positionality

A striking feature of academic work is that for any individual academic it consists of not one role but many. The Humboldtian vision of the integral unity of teaching and research was a myth even in its own day, although one that continues to shape many academic identities. Humboldt's idea of a university education was based on the assumption that the student undergoes a change in personality in the encounter with research, communicated through an activity called teaching. This was the meaning of *Bildung* – the intellectual shaping of personality. Newman, although hostile to research, also had a view of the unity of knowledge as based on an underlying truth which was communicated to students by academics. This vision of a liberal education today survives in undergraduate colleges in North America, where teaching is largely separated from large-scale research. But for the greater part, the idea of a liberal education is no longer a meaningful characterization of what goes on in the research-led university.

The reality for most academics is that they have to perform many roles, ranging from teaching to research to administrative roles and entrepreneurialism. The result is that the academic is pulled in many directions and many academics have difficulty in performing all these roles. Young academics in particular are under pressure in that the rewards are primarily for research, yet other roles increasingly have to be performed to a high standard. In terms of identity formation, the multi-positionality that results from role differentiation, does not necessarily lead to multiple identities, for not every role leads to identification with it. The majority of academics would appear to identify with teaching and research, preferring to leave administration to the professional administrator. While there are many examples of academics taking on and identifying with their multiple roles, as the examples of dean, pro-vice-chancellor and vice-chancellor suggest, the majority of academics do not identify with their administrative roles.

The law and identity positioning

The law has become a major site of identity making. Many identities in contemporary society are constituted in and through the law. This is the case with a wide range of so-called identity politics, ranging from gender to multicultural politics. The law is not a neutral site but is productive of identities. Many identities are sustained by their capacity to be expressed in the legal categories of rights. Legal rights, such as those associated with human rights, have given ethnic groups and various minority groups a means of articulating identity.

Nowhere is this confluence of rights and identities more evident than in higher education, where the cultural politics of identity claims has been particularly vociferous. The outcome of many of these cultural struggles has been the transformation of cultural categories into legal categories. The result is less cultural recognition – as in issues of diversity and equality – than legal compliance.

There is no shortage of examples to illustrate what might be called the juridification of identity. Affirmative action policies are one example as is the notion of equality of opportunity, which has a very wide sphere of application, especially in UK universities. The recourse to the law is no longer confined to fairness in hiring staff but pervades virtually every sphere of academic life. Academics – staff and students – who tend to have a relatively strong consciousness of rights in comparison to other groups are increasingly empowered by the law. Thus it has come about that the context of litigation is present in the working lives of academics both as a weapon of identity to be used against their employers and as a trope of media self-projection.

The governance of identities

An interesting consideration in any assessment of academic identities is technologization. By this I mean the degree to which identities are shaped within the institutional apparatus of higher education by various kinds of technologies. As the earlier remarks above suggested, institutions such as higher education are difficult to imagine without taking into account the subjectivities out of which they are composed.

It is possible to see, following Foucault, higher education as a system of governance that creates a variety of subject positions out of which emerge a great variety of voices and identities. This system of governance, which forms the basis of the institutional logic of higher education, is realized in numerous technologies that pervade most aspects of academic life and continuous. As an institution that is, as already argued, multilinear and processual, the system of governance that has evolved in higher education is one that has been reflexively incorporated into the actual practice of academic work.

Communication and information technologies are integral to academic work and as these technologies evolve so too does the subjectivity and identity of the social actor. The system of governance is extensive and includes quality assurance and continuous training and performance monitoring, mentoring and the varieties of strategies that Gunnar Handal in his chapter discusses under the heading of developers. As is well known, quality assurance is less about quality – which would have to be defined – than assurance, which can be managed.

Another feature of quality assurance that has implications for subjectivity is its concern with process rather than content. Excellence cannot be measured by a fixed set of principles, so everything can be excellent (see Readings 1996). This de-referentialized aspect of the system of governance is the highly fragile context in which academic identities are formed. In the absence of rigid structures and fixed and settled ways of doing things, the system of relations that holds the academic world together is highly fragile. This fragility is easily transformed into anxiety or stress. Stressed academics are not necessarily those who work excessively, but those who are unable to cope with a context that appears to be forever changing and lacking stability.

Inside and outside

Identity presupposes a capacity to distinguish between inside and outside; the self knows itself in terms of a relation to an other. The logic of this is generally articulated in a narrative. There are many examples of collective identity narratives in academia (centenaries, annual conventions, various myths of origin). But the capacity of individual academics to articulate self-identities in narrative form is less clear-cut.

One of the difficulties in building academic identities today is that the terms of identity building are being rendered diffuse. Institutions may have their official collective identities but individual academics lack certainty as to their identity. As mentioned, academics have to occupy many subject positions and their identities are being constantly worked upon by a vast range of technologies of governance and are also being juridified. In this complex world, it is often difficult to distinguish between inside and outside. Higher education is no longer quite 'higher' in a way that it once was. But the erosion of inside and outside is most evident in the interface of higher education with the market and the state.

Market values have become more prevalent within the academy than in the past. Academics are increasingly having to confront the market, whether for funding or to maintain market competitiveness to recruitment. A feature of this market is its global nature, with many funding streams within higher education institutions dependent on a steady supply of overseas students willing to pay high fees. However, marketization of the university is often exaggerated with visions of a universal descent into academic capitalism and the McDonaldization of higher education (see Slaughter and Lesley 1997; Scott 1998). It should be noted that the trend towards privatization in higher education does not mean that all private higher education institutions are players for profit, as there is an important distinction between the private non-profit institutions and those who work for profit. In the UK there is as yet little evidence of privatization.

Academics in the humanities and social sciences dominate the current debate about the university. They often forget that the science-based academics have long been accustomed to the market and situating research wherever the money lies. Virtually all research in the sciences requires external funding, unlike humanities-based research, which is predominantly the product of single scholarship.

Networks and identities as flows

Academics are networkers and the social form of the network shapes much of the work done by academics. According to Manuel Castells, the global information revolution has introduced network-based forms of social relations into many domains of social life (Castells, 1997). A network is a set of interconnected nodes and is a tendentially open structure organized around the flow of communication. Networks are dynamic, reflexive, polycentric and susceptible to innovation. The kinds of identities associated with networks also take the form of flows in that they are less likely to be fixed as in traditional identities.

These new ways of working and social relations have been pronounced in academia and have major implications for identity and the very conception of the self. As researchers, most academics are located in a network; the scientific scholarly community is itself a global network, even if it is nationally organized in national higher education systems. The implications of this for academic identity have not been fully assessed. Castells suggests that the network society can enhance individualized identities, but it can also lead to the fragmentation of identities leading to identities of resistance. The informational networked society is empowering as well as alienating. Academics, who do not have specific working hours unlike many workers, can work from home and often commute long distances. As well as being a basis for greater autonomy, it can also erode the distinction between work and home.

The spatial context in which academic work is conducted has been disconnected from place. In so far as they can be conceived of in terms of the notion of the network, universities are fluid institutions lacking fixed reference points. As such they are more likely to sustain identities of flows than less reflexively organized institutions.

Conclusion

The institutional logic of higher education makes it a fertile ground for the production of identities. Indeed many new cultural and political identities have been cultivated within the context of higher education. Higher education is no longer the privilege of elites as was the case up until relatively recently. The democratization of higher education has opened the institutions of higher education to the political and cultural issues of the wider public sphere. One consequence of this politicization of academia has been a lack of clarity as to the identity of its institutions. Universities can no longer lay exclusive claim to the mantle of truth and have to compete with many epistemic actors, all laying claim to truth. Science is no longer able to offer certain answers, a development that forces universities to redefine themselves (Fuller 2000). The university has irretrievably lost its monopoly over knowledge in the broad sense of education, nor does it exclusively define science. While universities have suffered a major crisis in their collective identity, there is no shortage of possible identity projects within academic institutions.

The argument made here is that the changing nature of academic institutions, where roles are being constantly changed and subjected to new orders of governance and where nothing appears to be fixed, results in an increased emphasis on identity. This is not least a consequence of the fact that, as has been widely commented on, we live in a highly individuated age (Giddens 1991). The identities of academics, in their professional and personal roles, like identities more generally, are expressions of individualized life projects rather than products of specific roles. Many identities, and this is particularly true of academic identities, result from a creative engagement with institutional roles.

On the basis of the conception of institutions suggested by neo-institutionalist analysis and other sociological approaches to institutions discussed above, universities can be seen as sites of identity projects. Institutional processes – for instance, networks and reflexive modes of self-organization and monitoring – can provide the means for identity construction, through for example various technologies of governance and juridification. In particular new legal categories of rights have become a major site of identity projects for many social actors. In other words, institutions are as much shaped by social actors as determining them. This is not of course the way the situation is perceived.

The current period would appear to be a situation in which academics are experiencing pervasive change due to managerialism and commercialization and lack control over what they do. But a wider view would suggest a different interpretation. The changing institutional frameworks contain many social spaces in which identities are being shaped and where many identity projects are emerging. Although the language of identity is predominantly one of crisis and the erosion of ancient liberties, the reality is more complicated. Universities offer those who work and study in them many opportunities for the expression and recognition of their identities.

Chapter 10

Academic development
Identity and paradox

Ray Land

In search of a warrant

In the complex and differentiated spaces of modern universities perhaps one of the most problematic identities is that of the academic developer. The four 'positions' noted by Taylor earlier in this volume as likely to distinguish identities resonate in interesting ways with the forty or so interviews with academic developers on which this chapter draws. The first position which is ' "taken on" through shared practices that demonstrate faithful acceptance of given truths' immediately brings into view the concern, anxiety even, that many developers feel in relation to the evidence base of their practice, and the question of its robustness. Is their warrant for practice to act in the interest of students and enhance the quality of their learning? If so, does this immediately imply there is an existing 'problem', a deficiency of some sort, in the practice of their academic colleagues? Would such an assumption position them awkwardly in terms of possible collaborative endeavour? Or does their warrant reside in a body of pedagogical research evidence which they expect their colleagues, and managers, to acknowledge and respect? But how likely is it that these colleagues, in the light of such evidence, would subsequently adapt their practice, particularly when they might hold radically different disciplinary understandings of what constitutes reliable knowledge? Those engaged in different knowledge practices might feel cast in the role of followers under (in their terms) questionable leadership.

Academic development knowledge is often 'alien' or 'troublesome' knowledge (Perkins 2006: 39). If the warrant is developers' own professional experience and expertise within the teaching and learning domain, then this too is open to challenge in terms of its disciplinary specificity, inappropriateness or degree of currency. There is an issue here of academic developers still feeling the need to earn a right to be heard in higher education, to find an effective *voice* within the sector, let alone a critical voice.

So the identities of this group are very much constructed through the reflective doubt and scepticism to which Taylor's second position attests. Often developers' own beliefs and commitments in relation to the salience of teaching and learning within academic practice run counter to those whose practice is premised on different allegiances and has a different focus, such as research excellence or consultancy. Moreover the non-rational processes and commitments to which Taylor's third position refers may well derive from developers' own earlier, and often strongly formative, academic identities. Handal, in this volume, points out how these individual latent identities can interact unpredictably with their later identities as academic developers. Hence Taylor's fourth position, in which identity is seen as continuously 'under construction' in conditions of indeterminacy and complexity becomes an apt characterisation of the experience of academic developers. For developers, continually justifying their position, it also feels as if it is permanently under deconstruction.

Handal, drawing on Wenger (1998), also highlighted the important relation between community and identity (or what, for reasons discussed later, we might prefer to term 'subjectivity'). These acts of negotiation with other members of a higher education community of practice, these patterns of influencing and being influenced seem, in the narratives offered by individual respondents, to be crucial in the construction, performance and maintenance of developers' identities. Though developers hope that their development knowledge is both 'warranted and wanted' (Peseta 2005: 94), in their dealings with the institutional communities they operate frequently in difficult strategic terrain, and within complex organisational settings. This entails sensitive readings of cultural situations and often tricky judgement calls about whether leadership, expertise or intervention are desirable (or desired) – with an appropriate degree of direction and mission – or whether intermediating, collaborative or facilitative measures would be more appropriate. These negotiating stances highlight the risks faced by academic developers when their work 'shows up the inadequacies of what is currently being done while demonstrating, with some urgency, what still needs doing' (Peseta 2005: 94). This can easily incur responses from colleagues which in turn can all too easily be characterised as resistance. If developers demonstrate too great a concern with efficiency, quality or policy, this can be misinterpreted as too ready an engagement with managerialist discourses and neo-liberal agendas of performativity. Too much emphasis on pragmatics is dismissed as mickey-mousery. Too much emphasis on pedagogical research evidence is rejected as unnecessary jargon or edu-babble.

The following sections seek to give some indication of the nature of this slippery terrain and the kinds of resistances that can be incurred. From this, something of the complex, complicit and often compromised nature of the developer's role may emerge. It is in many ways a *paradoxical* identity, involving both domestication and critique, perceived as powerful and powerless, modernist and postmodern, both with and sometimes against the work of colleagues. It will be argued that a helpful distinction may be made between the notion of identity, with its implication of agency and a personal project, and that of subjectivity, constituted through discourse, power and negotiation. The latter is perhaps less stable, probably more fragmented and incomplete, arising from a continuing sense of loss, desire and misrecognition. Accepting and working with such modes of being forms the focus of the concluding section. This is, in the end, what academic developers are and do.

Domestication and critique

Taylor pointed out that identity work is ongoing work, historically constituted and socially situated and specific. As the university adapts to an environment of supercomplexity (Barnett 2000), characterised by volatile change, rapid and massive flows of information, and uncertainty and unpredictability in relation to enrolments and revenues, academics find themselves caught in an acceleration of the generation and proliferation of knowledge and the transgressing and fissuring of disciplinary boundaries. This environment is marked by fierce competitiveness and, senior managers and governments warn us, threatened by potential organisational decline unless there is a vigilant and constant drive for innovation and flexibility. To compete successfully, pressures mount on the higher education curriculum to become more finely geared to a globalised economy. Such a transition requires an expanded and more culturally diverse higher education system, involving access for previously marginalised groups on the one hand and an increasing intake of international students paying full costs on the other. In turn, this expansion brings with it calls for greater accountability for the increased government investment it has incurred as well as increased managerialism to achieve and maintain efficiency and effectiveness through reduced resourcing and increased numbers. As a response to this cauldron of change, higher education institutions, initially in the UK, the USA and Australasia, and now increasingly widely, established academic development units as a strategic and operational means of ensuring that academic staff could accommodate and cope with such rapid changes in practice and organisation.

Since its inception, the cultural, epistemological and ontological complexity of the academic development task has demanded a repertoire of approaches. I have outlined elsewhere (Land 2004) the variation in orientation or stances adopted by developers in negotiating this changing cultural and organisational terrain. These are indicated in Figure 10.1, roughly positioned against different organisational cultures in higher education. These orientations to academic development can be positioned in relation to two axes each representing polarised tendencies. The vertical axis charts the extent to which academic development practice might be seen as focused more directly towards meeting the personal needs of individual practitioners (academic staff or students) as opposed to being oriented more towards the requirements of the institution and its functioning at a systemic level. On the horizontal axis a domesticating tendency (after Wellington and Austin 1996) indicates practice that is principally concerned with encouraging or developing behaviours

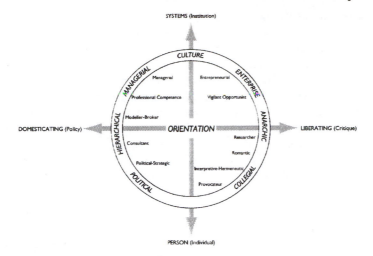

Figure 10.1 Orientations to academic development (Land 2004).

both in self and in others that conform with the expressed 'official' or explicit purposes or mission of the institution and its prevailing normative cultures (overt or covert). A liberating or critical tendency on the other hand would indicate practice that ran counter to such prevailing purposes and cultures and sought to transform them. Many developers recognise the need for both approaches at different times and in different contexts. However there is considerable variation amongst developers in terms of where they feel most at home on this compass model, and their self-positioning is strongly reflective of identity.

Resistances

> How all occasions do inform against me.
>
> (Shakespeare, *Hamlet* Act II Scene ii)

Taylor's chapter refers to how identity can arise from conflict, and engagement with 'a real or imaginary enemy' (von Busekist 2004: 84). The provenance of academic development at the particular historical moment discussed above has rendered its reception problematic and open to resistance. The notion of resistance to change has long been a matter of concern to education developers involved in policy implementation. How, and by whom, does 'resistance' come to be identified, located and represented? And how might strategies be devised to 'overcome' such perceived resistance? The ways in which change and resistance come to be represented is a non-trivial issue for developers. There is an accompanying need to deconstruct such notions of resistance, in the hope of reframing these problematic situations in ways that may allow more movement or productive collaboration with colleagues.

An alternative interpretation of the 'problem' of resistance is, of course, to see the characterisation of the resisting 'other' as a necessary part of the identity construction and maintenance of developers who wish, perhaps for the benefit of their own longer-term career trajectories, to associate themselves with discursive stances on change. Academic developers, unlike, perhaps, other professional groups within higher education, have no vested interest in maintaining the status quo. Though they are in a number of respects a fragmented tribe, dwelling in quite different neighbourhoods of a divided village, one feature which the great majority would appear to have in common is an identification with the notion of change. Though many are uncomfortable with being prescriptive about the direction of development, nonetheless most recognise that some process of change must be negotiated, some form of engagement entered into and supported, if their role is not to be superfluous.

There is amongst developers considerable variation in terms of this self-alignment with change. Whereas some are focused on the more problematic goal of longer term organisational and cultural change, and exhibit the stamina, patience and persistence needed to see it through, others can be characterised by their academic colleagues, and managers, as identifying more with quick fixes, passing bandwagons and fashionable trends. Such affiliation with novelty and the promise of new ideas and perspectives is perhaps not surprising amongst a group which feels that it needs to make some form of organisational impact or difference, within a definable, perhaps critical period of time and in a context where, despite an overheating external environment of supercomplexity, the prevailing internal tendency is towards conservatism, continuity and tradition.

Perceived resistances (for these may be developers' constructions of 'otherness') have taken many forms. The academic development project, for example, may be interpreted by academics as a threat to academics' own disciplinary identity. Academics are almost always concerned with the substance of what they teach even if their rationale for how they teach it seems less thought-through than developers might wish. Their disciplinary field is a major determinant of their subjectivity. Consequently they tend to be more amenable to context-specific theory that addresses their disciplinary context than to the prevailing discourse of academic development, which until quite recently has been more inclined to generalisable theory. The latter, in the opinion of discipline-based academics, can be seen to serve the interests and career trajectories of educational researchers and academic developers and hence can prove a site of tension and resistance (Webb 1996). Rowland (2000), long a scourge of generic theories of teaching devoid of any disciplinary context, and of teaching 'experts' whose expertise, in his opinion, lacks any coherent subject matter, advocates a discipline-based approach, but one which emphasises social context, frameworks of values and critical scrutiny.

Many academics consider higher education teaching a relatively private matter conducted, with one's students only, behind closed doors. Developers can be seen as trespassing within this secret garden, intruding to render visible, and hence calculable, previously private practices. Exposing practice to the light in this way offers development possibilities but is inherently highly risky. In these ways, academic developers can become identified with the practices of audit and surveillance, and the performative work required to deliver a neo-liberal agenda. Their work, with its frequent requirement for reflective practice and the recording portfolio is seen as akin to that of the confessional, or the therapist. Elsewhere (Land 2006) I have used Milton's *Paradise Lost* allegorically to indicate ways in which the shadowy, often transgressive, carnivalesque and creative spaces of (disciplinary) Pandemonium can be seen as rendered visible and hence calculable by the light of (managerial) Authority. Where the sympathies of the intermediating angels of academic development lie in this process raises interesting questions of allegiance.

There remains too the continuing risk of a deficit model being adopted by academic developers. As McWilliam points out (2002: 190):

> It is simply that, because development is always predicated on the idea that someone is knowledge-able while someone else is knowledge deficient, such communication cannot be a conversation among equals. The developer's knowledge is already assumed to be what leads to progress, not the knowledge of the developee.

An assumption perceived to be equally patronising is that the work of many academics is misaligned in some way and needs to be re-aligned, re-routed or re-designed. Academic developers are perceived as instrumental in this work of reorientation, reordering the performance, indeed the subjectivity, of the academic for more corporate and managerial times. Such encounters breed collegial distrust.

It is interesting to speculate what may account for resistance to participation in academic development activity. It may be that centuries of distinction between print and oral cultures in higher education have led to university hostility to pedagogy, with pedagogy traditionally regarded as a predominantly oral practice and therefore of low status (Waquet 2003). We might speculate, alternatively, that resistance to participation in academic development derives from the busy-ness of academics and their lack of time. In this instance, the developer is perceived less as a source of support and more as yet another call on their scarce time, hence as a potential stressor.

The denigration of teaching, and hence the academic development which is designed to enhance it, might be attributable to the research/teaching divide, and the fact that university priorities are determined almost entirely by the research agenda. The declared policy commitments of universities to teaching are often viewed by academics and developers alike as little more than lip service. There is a well recognised 'underlying game' that teaching and research are likely to be in conflict with each other and that the highest aspiration of most managers and academics is still to be in the premier league of research universities. Hence academic developers are seen not just as a distraction from the primary pursuit in terms of time (an opportunity cost), but also as an institutional cost that could be better deployed.

The contested nature of pedagogical research evidence mentioned earlier might also be seen as a source of resistance. One respondent, based in an ancient

UK university, referred to her own academic development evidence base as 'a rather flabby field'. Lindsay (2004: 280) refers to the field dismissively as 'Academic developmentology'. He sees it as a form of dogmatism which manufactures credibility not through analysis of empirical evidence but through setting itself against conveniently dismissable heresies. Most developers would reject such blanket dismissal but certainly are acutely aware of their lack of a collectively agreed research canon. They acknowledge too the comparative immaturity and paucity of their research arsenal compared with the hefty artillery of other more established research communities, and the absence of a shared professional conviction in regard to pedagogic values and knowledge. In defence they point to a rapidly burgeoning and energetic research community in their field over the last two decades.

Engagement around educational change may well lead both parties into a state of what Meyer and Land (2005) have termed *liminality*, a transformative state that engages existing certainties and renders them problematic and fluid. In this way change through educational development might be seen as another form of 'troublesome knowledge' (Meyer and Land 2006) that can be unsettling, entailing a sense of loss, a stripping away of an older professional or academic identity and the reconstitution of a new one. This transformation can be protracted, over considerable periods of time, and involve oscillation between states, often with temporary regression to earlier status. Within liminal states, anticipation of a new subjectivity, in this case a changed professional identity, gives rise simultaneously to both desire and apprehension. It would appear however, that once the state of liminality is entered, though there may be temporary regression, there can be no ultimate full return to the pre-liminal state, nor to the earlier subjectivity. Such environments of educational change and development involve encounters with new conceptual thresholds, unfamiliar discourse and knowledge practices, and shifts in existing power relations. These can provide keys to the ways in which the subjectivity of both academic developers and their academic colleagues undergoes reconstruction and transformation.

Identity and subjectivity

In the light of the perceived resistance discussed earlier, it is interesting to note the important distinction made by Bayne (2004: 82) between identity and subjectivity. As she points out, 'identity formation assumes an element of agency and of self-construction which is appropriate to the conscious exploration of alternative personas'. This distinction hinges on the possibility of agency, choice and principled autonomy, and would seem apposite to the case of academic developers. Like Taylor earlier in this volume, Bayne (p. 83) also draws upon the influential work of Castells, but contrasts his view with that of Poster:

> As Castells suggests, 'for most social actors, meaning is organized around a primary identity (that is an identity that frames the others) that is self-sustaining across time and space' (Castells 1996 p.7). By contrast, as

Poster points out, constitution of the subject is not a matter of conscious agency, in that it occurs through our immersion in our particular social and discursive contexts. Subject constitution therefore comes about in part via 'particular configurations of self and media' (Poster 2001 p.8).

Seen from this perspective, the varied value orientations of developers discussed earlier (Land 2004) would seem to fall into the category of 'identity', in that they might be seen as manifestations of the agental self, consciously adopted stances, elective affinities, personal projects even. It might be appropriate to consider these as *performances* of identity, or multiple identities. The condition of subjectivity, however, is an effect of being caught, and configured, within the operations of power (Hall 2004). As Belsey notes, the subject is 'the site of contradiction, and is consequently perpetually in the process of construction, thrown into crisis by alterations in language and in the social formation, capable of change' (Belsey 1980: 65). In relation to their academic colleagues, it is the fact that the subject is a process, of course, that gives rise to the possibility of transformation. On this idea that as subjects we are never quite complete or finished rests much of the faith of academic developers. However what might appear as limitless opportunity for professional renewal from the developer's perspective might seem more like meddling in others' subjectivities to their colleagues.

Identity and misrecognition

In the case of academic developers themselves, however, the condition of subjectivity is often a troubled affair. The resistances discussed earlier can give rise to dissonances, discomforts and disjunctions that stem from a sense of complicity, or insecurity. They can lead to a relationship of 'them' and 'us' between academics and academic developers. The apparent conferment of power on academic developers by managers can, from the perspective of the developers, be experienced as powerlessness. Valerie Clifford (2004) characterises this experience as akin to 'tumbling around in a washing machine that is in constant cycle.'

I swirl around in an ideological soup that tugs at and mis-shapes me, that bumps against my colleagues and threatens my integrity. Faculties demand to talk within their own comfort zones, service level agreements have me supporting my clients and monitoring my productivity, electronic learning management systems place modes of delivery at the centre of pedagogical decision making, the delivery of compulsory accredited courses to probationary staff stacks up hostility in the institution and robs us of 'spaces' for other (radical) possibilities, institutional strategic directions pile on top of each other, layering demands on the integrity of my own strategic directions. I need to reconstruct my own identity in collaboration with my colleagues to recommit to our ideologies and refocus our energies in constructive response to the institution.

(Clifford, cited in Clegg *et al.* 2004: 33)

There is a clear disjunction here, a gap in desire, between the actual *subjectivity* experienced by the developer, which is viewed as an imposition or distortion, something which 'mis-shapes' her, and her desired *identity* of 'integrity' and greater control, which the subjectivity 'threatens'. The attainment of the desired identity will require her to 'reconstruct' her identity, to 'recommit' and 'refocus'. There is a perceived mismatch here or misrecognition. Earlier in this volume Taylor referred to Lacanian theory, in which the notion of 'oneness' or human unity is critiqued. Within Lacanian theory the human ceases to be a unified, stable entity and conceptions of singleness, completeness and indivisibility of the self function more like an ideology, the purpose of which is to ease the restlessness and ultimate unattainability of human desire (Lacan 1977). Something like the restless desire for completeness that Lacan saw in the child's 'misrecognition' of itself in the 'mirror phase' as it enters into language may well characterise the unease experienced by developers in their discursive formation amidst the competing discourses of higher education, as they too seek some form of certainty, a narrative of the (developer) self with which they might feel comfortable and secure. But, as with Lacan's subjects, this self-fashioning would seem ultimately to be unattainable, 'a form of self-deception, an alliance with the ego's imaginary identifications of wholeness and unity which vainly tries to master and end the restless movement of desire' (Usher and Edwards 1994: 73). Between the developer's desire for completeness and the discursive formations on offer, there would always seem to be a degree of misrecognition.

Moral economy and insider resistance

Developers' subjectivities, then, are constructed partly by the flows of influence, discourse and power in which the subject finds him or herself enmeshed. A growing number of developers are becoming aware of the institutional representation of academic development as a moral good which, discursively, it becomes difficult, in effect deviant, to challenge. The discourses which support this representation might be, for example, those of enhancing the student experience, widening participation, increased access, flexibility of provision and greater employability. In a recent conference paper Peseta coined the term 'moral economy' to characterise the imbrication of developers within such discourses (Manathunga *et al.* 2006). It is not that the developers concerned are necessarily opposed to the broader aims of such developments but they are concerned at the way their own practices might be mobilised, or perceived to be mobilised, in what tend to be mainly domesticating agendas, with insufficient space to critique and surface the contradictions and incoherences of the ideologies inscribed within these agendas. This clearly jars with their own sense of identity and their own affiliations to radically different discourses, in this case the more emancipatory discourses of post-colonialism. Peseta (2005) and her fellow developers in the CAD Collective (Challenging Academic Development) use the term 'insider resistance' to capture their sense of dissonance and as a project to challenge the ways in which particular neo-liberal discourses are being presented within higher education as normalised truths or self-evidently correct practices.

More specifically they voice an unease that they may be complicit in the advent of a new rationality and morality. This, according to Shore and Wright (2000: 57), is 'designed to engender amongst academic staff norms of conduct and professional behaviours. In short, they are agents for the creation of new kinds of subjectivity: self-managing individuals who render themselves auditable'. McWilliam (2002: 199), similarly, sees this as complicity in the production of the 'malleable-but-disciplined' individual that is so necessary to enterprising culture.

> In universities, professional development activities provide scripts for turning ourselves into better (more professional) academics. Inasmuch as we make sense of our academic selves by reference to these bodies of knowledge, they produce or constitute us. It is in this sense that professional development can be read as both a site of knowledge production and a system of power relations.
>
> (p. 190)

This perceived manipulation of the subjectivities of colleagues is in tension with their own identity claims. These developers express concern that as a professional group they are becoming caught up in a form of colonial endeavour. They experience a form of misrecognition with the neo-liberal identities on offer to the developer and seek a working distance from those complicities whilst establishing effective (and safe) spaces in which to explore and foster alternative educational values and practices.

Conclusion: in praise of folly

> This fellow's wise enough to play the fool,
> And to do that well craves a kind of wit:
> He must observe their mood on whom he jests,
> The quality of persons, and the time,
> And, like the haggard, check at every feather
> That comes before his eye. This is a practice
> As full of labour as a wise man's art.
>
> (Shakespeare, *Twelfth Night* Act III Scene i)

We have seen then something of the tricky discursive terrain which academic developers must negotiate. We have seen too that the identities they adopt are also discursively positioned and compromised in various ways. These identities are often paradoxical and cannot remain neutral. Handal earlier in this volume drew a comparison between the academic developer and the figure of the clown. In the light of the complex identity states and subjectivities we have been discussing, it is in conclusion briefly worth revisiting the ludic tradition of the court jester. This is another figure of paradox, the Sage-Fool, who must always tread a careful and difficult line between trust and rebuke.

The Fool entertains but also warns. Welsford (1968) refers to the professional buffoon as 'a slippery customer' (p. 3) and points out the origin of the tradition in what Plutarch referred to as *Parasites*, gate-crashing the wealthy houses of the Hellenic world in search of a free lunch (p. 4). However she also notes

> the accepted convention that it is the Fool who speaks the truth, which he knows not by ratiocination but by inspired intuition. The mere appearance of the familiar in cap and bells would at once indicate to the audience where the 'punctum indifferens', the impartial critic, the mouthpiece of real sanity, was to be found.
>
> (p. 267)

Interestingly Welsford's research reveals a constantly recurring tendency for fools and learned men to be brought together in dialogue. We find bishops, princes and poets laureate at cross-purposes with jesters, and within higher education we find that as late as the eighteenth century professors of European universities could augment their incomes by (literally) playing the fool at court. One Friedrich Taubmann of Wittenberg University, for example, was in the early seventeenth century appointed by Prince Anspach as 'Poet and Professor and Merry Councillor'. He was variously described as 'our prince's indispensable guest', 'a shameless beggar', and 'a learned Latinist'. Yet significantly, though he was employed, perhaps a little like Handal's 'critical friend', as a 'merry companion' (*lustiger Gesellschafter*), he held no fixed salary, no permanent office or regular position in the household. He exerted influence but had to tolerate insecurity. He was, says Welsford, 'both a butt and a wit' and 'a skilful improviser' (p. 23). We might not relish a return to Taubmann's conditions of employment, yet there is something in the fluidity, licence, complexity, insecurity, risk and paradoxical nature of Taubmann's role that would be familiar to us as academic developers. Though we might construct heroic identities for ourselves, and indulge in the occasional victory narratives or innovation claims, at the end of the day we are forced to recognise the multiplicity, complicity and occasional duplicity inscribed within the developer's subjectivity. The ideal of unity and completeness is illusory. We have to settle for paradox.

> Within us are contradictory identities, pulling in different directions, so that our identifications are continually being shifted about. If we feel that we have a unified identity from birth to death, it is only because we construct a comforting story or 'narrative of the self' about ourselves.
>
> (Hall 1992: 170)

As a comforting story, a narrative of the self, we might find worse models than the wise, patient and eminently resilient Fool.

Chapter 11

The role of professional associations in the formation of professional identity

The US experience

Victor M. H. Borden

The identity of managers within higher education institutions is closely linked to how the domain of management relates to the academic mission. Those who lead academic operations, such as deans, department chairs, and research center directors, reside at one end of this continuum, where identity as a manager is often eschewed, or at least superimposed on and often secondary to identity as an academic leader.

At the other end of the spectrum are those who manage generic administrative areas, such as physical plant and purchasing, where the managerial identity is non-problematic but where there is typically little or no connection to the academic domain and identity. Along the continuum, there exist a range of lead/managed academic, institutional, and student support operations, including registration, libraries, information technology, planning, and residence halls. Within this large 'gray area,' academic leadership and managerial identities blend in varying proportions.

Professional identify formation is a socialization process that involves both the acquisition of specific knowledge and capabilities required for professional practice, as well as the internalization of attitudes, dispositions, and self-identity peculiar to the community of practitioners (Hall 1987). Our interest in this chapter is in the latter, attitudinal components and especially self-identity, that is, individuals' 'reflexive understanding of their own biography' (Giddens 1991: 53), albeit as specifically related to their roles as academic or administrative managers within higher education institutions.

Academic and administrative managers come to their roles through varying paths. Traditionally, many have been plucked from faculties based variously on self-interest, recognized capabilities, and/or more seemingly random processes. Increasingly, professional pathways have emerged through which individuals rise through the ranks from entry-level, specialist through senior-level, managerial roles. Ibarra (1999) identifies three tasks in the transition of professionals through these professional pathways into the senior roles: observing role models to identify potential identities; experimenting with provisional selves; and evaluating experience against internal standards and external feedback.

Where do emerging academic professionals engage these tasks of professional identity formation? Within the United States higher education sector, higher education professional associations are an increasingly important venue for identity formation among those who manage or lead academic and administrative units within higher education institutions. This chapter provides both a personal and a professional view of identify formation among US higher education professional managers and administrators, focusing on the role and scope of professional associations in professional identity formation.

A personal view

When my son was in his third year of primary education, at the unripe young age of 9, he had a school assignment for which he had to choose a profession, dress the part, and do a brief presentation. With no influence from his father, he donned a button-down shirt and tie, put a calculator in his shirt pocket, and went as an 'institutional researcher.' Flattering though it was, I realized it reflected his love and admiration for me rather than a career choice. Indeed, at the time, his actual career aspiration was to work in 'the pit' of a quick oil and lube establishment.

When I was his age, I also did not aspire to direct an institutional research office at a university. I do remember that, at the slightly more advanced age of 12, I wanted to be a sports statistician, specifically covering the sport of baseball. As it turns out, my work as an institutional researcher is in many ways similar to that of a baseball statistician – collecting and analyzing data regarding a team activity. But, rather than for a baseball team, I do this for a team of higher education administrators.

Like many higher education managers, I did not set out to be what I am. Rather, I came upon the opportunity and found that it suited me well. It combined the knowledge, skills, and abilities that I had and was further honing in pursuit of a doctoral degree in social psychology, with an applied context that satisfied my desire to see my efforts result in immediate consequences. It also allowed me to work within the university environment that I found to be so enriching and inspiring.

Having started my institutional research career at a large institution, I was part of an office that included a director, three other professionals, and two clerical staff. Our office team shared an identity related to our role (providing research and analysis to support strategic and tactical decision-making) as well as our place within the organization (academic affairs). More professionally advanced colleagues exposed me to the statewide, regional, and national networks of professionals who served similar functions at their respective higher education institutions. Through local and regional conferences, I was socialized into the profession. Although I did not gain much ground in being able to explain what I did to my parents and neighbors, I found a group of colleagues with whom I did not have to explain myself, although we spent significant amounts of time comparing notes on our roles, responsibilities, and methods.

I worked closely during these early professional years with colleagues in enrollment service, academic support, student support, and information technology units. We conferred about complex issues and, in the process, shared our experiences as working professionals within a higher education institution. Several projects involved traveling as a team to visit colleagues at other institutions or in other business sectors to determine ways to address an issue or improve a process. The formal and informal interactions, especially during periods in which we lived and work together, shaped our respective identities as higher education professionals of varying types.

When I began my second position as an institutional research professional, I came under the tutelage of a mentor who, at the time, was reaching the pinnacle of his involvements with the national professional association most germane to our work: the Association for Institutional Research. He supported my further involvement in this association as he served first as the chair of the annual forum, then as vice-president and president of the Association. I volunteered to provide technology support at the forum and continued my involvements through a range of roles until ultimately I had the opportunity to serve in the same capacities as had my mentor, as forum chair, vice-president, and president.

My personal career path includes many defining moments, such as my work with the Association for Institutional Research, that have contributed to my professional identity. My third post added a tenure-track academic assignment on top of my administrative position. This dimension allowed me to become a more active contributor to the literature of my profession and to become a mentor to others through academic and professional teaching and advising opportunities. Several years ago a few colleagues joined with me to form a band that performed parodies of our profession, which added a unique dimension to how others in our field viewed us and so how we viewed ourselves.

Each of the thousands of higher education professionals with whom I have interacted over the past 25 years has a unique story to tell about the development of her or his professional identity. In my first year of graduate school, I shared an office with a colleague, Dr. Margaret Madden, who ultimately followed an administrative career path albeit after beginning in a more traditional academic staff post. Whereas I moved directly into a professional post and later added the academic dimension, she rose through the ranks of the faculty to become the provost at a state university. Whereas I chose to affiliate with the professional association related to my substantive work, she maintained close ties with our disciplinary organization, the American Psychological Association (APA). More specifically, she became a very active contributor to Division 35, the Society for the Psychology of Women, ultimately serving as president. In her presidential address, Madden (2005) described how she used a model that she and colleagues developed for feminist psychology to 'understand and develop [her] identity as a feminist/social psychologist/academic administrator' (Madden 2005: 3).

At the other end of the spectrum, I have had the opportunity to work with colleagues who developed their professional careers in a variety of business and industry sectors before joining the ranks of academic administration. This has been especially notable among the more generic aspects of university administration, that is, those functions that are less unique to higher education and more generally found within a variety of sectors, including, for example, information technologies, physical plant, human resources, and financial operations. But it is also true within more higher-education-specific units, such as admissions and student records offices, as well as in my own profession, institutional research.

As implied through the stories told to this point, whether managers within higher education institutions view themselves as academics, business people, both, or neither depends on the individual: his or her background, dispositions, experiences, and circumstances. The degree to which there is commonality in identify formation then depends on the degree to which background characteristics, dispositions, experiences, and circumstances are shared and, more importantly, reflected upon and incorporated into one's self-identity. Before considering the role of professional associations in this process, we will take a short diversion to articulate more precisely the domain of interest and its prevalence.

Definitions and prevalence

In Chapter 5 of this volume, Celia Whitchurch describes the domain of interest, professional administrators and managers, according to definitions used by the Higher Education Staff Development Agency (HESDA). Specifically, she cites the 38,000 individuals representing 8 percent of the total workforce that fall within the category 'administrators and managers.' The US Department of Education collects parallel statistics through the National Center for Education Statistics. The Fall Staff Survey is completed by virtually all – more than 4,200 – US postsecondary degree-granting institutions, including those in the public and private sectors. The Staff Survey requires institutions to first categorize staff according to whether they are professional or nonprofessional. Professional staff includes subcategories of executive/administrative/managerial, faculty (instruction and research), other instruction and research, and other professional. The nonprofessional ranks include subcategories of technical/paraprofessional, clerical/secretarial, skilled crafts, and service/maintenance.

Results from the Fall 2003 survey reveal a total of 3.2 million employees in degree-granting institutions, among which 2.2 million, or 70 percent, are professional and the remainder nonprofessional. The 1.3 million faculty members and other instructional staff constitute 46 percent of the total workforce and 65 percent of the professional ranks. Thus the combination of executive/administrative/managerial and other professional, numbering over 800,000, accounts for 35 percent of the professional ranks, and 25 percent of the total workforce.

From a narrow perspective, one might define our domain of interest as the executive/administrative/managerial ranks, perhaps excluding the senior academic and institutional executives, such as dean, vice-president/chancellor, and president/chancellor (i.e. the chief executive officer). The entire category accounts for 185,000 individuals, representing just fewer than 6 percent of the total workforce and so with the exclusion of the most senior among them, the prevalence of our domain of interest would be reduced to no more than 5 percent of the higher education workforce. However, as the stories that begin this chapter imply, identity formation among this group is in large part influenced by career paths, which for many US professional administrators and managers involves prior time in the positions included within the 'other professional' category.

The definition for the 'other professional' category, which represents over 600,000 higher education staff, describes 'all persons employed for the primary purpose of performing academic support, student service and institutional support, whose assignments would require either a baccalaureate degree or higher or experience of such kind and amount as to provide a comparable background' (NCES 2004). Job titles encompassed in this category include Human Resource Specialist, Computer Programmer, Budget Analyst, Counselor, Lawyer, and Registered Nurse. More generally, such individuals may be described as 'specialists,' implying an aspect of identity formation related to the socialization processes associated with the specialty.

From a broader perspective, the professional specialists who lead and staff the support functions of US higher education institutions represent as much as one-quarter of the total workforce and cover a wide range of professional and disciplinary areas. Moreover, they are employed in a diverse array of postsecondary institutions, ranging from small, private, specialized institutions to large, comprehensive public universities. As with all human endeavors, the individuals occupying such positions vary greatly in their attitudes and disposition toward work. Some dedicate their lives and most of their waking hours to their careers whereas others do only what is required to maintain employment while focusing as much of their time and attention on other matters.

Communities of practice and professional identity formation

The socialization of practitioners through guided interactions with mentors and peers has been a central component of professional identity development for hundreds, if not thousands of years. From the craft guilds of the fourteenth century to the clinical rounds of today's medical school curricula, young apprentices learn far more than the skills and techniques of their trade through these interactions. They learn what it is to be a cabinet maker, a medical doctor, a primary school teacher, etc. The role of practice in professional identify formation is central to Bruner's (1990) distinction between 'learning about' and 'learning to be.' Ryle (1949) made a similar distinction between 'knowing that' and 'knowing how.'

The curriculum of practitioner programs has been strongly influenced by this

'Vygotskian perspective' in which professional learning and development are conceived as occurring within the context of evolving participation in a social context (Van Huizen *et al.* 2005). Lave and Wenger (1991) described 'situated learning' that revolves around the role of communities of practice. Wenger (1998) subsequently developed further the concept of communities of practice as entailing three dimensions: what the nature of the work is about, as it is continually renegotiated by members; how the community functions, that is, how members are bound in a social entity; and what capability it produces, or the communal resources that community members develop over time.

The types of social arrangements essential to learning one's craft and developing a professional identity as a practitioner, as warranted by the concept of communities of practice, require networks that typically must go beyond one's own work setting. Even in large higher education institutions, there are not enough practitioners of each kind (analysts, admissions counselors, auditors, etc.) to develop a significant community. More importantly, the particular circumstances of a single working environment limit the prospects for enriched learning and socialization on account of the relative homogeneity of tasks and environments. As a result, professional associations have come to serve the broader communal needs of higher education practitioners.

Professional associations and professional identity

Like their academic counterparts, the disciplinary associations or learned societies, higher education professional associations are the primary organizational forms of voluntary association across institutions. Russell (1996) contrasts the ideal learned society – an organization that facilitates the communication of knowledge created by its members and organized around a learned discipline – with an ideal professional association, which promotes the occupational interests of its members and the utilitarian effectiveness of its existing body of technical knowledge. The professional association achieves these objectives through a range of functions, including professional development activities, research and trade journals, codes of ethics, conferences, and, in some but not all cases, licensure and/or certification.

The prevalence in the United States of professional associations related to higher education professional (non-academic) functions is large and growing. An appendix to this chapter lists 30 such organizations, focusing only on those that are related specifically and exclusively to higher education functions. The list, though not exhaustive, provides a comprehensive view of the range of higher education administrative function supported through such associations.

It is important to note that there are a plethora of other associations or 'intersecting' communities that relate to other dimensions of professional identity. For example, a range of associations focus on institutions of a certain type, such as community colleges, urban and metropolitan universities, state colleges, independent colleges, and so forth. There are also associations that include higher education functions within broader contexts, such as those for educational research (pre-primary through postsecondary) and libraries (including academic but also non-academic, public and private). There are also associations that focus on certain cross-functional aspects of postsecondary education, such as liberal education and problem-based learning. Finally, there are hybrid associations that bring together academic staff from departments that teach about a functional area and those that practice the function. Examples of these include the associations for student affairs professionals (e.g. the National Association of Student Personnel Administrators and the American College Personnel Association), which include membership from many academic staff in student affairs departments of higher education programs, as well as the Association for the Study of Higher Education (ASHE), which serves higher education researchers from academic department and applied settings.

All of these professional (and academic) associations play an important role in professional (and academic) identity formation. Individuals can pick and choose which types of networks to join and can move in and out of these networks as desired to pursue interests and enrich learning and experience. The networks are especially useful when one takes on a new post with unfamiliar roles and responsibilities. Through workshops, conferences, participation in listserv communities, and by reading the available trade literature, one can come quickly up to speed. Perhaps more importantly, one can interact with colleagues as needed to gain advice and guidance on daily tasks and activities.

Professional associations also provide important links between practitioners and affiliate or associate members who develop commercial solutions to administrative problems. This includes the myriad software vendors who sell automated systems for administrative functions, but also testing companies, architectural firms, accountants, publishers, etc., as relevant to the function. These members and their companies play an increasingly important role in validating the professional nature of the practitioner's role. They customize their wares and their marketing strategies to court the prospective practitioner and to make them the advocate for their products within their institutions. In so doing, they provide potential leverage to the practitioner for engaging in high-level institutional decision-making. As a result of the interactions between commercial vendors and practitioners, the vendors become more socialized into the profession and begin to contribute substantively to conference programs and workshops. Not surprisingly, a significant number of practitioners join the ranks of commercial vendors and, less frequently but still commonly, vendors give up their commercial roles and join the ranks of the practitioners.

When attending a conference of one of the professional associations listed in the appendix, one can walk away with all sorts of takeaway gifts and souvenirs from the vendor participants. In addition, most of these associations have their own identity product line, including shirts, caps, folders, luggage tags, clocks, etc. with the association logo. The less expensive of these items are given away to members and prospective members, thereby spreading the name and identity further. Attendees to the annual conference receive tote bags or attachés with the identity logo to use at the conference and upon return to their respective institutions.

Given the high cost of conference attendance, there are a significant number of staff within a functional area who may not have the resources to attend the annual national conference. Regional and state affiliates provide more cost-effective events for these individuals. Moreover, the development of web-based professional development activities, such as web-based seminars or 'webinars,' has widened access considerably.

Conclusion

The formation of professional identity is a complex, multi-faceted process that is shaped by a wide array of personal, social, and environmental factors, and evolves continuously over time. Chapter 5 of this volume describes how evolving higher education organizational climates in the UK have influenced and been influenced by the changing identity of professional administrators and managers. This chapter has focused on the impact of professional associations in the US on professional identity formation among the leaders and professional staff within administrative units. In as complex a manner as each of the chapters suggests identity formation occurs and evolves, reality encompasses both.

In the UK, the US, and virtually all other countries that have higher education systems, individual practitioners, be they instructional staff, administrative managers, or professional specialists, have their professional identities shaped through their interactions within their work units, more broadly among their institutions, and with all the professionals of like and unlike ilk with whom they interact. Structural characteristics of each of these environments shape these interactions, whether or not they are intentionally designed to do so.

In closing, it is useful to reflect upon the degree to which reflexive navigation through communities of practice shapes professional identity formation relative to other possible influencers. This can be taken as a matter of quantity and salience. That is, the influence of interactions within communities of practice on professional identity development can be viewed entirely as a function of the time and attention that an individual directs towards these experiences relative to other experiences that can influence professional identity development, such as institutional customs and rituals. However, this view suggests that identity formation is a largely reactive process. Other views of identity formation place more emphasis on the proactive or agentic nature of individual inquiry and activity. Marshall (2000) provides a distinction between four aspects of agency: the human capacity to be intentional; the resources that an individual has to engage in intentional behavior; the behavior that reflects intention; and the social and physical environments available to the individual to act within. The discussion in this chapter relates to all of these aspects but does not provide much insight into the motivational aspects of identity development, such as why a person chooses a specific path and, once in the path, why they choose to engage in certain professional experiences.

I am both an institutional researcher and a member of the psychology faculty, but I identify more with the former than the latter. I have attended two conferences of the American Psychological Association – one national and one regional. I have attended the last 19 consecutive national fora of the Association for Institutional Research and more than twice as many state, regional, and international conferences of affiliated groups. Do I self-identify as an institutional researcher because of all my experiences within the profession, or did I pursue those experiences because of my identity? The causality is inexorably intertwined.

Appendix

The following list includes US-based professional associations that serve higher management functions, excluding direct academic management. Associations were selected based on an exclusive focus on higher education academic, student, and institutional support services. The list is comprehensive but not exhaustive. Excluded from this list are academic disciplinary associations for higher education and associations that serve broader institutional-level purposes, as well as associations that include higher education within broader domains.

Association name	Mission	Scope
American Association of College Registrars and Admissions Officers (AACRAO – www.aacrao.org/)	To provide professional development, guidelines and voluntary standards to be used by higher education officials regarding the best practices in records management, admissions, enrollment management, administrative information technology and student services	More than 9,000 members representing approximately 2,300 institutions in more than 35 countries
American College Personnel Association (ACPA – www.acpa.nche.edu/)	Supports and fosters college student learning through the generation and dissemination of knowledge, which informs policies, practices and programs for student affairs professionals and the higher education community	Nearly 8,000 members representing nearly 1,500 private and public institutions from across the US and internationally
Association of Collegiate Conference and Events Directors – International (ACCED-I – www.acced-i.org/)	To improve, promote and recognize excellence in the collegiate conference and events profession	1,300 members representing 600 institutions
Association for Institutional Research (AIR – www.airweb.org)	To benefit its members and help advance research that will improve the understanding, planning, and operation of higher education institutions	Over 3,100 members

Association name	Mission	Scope
Association of American University Presses (AAUP – http://aaupnet.org/)	Dedicated to the support of creative and effective scholarly communications	129 university presses
Association of College Administration Professionals (ACAP – http://www.acap.org/)	Providing professional development and information resources to a variety of college administration professionals	Over 3,000 college administrators
Association of College and University Auditors (ACUA – http://www.acua.org/)	An international professional organization established in 1958, that provides an arena to discuss mutual professional problems and to generate new ideas and methods concerning the profession	Over 500 institutional memberships
Association of College and University Housing Officers – International (ACUHO-I – http://www.acuho.ohio-state.edu/)	To contribute to the improvement and coordination of the various aspects of student residence halls and apartments, food service, developmental programming, administration, conference services, plant operations, maintenance and related programs at member institutions on an international scale	Over 5,800 individuals, from over 900 colleges and universities
Association of College and University Telecommunications Administrators (ACUTA – http://www.acuta.org/home.cfm)	To support higher education institutions in achieving optimal use of communications technologies	Nearly 2,000 individuals at 825 institutions of higher education
Association of Higher Education Facilities Officers (APPA – http://www.appa.org/)	Dedicated to the maintenance, protection, and promotion of quality educational facilities	Over 4,700 individual members
Association of Research Libraries (ARL – http://arl.cni.org/)	Influences the changing environment of scholarly communication and the public policies that affect research libraries and the communities they serve	123 academic research libraries

Association name	Mission	Scope
College and University Personnel Association (CUPA-HR – http://www.cupahr.org/)	Serves higher education HR professionals and their institutions by providing high quality resources that sustain performance, enhance capabilities, increase effectiveness, expand career options, and support efforts to advance and promote the HE-HR profession	Over 6,500 members in more than 1,500 colleges and universities
Council for Advancement and Support of Education (CASE – http://www.case.org/)	Advances and supports educational institutions around the world by enhancing the effectiveness of the alumni relations, communications, marketing, fund raising, and other advancement professionals who serve them	More than 3,200 colleges, universities, and independent elementary and secondary schools in 55 countries around the world
Council of Graduate Schools (CGS – http://www.cgsnet.org/)	To improve and advance graduate education	Over 450 universities in North America
EDUCAUSE (http://www.educause.edu/)	To advance higher education by promoting the intelligent use of information technology	More than 2,000 institutions with 15,000 active members
National Association of College and University Attorneys (NACUA – http://www.nacua.org/)	To advance the effective practice of higher education attorneys for the benefit of the colleges and universities they serve	Over 3,000 members at 1,400 campuses of about 660 institutions
National Academic Advising Association (NACADA – http://www.nacada.ksu.edu)	Champion the educational role of academic advisors to enhance student learning and development in a diverse world	Over 8,200 members
National Association for College Admission Counseling (NACAC – http://www.nacacnet.org)	Dedicated to serving students as they make choices about pursuing postsecondary education	Over 9,000 members
National Association of Academic Advisors for Athletes (N4A – http://www.nfoura.org/)	To cultivate and improve the opportunities for academic success for student-athletes in universities and college by providing informed, competent, and holistic advising	Over 550 members

Association name	Mission	Scope
National Association of College and University Business Officers (NACUBO – www.nacubo.org/)	To advance the economic viability of higher education institutions in fulfillment of their academic missions	More than 2,500 colleges, universities, and higher education service providers across the country
National Association of College and University Food Services (NACUFS – www.nacufs.org/)	To promote the highest quality of foodservice on school, college and university campuses by providing members with educational and training opportunities, technical assistance, scholarships, industry information and research	Over 600 institutions and over 450 industry partners
National Association of College Auxiliary Services (NACAS – www.nacas.org/)	To enhance the profession of auxiliary and campus support services in higher education	950 colleges and universities
National Association of College Stores (NACS – www.nacs.org/)	Represents and supports higher education retailers by providing valuable programs and services, and by facilitating strategic partnerships that ensure college stores are essential to their campus constituencies and the higher education retail channel	More than 3,200 college stores plus 1,200 associate members
National Association of Student Financial Aid Administrators (NASFAA – www.nasfaa.org)	Supports financial aid professionals at colleges, universities, and career schools	Nearly 3,000 institutional members
National Association of Student Personnel Administrators (NASPA – www.naspa.org/)	To provide professional development and advocacy for student affairs educators and administrators who share the responsibility for a campus-wide focus on the student experience	Over 1,200 institutional and 8,000 individual members
National Career Development Association (NCDA – www.ncda.org/)	To promote the career development of all people over the life span by providing service to the public and professionals involved with or interested in career development	4,200 members

Association name	Mission	Scope
National Orientation Directors Association (NODA – www.nodaweb.org/)	To provide education, leadership and professional development in the fields of college student orientation, transition and retention	1,032 professional and 312 student members
Professional and Organizational Development Network in Higher Education (POD – www.podnetwork.org/)	Developing and supporting practitioners and leaders in higher education dedicated to enhancing learning and teaching	Nearly 1,500 members
Society for College and University Planning (SCUP – www.scup.org/)	A community providing its members with the knowledge and resources to achieve institutional planning goals	Over 5,000 individual members
Society of Research Administrators (SRA – www.srainternational.org)	Dedicated to the education and professional development of research administrators, as well as the enhancement of public understanding of the importance of research and its administration	Over 3,600 individual members

Part III

The students' views

Universities are places, perhaps above all, for the formation of student identities. Especially through their curricula and their pedagogies, but also through all the other experiences that they make available, the identity of students may be powerfully formed. This is not a new reflection. Just such a consideration has underlain much of the history of the idea of the university, as worked out from Newman's liberal Idea of the University, or in the German idea of *Bildung* or the American idea of higher education as public service.

However, the spread of chapters in this book bear testimony to contemporary dimensions of identity formation in universities. And the two chapters in this section demonstrate how the challenges of identity formation are reflected in the student experience at this time. (For ease of reference, I shall use simply the shorthand 'Ahearn' to refer to the chapter jointly contributed by Alison Ahearn, Oliver Broadbent, John Collins and Eirini Spentza.)

In these two chapters, we glimpse several layers in the structuring of student identity: student–student; student–staff; student–university; and student–wider society. All of these layers are working at once. And we also glimpse in both chapters indications of significant differences across disciplines and across universities. But we see here, too, that the matter to hand is more complex still. Susan Lapworth draws attention to the way in which the boundaries of identity formation are themselves weakening, if not actually dissolving. Particularly, perhaps, on courses that are attracting large numbers of mature students, especially courses that are focused on aspects of professional life, students may have more understanding of issues than their tutors. But there are more general movements at play here: Lapworth points out that the projection of students as 'customers' is a sector-wide policy. So the weakening of 'difference' may be a universal matter across higher education.

However, that sense of the dissolution of boundaries, of a sense of students and tutors as 'them and us', is surely absent from Alison Ahearn's chapter: all three (undergraduate) student contributors reflect on their experience in ways that acknowledge a sharp and implicitly valued difference between themselves and their lecturers. But *this* consideration is again only testimony to the marked differences of identity formation across students in today's higher education.

On the strength of these contributions, any weakening of boundaries is even accompanied by a strengthening of boundaries. Both chapters offer evidence as to the formation of strong communities among students, both within their department (within the actual course in Lapworth's chapter and across the year groups in Ahearn's offering) and also particularly in the university itself, through the student clubs and societies and the students' union (Ahearn).

The university may after all still be an institution that is predisposed to the formation of communities. And it just may be that it is forms of community among students that are a particularly strong form of community. The two chapters here also, surely, reflect the complex interactions between the identity formation of individuals and the rich interactions between those individuals and communities. No student – in the becoming of a student – is an island.

It turns out, then, that both chapters are testimony to the ways in which the support of communities can aid identity formation; and an identity that may still reflect the idea of a university as a site of personal and worthwhile human development.

Chapter 12

A crisis in identity

The view of a postgraduate student of higher education

Susan Lapworth

Introduction

I am a professional university administrator who fits neatly into the account provided by Celia Whitchurch earlier in this volume: my professional identities are multiple and fluid. I undertook the MBA in Higher Education Management offered by the Institute of Education as a part-time student from October 2003 to September 2005. It is this new identity as a part-time postgraduate student that I intend to consider here, although it will become clear that my identity as 'student' is inextricably linked to my identities as 'university manager'. I will also suggest that my own multiple identities cannot be considered without forming a view of the identity of the contemporary university.

I intend to take a discursive approach to the consideration of identity: here, identity is constituted in and through both language and practice. I will begin by considering the markers of difference that might allow the identity of 'student' to be fixed. In this context, I will examine the experience of being a student on the MBA in Higher Education Management. This will lead to a consideration of a penetration of management discourse into the academy and the implication for me, as both a student and a university manager, of an apparent tension between academic critical enquiry and the managerial. I will end by reflecting on whether the elusiveness of stable student identity might also indicate a crisis of identity for the university more widely.

Constituting student identity through difference

I want to adopt a simple model to consider my own student identity on the MBA: I want to think about identity as constituted through difference, as something that requires a classification system that separates 'us' – those who share a particular identity – from 'them' – those who do not. I also want to think about identity as constituted through both the symbolic and the social: the markers of difference exist both in terms of how relationships and practices are signified and the way in which they take form as concrete practices (see, for example, Woodward 2002).

The identity 'student' is constituted through such markers of difference. In the symbolic realm, the arrangement of the traditional lecture – students seated facing a teacher who stands on a raised platform – provides an easy example of the way in which the differences between the two identities are signified. The accompanying social practices – listening, note-taking, asking questions – solidify the identity of 'student' on one side of the boundary between student and teacher. In these examples, student identity is defined by both what it is – (hopefully) attentive learner – and what it is not – knowledge-imparting teacher.

The MBA programme was intended to be a collaborative enterprise; we were often told that the programme belonged to us and that we should work with the course team to shape our experience. This philosophy of collaboration was reinforced through the delivery of the programme in week-long residential blocks at a series of different UK institutions. Relationships and professional networks were built between students, the course team and a wide range of speakers. Despite this, the markers of difference that denote student identity are, at first sight at least, readily apparent. The earlier example of the symbolic and social characteristics of a lecture were certainly present. There was also a broader set of concerns relating to the traditional student learning experience: applying and registering for a degree, preparatory reading, engaging with lectures and tutorials, writing essays, and so on. These exclude those not participating in the student learning experience – 'them' – thereby stabilising through difference the category of 'student' as 'us'.

As a graduate student having been through the UK higher education system before, I felt that I would be able to navigate this range of symbols and practices without too much difficulty. I was familiar with my own preferred learning styles, and thought that I knew which areas of the curriculum would be of particular interest. In part, my expectations were confirmed, but there were also some surprises along the way. For example, I had not previously worked within a social science context and the disciplinary conventions, the literature and the method were all unfamiliar. In curriculum terms, I had expected that the module on managing financial resources would be dry, technical and difficult; it turned out to be one of the most interesting and useful areas of the programme, providing a real appreciation of the importance of widespread financial literacy within institutions.

These strands of a traditional experience – adjusting to the conventions of a discipline, finding new areas of intellectual interest – were accompanied by the tropes of a more contemporary student experience. Participation in the quality assurance regime through provision of regular feedback – on issues such as the suitability of physical teaching environment, promptness and legibility of lecture handouts, the quality and variety of the visiting speakers – was also there to mark out difference between the MBA cohort and the course team. I don't remember these issues being part of my experience as a student the first time around (although it is a long time ago: I first went to university before the 1988 Education Reform Act that began to dramatically reshape the sector) and it is worth considering for a moment whether this shift in experience results in a different construction of student identity.

The difference of being judged

Denise Batchelor has identified the way in which the student voice is infiltrated by 'impersonal commercial languages of consumerism and commodification'. I want to suggest that this idea of 'student as consumer' functions to blur the boundaries between the sharp 'us and them' categories I have discussed. This is particularly acute in relation to one of the key markers of difference that forms student identity: the symbolic and social practices of assessment. The act of judging academic performance, however collaborative the process up to the point of assessment, functions to contain academic identity as a separate category from student identity: those judging are different from those being judged. Even an increasing prevalence of forms of peer assessment does not endanger this exclusion, as these pieces of assessment are often formative rather than summative or are weighted so as to have negligible impact on final classification decisions.

My recollection of my earlier university experience is that assessment processes and the way in which summative judgements were made at a programme (or 'course' in those days) level were opaque and something of a mystery. Marks were not routinely provided, nor was there an expectation that extensive written feedback would be given. Students knew that they were 'heading for a high 2:1' rather than having their performance analysed through dozens of individual pieces of assessment attached to separate modules. The intended transparency of these processes today opens them up to scrutiny and critique. Whereas transparency and accountability might well have been long overdue in some areas, this has also resulted in a shift in the way in which difference is mapped out between the judged and the judging. Students pass judgement on the adequacy of assessment and the associated feedback and, although we maintain an absolute defence of 'academic judgement', even the security of this exclusionary boundary might be seen to be being eroded by some of the judgements of the Office of the Independent Adjudicator (see Office of the Independent Adjudicator 2006).

In the MBA context, a desire for clarity over assessment practices was certainly apparent. There were two strands of assessment for each module: an assessment of the syndicate group work measured on a pass/fail basis through both participation and group presentation, and a graded assessment of a more traditional written essay. Participants felt that there was a lack of clarity over the assessment criteria for the syndicate group work: each group routinely passed and we were all told that we'd done terribly well. It was difficult to see how a group might fail and some groups were keen for the kind of detailed feedback that might help them to improve performance in the next task. A suggestion during my last module that a system of peer assessment be introduced for syndicate presentations to provide more detailed discussion of performance resulted in uproar. The assessment process was seen as a confidential and private interaction between student and teacher rather than a public discussion of relative performance.

The essays also prompted extensive discussion, particularly in relation to the criterion that required appropriate use of the academic literature in the context of essay questions that were largely practice-based. My cohort was told very clearly during induction that we should not expect that everybody would get A grades for written work and that we should not be disappointed with Bs as the previous cohort had been. There were also several discussions about the variability in the nature and extent of written and oral feedback provided on essays.

I find it interesting that I'm able to write at length about the discussions about assessment throughout the programme; the staff–student liaison committee returned to the issue repeatedly during my time as a member. I believe that this may, in part, be attributable to the prevalent practice of inviting students repeatedly to provide feedback in various forms. The MBA was an excellent programme that prompted very little by way of genuine criticism, and discussion returned to an area of student anxiety: being judged. I don't believe that this concern is confined to the MBA; the data from the National Student Survey (see Surridge 2006) suggests that the category of 'assessment and feedback' routinely scores below other areas and it seems that, at the very least, the sector ought to be considering why this might be the case.

My argument here is that the discourse around assessment begins to invert the relationship between the identities of 'student' and 'teacher': those being judged are repeatedly asked to judge the adequacy of the judging processes and outcomes. If judging is one of the key markers of difference, then the boundary between 'us' and 'them' is more porous than before and therefore less able to fix identity. If we then take the 'student as consumer' identity, in which judging academic achievement is merged with the consumerist judgements of paying 'customers', the boundary that secures student identity is breached and the difference between those judging and those being judged begins to collapse. We can see that the identity of academic staff as those who judge is no longer capable of consistently excluding those who are judged.

Student identity on the MBA

I have set out some of the issues in constructing the contemporary student identity, but I now want to focus on how this might be conceptualised for those on the MBA in Higher Education Management: I want to argue that on this particular programme student identity is constituted differently. The student cohort on the MBA deliberately consists of a range of people with very diverse career backgrounds: professional administrators from central services and academic departments, academics, and academic managers. These people find themselves in their professional lives on the 'them' side of student identity; they are excluded by the markers of difference that have traditionally secured student identity as a coherent category. Despite this positioning, the MBA cohort did adopt the signifiers of student identity; we were students by definition and by practice.

In particular, we were post-experience, postgraduate students on a practice-based programme. Here, the idea of constituting identity through difference remains valid: the aspects of both the traditional and more contemporary learning experiences that I have already set out apply equally to the development of student identity on the MBA. However, a sub-set of the potential markers of difference appear to be less relevant than they might be in attempting to secure the identity of, for example, undergraduate students who live, study and socialise together on a campus throughout the academic year, have to navigate the complexities of loans and top-up fees, and worry about post-graduation employment prospects.

For us, different markers shaped our identity as a student cohort. We all brought varying professional experience to the programme, but assumptions of difference between, for example, academics and administrators quickly dissipated as a broader collective identity began to be constituted. We were united as a group by our desire to develop ourselves professionally and to broaden our experience of the field in which we work. This appeared to overcome the differences that demark our professional identities in the workplace and allowed us to develop a coherent identity as students within a common professional context. Sector-wide trends towards more specialised or niche master's-level provision might well result in an increase in coherence in student identity on these programmes as applicants make study choices that reflect their developmental aspirations in certain fields. However, my feeling is that the sense of collective identity on the MBA was particularly strong. This may be in part a result of the pattern of delivery, with us coming together for relatively short, intense periods and then returning to the workplace. In this way, personal relationships developed in ways that might not have been possible had the programme been delivered on one or two evenings each week.

Despite these apparent successes in securing a collective student identity on the MBA, I want to suggest that, in the context of this programme, the identity of 'student' resists being stabilised through difference. I believe that this resistance takes place in two ways: first, as a result of the identities of those delivering the material and, second, because of the other, non-student, identities within the cohort itself. The use of visiting speakers to deliver the majority of the material plays a significant role here.

The programme was developed and managed by a core course team made up of high-profile academics within the field, some of whom had extensive experience of managing higher education institutions. Although the course team contributed to the delivery of each module, drawing together themes and providing coherence, the majority of the content was delivered through the involvement of visiting speakers drawn from a wide range of specialisms: for example, pro-vice-chancellors for teaching and for research; academic experts in marketing or strategic management from prestigious business schools; professional university managers with expertise in particular areas; senior policy-makers from HEFCE; managers from other parts of the public sector. The breadth of experience, approaches, and disciplines contributed to a rich and complex experience. It also served to problematise the markers of difference that might otherwise secure the category of 'teacher'. The majority of those delivering material were not involved in assessment, and the differencing through judging that I argued earlier to be a key separator of student and teacher identity does not easily apply. Equally, the symbolic label 'academic' was not valid as not all of the visitors were academics who practised in a disciplinary context of direct relevance to the programme. The inclusion of non-academics in delivery – for example, registrars, sector-wide policy-makers, HE consultants, NHS managers – further resists the security of the identity of teacher. Expertise was gathered from contexts extending beyond the more traditional delivery of master's programmes by academics teaching within a particular research specialism. I want to argue that, despite the markers of difference functioning to constitute a collective student identity, the 'other' against which that identity secures its meaning – 'teacher' – was not a stable category on the MBA.

A further layer of this argument can be added: the diversity of identities on the 'teacher' side of the line replicated the multiplicity of professional identities on our side. The identities that we each occupied in our professional lives and that placed us in opposition to 'student' contributed to the blurring of the boundaries between categories. Those involved as students had informed views on a range of broader issues that might fall outside the student perspective on more mainstream programmes, for example, the effectiveness of pedagogical approaches, the bureaucratic dangers of quality assurance practices, and so on. More specifically, the expertise of the MBA student in some areas was greater than that of the 'teacher' – a professor of accounting provided *ad hoc* tutorials on understanding financial ratios, a statistician proved more adept with tools for statistical analysis. Here, the identities of those involved in delivering the material – academic, professional, manager – are replicated by those receiving it. The stabilisation of student identity through markers of difference in this context fails. Difference cannot be maintained and the process of exclusion of 'other' no longer functions.

I have already suggested that the idea of student identity as a homogeneous category has begun to break down under contemporary conditions. I now want to suggest that, in the MBA context, the exclusion no longer works at all. To take this argument a stage further, I now want to consider what the existence of an MBA in Higher Education Management might mean for the university more generally.

Management discourse in higher education

There has been a growth in the number of students completing MBA programmes over recent years from only 1,200 UK MBA graduates in 1986 to approximately 10,000 graduating students in 2000 (see, for example, Currie and Knights 2003 for an account of the development of the MBA). The increase of this type of professionally oriented programme reflects the discourse around the role of higher education in providing graduates able to work within the knowledge economy (see, for example, DfES 2003) and should not be seen as a surprising trend. Initially, MBA programmes were generalist management development programmes aimed at those in the private sector with some career experience. More recently, context-specific and specialised versions of the MBA – focusing on entrepreneurship or e-business, for example – have been developed. There has also been a development in provision focused on areas of the public sector, such as the NHS, local government and, in my case, higher education. This public sector orientation involves explicitly bringing the techniques of private sector management to the public sector; concerns about how to be a better manager are placed centre stage.

The rise in the public sector MBA may been seen as a response to – or a component of – the introduction of new public management (NPM) techniques and practices through the 1980s and 1990s. During this period, the principle of accountability in the public sector became more broadly conceived than strictly financial and expanded to include a keen interest in performance more generally: 'it has been argued that taxpayers have rights to know that their money is being spent economically, efficiently, and effectively – the three Es – and that citizens as consumers of public services are entitled to monitor and demand minimum standards of performance' (Power 1997: 44). NPM revealed a shift away from the traditionally unchallenged professional expertise of doctors or academics towards an increasingly managed environment equipped to respond to the imperatives of the three Es.

The higher education sector was not immune to these shifts in public policy. Others in this volume have already set out the changes to the sector over the past twenty years that have produced a contemporary environment that is more competitive, more internationalised, and potentially more turbulent and unstable. We might assume that the need to manage more and better would be unarguable and, within this discourse, that a focus on the good management of the university is inescapable. We can trace a series of interventions in this area by HEFCE, through for example hypothecated funding for leadership, governance and management (HEFCE 2003). The more recent creation of the Leadership Foundation for Higher Education, which is 'committed to developing and improving the management and leadership skills of existing and future leaders of Higher Education' (Leadership Foundation 2006), signals a drawing together of previously disparate strands of activity. In this context, it might appear to be a natural extension to create a sector-specific MBA to bring the tools of management into the academy. However, I want to consider whether this is such an inevitably natural and positive intervention.

The MBA in Higher Education Management was first offered by the Institute of Education in October 2002. It is aimed at participants from a range of backgrounds who are 'future holders of senior positions in higher education management' (Institute of Education 2006). The MBA programme that I followed consisted of a series of core modules in areas such as strategic management, the management of financial resources, the management of teaching and research, and institutional governance. There was also a range of optional modules covering more special-ised areas of contemporary higher education, including the quality process, inter-nationalisation, third stream activities, and lifelong learning. Towards the end of the programme, participants undertook either a real-life consultancy report based in an unfamiliar institution, or a more traditional master's dissertation. The fact that the vast majority of us undertook the consultancy project may reflect the practice-based ethos of the programme and the desire of participants to develop a broader range of skills and expertise. In its structure and generic content, there-fore, it looked similar to other MBA programmes.

The existence of a sector-specific programme containing the elements that would be expected from a more generalist MBA might lead us to assume that a particular kind of subject is recruited to the management discourse that is in-creasingly present in higher education: it might produce better managers tooled in the logic of management. One of the key markers of difference through which the university was able to secure its identity in the past involved the 'us' of the academic world being set firmly in opposition to the 'them' of the private sec-tor business environment: management was placed firmly outside the boundary that constructed academic identity. The logics of NPM, the language of manage-ment, and even the MBA in Higher Education Management, are now inside the academy. The boundary has become porous and the management language and practices that used to be outside and 'other' are now inside and elements in the way in which the university's identity is constituted. I'll return later to the impli-cations of this, but I want to pause for a moment and consider whether this logic of management is indeed inescapable within the academy.

Culture of critical discourse

Better management implies that it is possible to arrive at coherent answers to organisational questions if managers are sufficiently well equipped to operate in the contemporary environment. Barnett's concept of supercomplexity – in which the role of the university becomes one of 'organised inquiry for generating and for managing uncertainty' (Barnett 2000: 142) – should at the very least raise a sig-nificant degree of scepticism about our ability to manage with any degree of cer-tainty, with or without NPM principles or MBA programmes. Rather, it suggests that the challenge for those seeking to manage is to learn to operate effectively amidst conflicting, unresolvable frameworks that defy the tools and techniques of management.

Concepts such as supercomplexity, therefore, problematise the logic of man-agement. Currie and Knights (2003) set out a similar set of issues in the context of different pedagogical approaches to MBA programmes. They provide a model in three parts: disciplinary, staff development, and critical pedagogy. The disci-plinary strand involves the acquisition of a body of knowledge about – rather than for – management. They suggest that a perceived need to maintain academic standards in a graduate-level programme encouraged this type of approach. The staff development strand is seen as a response to student demands to make programmes more relevant and more professionally focused. Here, the use of case studies and role-playing encouraged participation. Finally, a critical pedagogy 'uses the work and non-work experiences of students to problematize rather than simply validate management theories and assumptions' (Currie and Knights 2003: 31) and students are encouraged to 'reflect critically on such knowledge in order to understand management and work as a social, political, economic and moral practice' (Currie and Knights 2003: 31). Currie and Knights argue for a critical pedagogy on the basis that it 'could help arrest the drift, on the part of both teachers and students, towards an instrumentalism that easily collapses into indifference' (Currie and Knights 2003: 28).

My own MBA programme consisted of components of all three pedagogical approaches in a reasonably easy balance. I would agree, however, that the temptation to view the programme as delivering knowledge and skills acquisition was there for some participants and visiting speakers, sometimes despite the efforts of the course team to underpin the delivery with a critical thread. Here, there appears to me to be a very real danger of recruiting subjects to the managerial discourse, thereby further embedding the logic of management in the university. I don't believe that this was the aim of the course team. Rather, there was an expectation of criticality on the MBA in Higher Education Management that might not be apparent in other contexts. Knights and Currie write in the context of a generalist MBA programme and we might want to consider whether or how this idea of criticality – or problematising knowledge – might be important in an MBA specifically focused on higher education. Here, it is important to remember that critical enquiry is central to higher education as both idea and practice: a 'culture of critical discourse' (Alvin Gouldner cited in Barnett 1992: 66) identifies the key high-level feature that unites higher education across disciplinary boundaries. My professional experience suggests, however, that there is little evidence of a 'culture of critical discourse' about management working practices in universities and that the 'highly structured and self-critical conversation' (Barnett 1992: 62) that organises academic life appears absent in the management of the academy.

However, by creating an academic programme – the MBA – populated by those from within the academy as both participants and deliverers, the possibility for critique of the management discourse is opened up and the idea of the academic as a manageable commodity is challenged. I want to suggest that, as we expose management ideas and practices to the culture of critical discourse, they are problematised. In other words, the academic function renders the principles of management less inevitable and each of the two different discourses – critical enquiry and management – is revealed as increasingly open to the logic of the other.

The MBA operates amidst this apparently contradictory landscape. There is a tension between the implied outcome to produce better managers, suggested by the existence of a sector-specific MBA, and the unmanageable nature of higher education. At its best, the programme provided a critical (and sometimes quite argumentative) engagement with both the idea of the contemporary university, and the concepts and practices of management. For me, this problematising process for both the academic and the managerial discourses sits at the heart of my experience and, as a result, my identities as 'university manager' have been challenged and reshaped. As a student in this context, and as a university manager in the broader context, I experienced a degree of dislocation that presented something of a crisis of identity.

The identity of the university

I want now to return to the problems around securing identity that I raised in relation to student identity and argue that these are a manifestation of a crisis of identity for the university more widely.

I have already suggested that the logic of management has breached the boundary between the university and the private sector. In doing so, the 'us' identity of the university is no longer secured through opposition to the external 'them' of management. At the same time, the sector itself has expanded and become more diverse; the relatively homogeneous pre-1992 sector no longer holds sole claim to the identity 'university'. The symbolic and social markers of difference that used to exist to secure identity – the legal power to award degrees granted by a university's charter and statues, titles such as Vice-Chancellor or Registrar, delivering and being funded for a dual mission of teaching and research – no longer provide a water tight category of 'university'. Other kinds of institutions – the former polytechnics, and other specialist institutions – all now have access to the symbolic title 'university' without necessarily partaking in the social practices that used to securely constitute the identity. The category 'higher education' extends even further beyond this enlarged group of institutions with university title: it is broad and defies easy articulation or definition. The ability of the symbolic and the social to denote difference and thereby circumscribe identity has been eroded. The elements that had traditionally existed inside the identity 'university' are no longer secure and those elements that had existed outside the exclusionary limit are now inside; the boundaries that seek to stabilise identity are increasingly porous.

This inability of the traditional markers of difference to exclude 'other' produces a crisis of identity for the university and, in turn, for those working within it. For academics, there is a temptation to resort to essentialist claims to identity, and the mythical golden era set out by Burgess is invoked. Students, as 'members of the university', are positioned amidst this fluidity but for them there is no collective recollection of a golden age on which to draw. The new forms of student identity that I discussed earlier – the 'student as consumer' issues – begin to coalesce without challenge.

I would not want to give the impression that the higher education sector is identity-less. A redrawing of boundaries for this enlarged sector can also be seen to be taking place. New interventions in both the symbolic and social realms have sought to cohere and stabilise the university's identity, for example, the government's widening participation agenda, a focus on employability, or the QAA dogma of broad comparability of standards across the sector. Here, all parts of the sector are equal and higher education as a contained category is preserved. My MBA student cohort represented the heterogeneous nature of the contemporary sector: the range of institutions represented included Russell Group to post-1992 universities, specialist institutions and a private American institution. There was a wide geographical spread and following cohorts included participants from overseas institutions. The 'higher education' label captured us all regardless of our differences. However, I would suggest that it is necessary to ask where the new limits to this identity might be found; as the boundary necessary to secure identity is forever pushing outwards and collapsing difference to allow new areas into the 'higher education' sector, it becomes increasingly difficult to determine who is 'us' and who is 'them'. The process of continuous change creates a fluidity in which attempts to stabilise – through, for example, the clustering in the sector that gives us the Russell Group or the 1994 Group – continually fail; the identity of the university is in crisis.

My argument here underlines the university as a site for contestation and for practices that remain open-ended and unresolvable. The role of the MBA is not, therefore, to produce a set of better managers able to recite from the HEFCE strategic planning guide or to understand the complexities of off-balance sheet accounting; rather it is to develop a set of subjects able to mediate and translate between the academic and the managerial in a context where identities consistently defy solidity. Rather than further embedding managerial discourse in the academy, the MBA seeks to return to the academy those with a greater capability to articulate the nodes of the management discourse and identify the areas where these touch the academic. I want to suggest that the MBA, therefore, constitutes identities – both student and professional – capable of intervention in the crisis of identity of the university.

Conclusions

I have provided an account of student identity as discursively constituted through difference. In this context, attempts are made to fix or stabilise identity within boundaries that exclude 'other'. I have argued that, although there are clear markers of difference that might allow the identity of student to cohere, under contemporary conditions the category resists stabilisation. The symbolism and practices of assessment highlight the increasing difficulty of stabilising identities as the boundaries against which 'us' – student – and 'them' – teacher – are constituted become porous. I have also identified a particular set of issues in relation to student identity on the MBA in Higher Education Management. Here, despite a clear sense of collective identity as a student cohort, the secure relative identities of student and teacher breakdown and the discursive process that constructs difference fails.

The sector-specific nature of the MBA also draws attention to the way in which a culture of critical enquiry functions to problematise the nature of the management discourse in higher education. Celia Whitchurch has identified this tension between the competing logics of the academic critical enquiry and of management as '[the/a] key problematic for universities, whereby academic and management agendas are seen as competing narratives inducing a "cultural malaise"' (Chapter 5 of this volume). I have suggested that the existence of the MBA provides for a critique of the management discourse as subjects able to challenge management imperatives are constituted. My experience as a student led me to challenge my assumptions as a manager; I try to manage less and better and to seek areas where the two discourses meet productively. These are necessarily contingent moments in time where meaning can be stabilised momentarily. I have argued that, through reconstituted subjects such as me, the MBA provides an intervention in the crisis of identity of the university rather than representing its cause.

Chapter 13

Being an undergraduate student in the twenty-first century

Alison Ahearn, Oliver Broadbent, John Collins and Eirini Spentza

Introduction by Alison Ahearn

This chapter presents three stories of the student experience, told by students from the same department at Imperial College London, allowing readers to make their own comparative analysis with ease. Oliver Broadbent, John Collins and Eirini Spentza were invited to contribute to this chapter because they have been serious students who were notable as student leaders at department, faculty and/or college level. Each student is describing the same course at the same time, yet their experiences are highly coloured by their personal concept of what a university education ought to be. Thus we see a political model of education, a social model of education and a personal transformative model described in this chapter. Each student gives stinging and trenchant criticism of their institution where its characteristics detract from the student experience, yet each professes great enjoyment and personal development from their education. It should be noted that these students, although elected by their fellow students as representatives, are not typical students: they handle an enormous workload in their degree with an enormous workload in their extracurricular work as student leaders. (As an indicator, their workload far exceeds that of Imperial's pre-clinical medical students.) Each of them can point to the changes they have made for other students: the schemes they created, the events they ran and the changes they wrought to the system. These are not the views of onlookers in the education system, but of participants who care. Their only priming before writing their contributions was a brief meeting with the editor, Dr Di Napoli, where they were informed of the nature of the book and invited to ask questions.

A twenty-first century student: Oliver Broadbent

I am about to start the fourth year of my civil engineering degree at Imperial College but it is my second undergraduate degree. My first degree was in chemistry at Oxford University, graduating one year before starting this second degree. As I have studied science-based degrees at two different universities it has really become apparent to me just how different the student experience is at these two institutions.

For me, how students develop into rounded individuals is as important as, if not more important than, how students develop academically at university. The majority of the facts crammed for those final exams will be forgotten as quickly as they were learned, but the person you become shapes your outlook, lifestyle and actions for many years after. That personal development I believe happens within the context of a student community: the broader the community, the more diverse the group of people within it and the greater the opportunity to learn from others and become better informed.

The student community can also be a melting pot of ideas. It was certainly the case for me that I came to university without any of my beliefs – be they political, philosophical or ethical – ever really having been tested. At university, there is the opportunity to really broaden awareness of issues in society just through talking to people who study a different subject. Above all, if that community is strong then awareness of the issues that are affecting that community is much higher. And where there is debate, people are much more willing to speak out about the issues that affect them.

It is clear to me that geography can have a significant impact on the strength of that community. Imperial College students' accommodation is spread all over west London. By contrast, the student population at Oxford is concentrated in a very small area of the city. It is much easier to feel part of a student community when everywhere you look there is another student. It is a view shared with friends who study at universities across the capital, that the city dilutes the student experience.

The level of student political activity, I believe, plays an important part in shaping the outlook of the students who study there. Whereas Oxford offers a full range of courses, Imperial College is a science university without any full-time undergraduate courses in the arts and humanities. As a result I think there is less awareness of political issues. That Imperial College Union has only just joined the NUS shows a lack of appetite at Imperial for speaking about student issues. For instance, strike action by academic staff at other universities received little attention, it seemed to me, at Imperial. Most significantly, the college has just pulled out of the University of London. Far from empowering Imperial students to go their own way, I believe it will further isolate them from the rest of the students in London, the issues that affect them and in doing so further dissuade them from speaking out themselves.

Whereas I think a feeling of belonging to a group of students is lacking at Imperial, the feeling of belonging to a profession is much stronger on my civil engineering course than when I was studying chemistry. I concede that a civil engineering degree is more vocational than a chemistry degree and so this sense of belonging is to be expected. This professional orientation has obvious benefits down the line for those who want to pursue engineering, but I think it comes at the cost of weakening the sense of commonality with other students. Students who are treated as young professionals may be more likely to speak up on issues such as the relevance of teaching material to their career path, which may be a point of discussion between them and their colleagues on the course, but far less likely to speak out on broader, more traditional topics for student discussion: human rights, socialism, peace movements, CND even – all topics that are very 'studenty' and not very 'young professional'. In short, this professional alignment, be it within engineering or, often, finance, serves to cut short student debate, potentially confining personal development to the realms of the profession that awaits at the end of the course.

Moving away from the topic of personal development and onto academic development, I can make a more direct comparison between these two universities. At Oxford, lectures are backed up to some extent by tutorials, either one on one or in small groups. At Imperial, lectures are also backed up with tutorials but the definition of tutorial here is a little different, typically involving splitting the entire class of 90 students between two rooms and students working through question sheets with lecturers or PhD students on hand to answer any questions. It is my observation that, because the individual contact is so much less at Imperial, the lectures have to be much better written to achieve maximum understanding and coverage in the minimum amount of time. It is for this reason I believe that the quality of the lecturing at Imperial is better than that which I experienced at Oxford. The teaching is more comprehensive but as a result the learning experience is quite different. The cliché of stuffy Oxford dons asking questions that are a little too difficult to answer is not that far off the mark in my experience, but what I think this more adversarial way of learning does is force students to think harder and develop the mental agility to deal with the stress (and it is a stress!). At Imperial, because there are not the resources for every student to seek help from a lecturer, the questions asked have to be that much more 'do-able'. In a sense, at Imperial, the work is set out for you and you just have to do it. It is not to say that it is a pushover, but the real challenge for the attentive student is just getting through it all. I have to say that, although I sing the praises of the tutorial system for the academic development it can bring about, I have been far more successful studying under the Imperial regime.

With the advent of league tables, and tuition fees, it seems universities can leave nothing to chance. The risk of a student studying for four years and getting low marks or failing, affecting league table positions, seems to be offset at Imperial by testing students at every available opportunity. That way, anyone who falls by the wayside can be helped along or kicked out before they risk falling in the final furlong. It is unfortunately a trend that severely restricts the opportunity for unsupervised learning – the opportunity to pursue lines of study that are of interest. Children learn by playing. Maths students can learn by messing around with derivations and seeing what sort of interesting results come up. It is a crude example, but this sort of learning is not possible when students' time is so filled with the hoop-jumping that is continuous assessment. On the other hand, I think that the Oxford system of Finals, in which the level of degree depends solely on the outcome of these exams, is not progressive and is unduly stressful. If students are to develop mentally and academically, they need to be given the time to learn.

For all its excellence in the courses that it teaches, the Imperial student experience is limited by its location, the almost institutional lack of engagement by students with student issues, and the stifling workload. But I must say that I have thoroughly enjoyed studying at Imperial despite the criticism that I have levelled at it.

A twenty-first century student: John Collins

My decision to attend Imperial was determined by two key factors: firstly, Imperial was and still is regarded by industry employers as the best technical university in Europe. Secondly, Imperial is located in the centre of Europe's largest city.

Schoolteachers and family tried to dissuade me from choosing Imperial, seen as a stressful environment for any young person, especially one who had experienced a turbulent education like mine. And they were right: Imperial can be incredibly stressful at times; but for this reason, and because of the high quality of people that are drawn to the institution, I believe Imperial has given me a great start to my professional life as an engineer.

At age nine I was judged by my Local Education Authority to have special educational needs that could not be met within the state system at that time, so my secondary education started at a small Rudolf Steiner School where the staff-to-student ratio was two to one, school food was grown on site and teachers set no homework. Thence to a progressive independent boarding school with teachers and pupils on first-name terms and the school largely governed by a staff–student council. Plus a gap year with a small Scottish charity, pioneering an English teaching project in Africa. My education was anything but conventional.

Thus my arrival at Imperial came as a huge shock, largely because of the two factors that had persuaded me to study there in the first place. London felt much larger than it looked on a map. And the high intellectual standard demanded by academics, coupled with a highly competitive culture, was completely unlike anything I had experienced before. Furthermore, compared to school, there seemed little community spirit and social cohesion within my department and around the campus. Initially it was only in my hall of residence that I felt that I was actually meeting normal, balanced human beings.

Like many young fresher students, I did not hold back from throwing myself into several clubs and societies at Imperial. It is my perception that the social life of most other British universities is largely based around student bars and night-clubs, whereas at Imperial the majority of students form their social groups within their departments, halls of residence and the diverse range of clubs and societies that are subsidised by the student union. The social scene within these often tiny societies is diverse, sheltered and, in my opinion, could be much more inclusive. Whereas there may be a wider sense of collective identity at other universities, at Imperial there seems only to be a disparate range of social groups who are often reluctant to interact with each other.

The decentralised nature of these social groupings produces two key characteristics that make Imperial very different from other universities. First, it seems to widen participation in extracurricular activities; Imperial College Union runs over 250 societies and nearly half of all Imperial College students are registered as members of at least one club (this is nearly four times higher than the national average). Second, it has been accused of creating 'cliques' and 'ghettos', which weave unfriendliness into the social fabric of the college, although this assessment may be an exaggeration as the college and student union still run successful bars and social events on the campus. But rising numbers of students from alcohol-free backgrounds, along with the closure of the largest student bar on the campus, have significantly challenged the established British student stereotype at Imperial College.

I spent my first three years in a hall of residence on campus at South Kensington. Life in a ten-storey concrete tower block felt claustrophobic at times, but I valued my opportunity to live in London's most fashionable and expensive district. I recall in my first year being distracted from my studies in my room by a noisy crowd and sound of helicopters; a short walk to Hyde Park revealed political leaders addressing an enormous crowd after an anti-war march attended by 2 million people from across the world. In my second year I remember vividly my walk home being delayed by the American president's motorcade. Third year saw me on an empty tube train to college during rush hour; it was the day after the 7 July terrorist attacks on London. Sometimes, when you live in the centre of London, you feel that you are living in the eye of the storm. In contrast, my final year spent living in the suburbs, 90 minutes from campus, felt quiet and spacious and completely different.

I was much involved in the student union: in my third year I represented all of Imperial's 5,500 engineering students at a faculty level, which let me see the student experience across Imperial's nine engineering departments. Contrasts were obvious. The civil engineering course is regarded by many to be more practical and kinaesthetic in approach, whereas the materials, computing and electrical engineering courses are seen as far more theoretical. All courses are equally challenging, both intellectually and emotionally, but some are more theoretical than others. I observed some effects of this.

Interestingly, one of the most important factors that seemed to affect students socially in my department was the course syllabus itself. As a civil engineering undergraduate, I had group field trips and group project exercises, the most notable example of which was the 'Constructionarium' week in my third year, in which undergraduates use engineering methods and practices on a construction site to build large structures such as footbridges, dams and piers. Aside from the educational value such a task brings, there is the added bonus of social cohesion that develops from the teamwork involved in implementing intense tasks. It has been noted by many students that geologists, biologists, medical students and civil engineers are seen to be more sociable than, say, computing and chemistry students, and it could be argued that the field trips and regular group tasks that commonly feature in these departments' courses contribute to this phenomenon.

I had always expected that my learning experience at Imperial would be very different from school and I was not surprised to find that the burden of responsibility for my educational progress rested almost entirely on my shoulders. I was given limited tuition in 'Learning to Learn' during the first few weeks of the first year; however, it was only after completing the first year exams that I had a clearer idea about how much commitment and time would be required from me if I wanted to succeed. That said, it is obvious that engineering courses in general are amongst the most structured degree courses available in the UK today and at times I benefited from over 30 contact hours each week.

I found my second year at Imperial very challenging indeed. This is the year when the bulk of course theory is taught and I must admit that I was highly unsatisfied with the quality of teaching I was receiving at that time. It seemed to me that, whereas it was difficult for me to understand the pure maths and mechanics that were being taught by leading academic researchers, to those lecturers the course material seemed like uninspiring kindergarten maths. For me, the gloom of the second year was compounded by the new routine of living a great distance away from the college and commuting into London for a 9 a.m. start every day. I eventually negotiated a room in halls for the second half of my second year.

With the exception of the second year, I would say that my learning experience at Imperial College has undoubtedly benefited from high quality teaching, educational resources and facilities. Furthermore, I have seen evidence that many of these facilities such as the libraries, computing facilities and sporting facilities have improved during my time at the college. However, there seems to be a belief amongst international students that the quality of Imperial's facilities still trails behind the quality that would be expected from a similarly prestigious American institution. A cursory glance at any international league table confirms this suspicion; Imperial is probably the best technical college of its kind in Europe, but Europe has fallen far behind America over the last several decades (Institute of Higher Education, Shanghai Jiao Tong University 2005). This fact has formed the backdrop to a controversial debate about the future of higher education funding, which is still taking place in Britain today.

The student body has been forced to accept that, if Imperial is to raise its standards higher and compete with the world's best universities, then the contribution from the student to his or her education must increase. Interestingly, at a recent student council meeting several council members expressed the view that the students' union should not oppose any increase in tuition fees should they be proposed in the future. For any student union, this would be an extraordinary position to adopt and I should stress that Imperial College Union policy still maintains that the financial burden on students should not be increased. However, the fact that many students feel confident enough to oppose this view is extraordinary and possibly symptomatic of wider culture at the college. I still believe that, in spite of its flaws, Imperial does represent excellent value for money and, given the relatively low financial resources that are at Imperial's disposal when compared to its American rivals, it is commendable that this university has been able to maintain its place in the world's top 20 best institutions for so long.

It was not until I reached the third and final year of my undergraduate degree at Imperial that I really began to appreciate the sheer class of the academic researchers who work at this institution. When I came to take my final year modules I was surprised to find that very few textbooks are available for these courses, simply because they had not yet been written. Instead I was given the opportunity to learn exciting topics such as earthquake engineering and transport planning from first-hand experiences of our enthusiastic final year lecturers, who seemed to regard the teaching of these courses as an opportunity to impress upon us the value of their life's work. Additionally, it was really only towards the end of my time at Imperial, as I started to recognise the value of these lecturers and the strength of the Imperial brand on my CV, that I began to feel satisfied that I had made the right choice in coming to this college. The first few years of Imperial life are difficult, alien and cold; but as the degree develops and social groupings strengthen, the student experience becomes world class.

A twenty-first century student: Eirini Spentza

On 26 September 2002 I left Greece, my home country, to move permanently to London in order to study civil engineering at Imperial College. The decision to leave my country to study abroad was a difficult one and one made knowing that it will forever affect my future life. The particular choice of studying in England at Imperial was a much easier choice to make, thanks to the worldwide reputation of Imperial as a leading institution in my field of interest, engineering. These choices made at the very early age of 17 were decisive steps forever influencing my life thereafter, but I can gladly say four years later that I have not regretted them, and have greatly benefited from the environment in which I spent my university years.

As a European Union student, I found fitting into life in London challenging but I suspect not as challenging as for other international students. The great passage into adulthood undertaken by all young people when they first leave their homes had to be achieved in a foreign environment, but was facilitated by the existence of a very large number of Greek students at Imperial and in London universities in general. The college itself was helpful in that respect, since in our department in particular much attention and pastoral care is given to the first-year students if needed. Adapting to the method of working caused no issues for me; I found that the style and method of teaching and type of work required resembled very closely the International Baccalaureate system which I had followed during the last two years of school in Greece. In spite of all these assisting factors it must be said that it took me the whole of my first year to really adapt to this new way of life.

I realised that I was finally feeling comfortable and at home in the university when at the beginning of my second year I felt that I wanted to get involved in common activities, and chose to become year representative. Since then the student union has become a large part of my life, consuming ever-growing amounts of time and effort, and is the aspect of student life at Imperial that I enjoy and appreciate the most. The experience of being a student representative in my second year led me to take on a very challenging role for me, which was becoming chair of CivSoc, the departmental society in civil engineering. Taking on this role forced me to come to terms with many of my own insecurities and inherent shyness and develop the leadership skills necessary to run a vibrant and growing society such as CivSoc. In my fourth year, eager to keep the link to the student union, I took on the role of welfare officer for the engineering faculty, and through that role was involved extensively with a college initiative to support and encourage female students to stay in male-dominated environments as part of the Women in SET project. Being involved with the student union at Imperial, which is one of the largest and most active in the country, led me to develop as a person and acquire skills and experiences that I could not have acquired otherwise.

The civil engineering course at Imperial has been an asset in itself. Acknowledged to be a difficult degree, it involves many challenges. Graduating with first class honours required a lot of endurance, stamina and steady nerves since the workload is heavy and the expectations endless. However, it is a well organised course, with a large emphasis on coursework and particularly on group projects, which I approve of. My only criticism at the end of the four years is that some of the work seems to be assigned only to increase the pressure on students, and the workload is not always directly related to the amount of knowledge or insight gained; a different structure of certain pieces of coursework could result in us learning more in the same number of hours. The quality of teaching however is very good overall, and the attention, help and support supplied by the lecturers is significant and accelerates the learning process.

The main difference when comparing the education system in England with that of Greece in particular, or of various other European countries, is that the English system functions more like a school in that much close attention and supervision is given to students. This is facilitated by the relatively small number of students in each year, which leads to a manageable department with close relations between staff and students. The system used, whereby students must pass the year overall rather than individual modules, leads to clearly defined year groups and a sense of belonging to that year group, which is enhanced by the large number of common activities and projects undertaken.

Working closely in a group was initially challenging for me since group work is not central to the Greek education system. However, after the first two years I became so accustomed to this way of working that undertaking the few individual projects required seemed laborious and trying. The philosophy that has developed over the years is that, if one is going to be working as much as we do, it might as well be together with someone else rather than alone. Indeed, what I recall now most vividly from the four years at Imperial is working in large groups late at night in a computer lab.

The day-to-day routine of the course however was broken with the annual field trips which were invariably very enjoyable and a great way for us to bond as a year group. The first-year surveying field trip and second-year geology field trip are memorable experiences in their own right, but the Constructionarium in the third year has been for many the most significant part of the entire course. The Constructionarium takes place in the National Construction College in Norfolk, and involves us getting first-hand experience of construction work on site and project management, by building our own mini projects. The projects are not as small scale as they sound; in my year the accomplishments of the week involved a dam, a 10 m long bridge and a 40 m long stadium (for reference, 40 m is roughly equivalent to the height of a 12-storey building). The week involved everything from managing the finances and budget to pouring concrete, making formwork and digging. For me it has probably been the most stressful week of the entire course, but also the most rewarding. This experience was invaluable since it showed me the joys and woes of construction and made me really feel like a civil engineer.

Overall, the four years I spent at Imperial have been tiring and frustrating at times but mainly exciting, challenging and immensely rewarding, opening up opportunities that I could not initially envisage. I have graduated a different person from who I was when I entered, and hopefully better educated, more skilled and knowledgeable and better equipped for all aspects of life; and since I loved being at university so much I have decided to stay for another four years to do a PhD.

A final comment I would make concerns the direction that I see education in England taking in the future. It has been evident at Imperial during the past four years that the college is focusing more and more on running the university as a business in order to overcome financial hardships and increase income. Although this attitude is called for by practical constraints and the competitive market that has become higher education, the possible consequences for the education system are worrying. I would not like to be in a university environment where education and knowledge are thought of exclusively as products to be sold that will enable students to earn higher wages; there is a high value in education and knowledge in itself and we must not lose sight of that fact in the future.

Conclusion by Alison Ahearn

These student pieces reveal very different conceptions of what university life should be about: for Oliver, the student should be politically aware and concerned with 'student issues': a model of university as the place where one forms ideals and champions them. For John, university belongs to a social model and he considers, at some depth, the systemic causes of the multitude of niche social groupings found at Imperial compared with more generalist universities. Both see the arrangement and organisation of their studies as having an impact on their learning and their learning opportunity, but each views it through either the political or the social model of learning. Eirini looks at her education as transformational in a different way: a result of a series of serious choices, personal development and an upwards spiral of confidence, skill, knowledge and opportunities.

It is apparent from these pieces that the students see a modern university education as part of a life process rather than a commodity: trenchant criticism is matched by a passion for being challenged. The social, political and personal development is to the fore of the stories of experience, with technical learning described in terms of admiration for the expertise of the lecturers, particularly in the specialist senior years of the degree. The value of the extreme learning events, such as the Constructionarium, is perceived as extending well beyond any technical knowledge of engineering. Perhaps this is the element in common amongst the students: they are alive to the added value of a university education and are protective of it, wishing to shape it for others and protect it from being reduced to a mere commodity.

Postscript

Chapter 14

Academic identities and the story of institutions

David Watson

Social anthropologists and moral philosophers would agree on one thing (if not much else): that personal identity is tied up in a narrative, or life course. Scaling up this insight to the study of institutions is, of course, complex, but this is where the discipline of history is of most use. As Richard Evans demonstrates in his masterly *In Defence of History*, even the most complex problem can be approached through a technique of multiple analyses. He outlines the 12 linked narratives which he employed to investigate the Hamburg cholera epidemic of 1892: from the 'amateurish nature of the city administration,' through examinations of political inequality, poverty, environmental conditions and nutrition to the state of medical knowledge and practice, the course of earlier epidemics and so on (Evans 1997: 144–6).

Reading the earlier essays in this book together gives an impression of the Evans technique at work. We have here a series of personal and professional perspectives, each of which contributes a 'story' to the rich anthology of stories that is the modern university. All of these people relate to the whole institution in different ways. They may want different things *from* it. They may want different things *for* it.

In *Managing Strategy*, I prayed in aid the Dean of Westminster on this point:

> An organisation exists to get something done and requires management while an institution is less concrete and is largely held together by people in the mind as part of their frame of reference. An institution is composed of the diverse fantasies and projections of those associated with it. These ideas are not consciously negotiated or agreed upon, but they exist.

> (Watson 2000: 97)

Universities are very peculiar places. They are professionally argumentative communities, with very flat structures. Think about the current discussions of 'academic risk,' and the power of the individual lecturer making an assessment or a researcher choosing and then conducting a project. More or less everybody is authorised to have an opinion about everything.

Vocabulary

The lexicon of 'soft' or contested concepts which has been built up through the earlier chapters indicates just how provisional academic identity can be. Here's an A to Z list from which another academic 'devil's dictionary' might be created (see Nelson and Watt 1999). I have deliberately not chosen some of the usual suspects (like 'accountability', 'art', 'autonomy', '*Bildung*', 'competition', 'criticism', 'culture', 'freedom', '*habitus*', 'justice', 'knowledge', 'liquidity', 'narrative', 'negotiation', 'network', 'partnership', 'pastoral', 'regulation', 'standards', 'welfare' or 'wisdom' – for all of these, see the index).

Authenticity
Blame
Collusion
Domestication
Emancipation
Friendship
Gift
Health
Integrity
Jest
Kudos
Loss
Mutuality
Nostalgia
Opportunism
Power
Quality
Risk
Silence
Transformation
Underbelly
Voice
Work
Xenophobia
Youth
Zero-sum

These are all words replete with meaning and dripping with significance. Exploring what each means to the different members of an academic community shows just how complicated – how peculiar (in more than one sense of the word) – we are. I have in mind an exercise for the students on the MBA in Higher Education Management at the Institute of Education (this is the course whose moral compass is so eloquently described by Susan Lapworth – an MBA HEM graduate – in her chapter). *Offer a definition of each of these words in relation to the academic community to which you belong.* What more do we know, Evans-style, having heard them (all except the final three, which I made up, in the style of Simon Hoggart) used by our different witnesses?

Here is another illustration which acts as essay question in its own right. This is how my friend Jonathan Rée (a key figure for Denise Batchelor, in her discussion of 'voice') describes himself inside the jacket of his wonderful book on the history of the senses: ' "Jonathan Rée teaches philosophy at Middlesex University". *Discuss*' (Rée 2000). For the paperback edition the legend is expanded as follows: 'Jonathan Rée ("The Charles Dickens of philosophy" *Observer*) teaches philosophy at Middlesex University'.

Students on the MBA, in the course of tackling this exercise, have reflected on the order of the nouns, the choice of the verb, and above all the force of the preposition (echoing the German professor who declares that he does not work *for* his university but *in* it). It may only be one step from here to Howard Kirk in *The History Man*: 'this [the University of Watermouth on his first visit] is a place I can work against' (Showalter 2005: 74).

Hierarchy

People are organised in different ways inside universities and colleges. In ironic contrast to the 'flatness' alluded to above, most participants would imagine a hierarchy, something like the following. (Interestingly, it takes until Chapter 9 for any such systematic consideration to appear above):

* senior management;
* 'academic' (teaching) staff (or 'faculty');
* 'professional' support staff;
* contract researchers;
* clerical staff;
* manual 'workers'.

There are, I think, enduring differences between chartered and statutory universities in the UK here: the legacy of a strict demarcation between 'faculty' and 'administration' on the one hand, and common cause of all 'public sector HE' workers against the local authority personnel department on the other. Celia Whitchurch explores this legacy, and its continued impact on relationships between different categories of staff in different types of institution. Another divergence was in the ways in which individuals built their careers and developed esteem among their peers. In the 'chartered' sector, research ruled (although perhaps not to quite the extent that some have claimed – as in Lord May's constant reiteration that the

RAE has become 'the only game in town'). In contrast, in the 'public' sector, curriculum development and in particular (large) course leadership was a path to recognition and reward.

Like the other authors of chapters in this collection, I have been encouraged to be 'confessional'. My contribution to that aspect of the project is a fairly unoriginal observation: *at some stage in your career you discover who you are and what you can do.* There is a corollary: *this is rarely at the end.*

For me the critical stage was at Oxford Polytechnic, where the director took a gamble on me to sort out a mess: managing what was then almost an institution-wide undergraduate modular course. This had been one of the pioneers in the field but needed radical reform and renewal (see Watson 1989). I was appointed as its dean in 1981, and when I left (to become director of Brighton Polytechnic in 1990) I was a professor and deputy director of the polytechnic. The dean's role involved a mixture of academic development, people management and systems. Tackling it, I think, showed me what I could do, and what I enjoyed doing. And I've never had a harder job (in a particular way) since. I had previous experience in leading the 'diversification' of courses in the arts and humanities at a merged pair of former teacher education colleges (now part of Manchester Metropolitan University), and I subsequently had the privilege of leading what I believe to be one of the most respected universities in the system. But I built my career (which has certainly not precluded an attempt to contribute through research) as a teacher and as a curriculum developer. My experience was not unusual. At that time experienced and innovative course leaders were as much in demand (and wooed) within the polytechnic and college sector as RAE 'bankers' have come subsequently to be in the system as a whole.

This raises another question, of historical significance. Is higher education fundamentally about the curriculum (including the 'research-informed' curriculum) or is it simply about research? For the majority of our collective history, I would submit, it was about the former (see Watson 2007, Chapter 2). The 'merged' system has, of course, tilted towards the latter. At what cost?

Meanwhile, in terms of what is now called 'academic' practice, what happened in the late twentieth century was the discovery that such practice no longer belonged exclusively to the ranks of the so-called 'faculty.' The teaching, research and service environments are increasingly recognised as being supported and developed by university members with a variety of types of expertise (finance, personnel, estates, libraries, communications and information technology, and so on), each with their own spheres of professional competence, responsibility and recognition. To complicate the picture still further, Robert Burgess identifies how new subjects or professional fields, new courses and new modes of professional formation continue to diversify the narrative streams.

Most, but not all of the levels of the hierarchy are represented by voices earlier in this volume. 'What about the workers?' I wonder why the editors did not approach a porter or even a librarian (McAlpine *et al.*, in Chapter 8, do at least purport to speak for them).

There are also stories from some 'hybrids,' who fit in awkwardly: look again at Gunnar Handal's account of the 'academic developers' ('who exactly are we?'), and its gloss by Ray Land ('a fragmented tribe, dwelling in quite different neighbourhoods of a divided village'). Again, Whitchurch is a valuable guide to the new *species*: of 'niche builders', 'project-workers' and 'path-finders'. Victor Borden's autobiographical fragment illustrates the perils of professional pioneering (isolation, sectarianism, status-anxiety), as well as the collegial pleasures of success and eventual recognition.

An important question is 'where do students fit in?' In the UK, will greater exposure to undergraduate fees change the answer? For Burgess, the increasing recognition of the students' role in governance of institutions and evaluation of courses is one of the more progressive features of recent developments. To what extent does this complicate the fashionable discourse on 'students as consumers', by emphasising the relatively unfashionable concept of student 'membership' of their institutions? Laura Miller's probing of the basis of student 'contracts' is relevant here. So too is Marian Jazvac-Martek and Allison Gonsalves' exploration of the transitional (purgatorial?) status of the PhD candidate intending to pursue an academic career.

The 'university hierarchy' reminds me a bit of what is still the best book on baseball that I've read so far: Jim Bouton's *Ball Four* – one of the New York Public Library's books of the last century). Bouton's professional baseball club hierarchy goes something like this (Bouton 1970):

- owner;
- star player (sometimes called 'the franchise');
- manager;
- established players;
- coaches;
- marginal players.

If the allusion to higher education seems far-fetched, I can tell the story of a vice-chancellor having to tell his university council of the time when a Nobel-prize winner on the staff defected to an apparently better-endowed American university. The vice-chancellor had learned about it first from the *Daily Mail*. (Interestingly, the scientist in question has subsequently returned – it is suggested partly in response to new legislation outlawing age discrimination.) Taking the bottom three levels from Bouton (which is where most of his story takes place), think about the analogy with the short-term contract researcher: who pushes him or her around, and why?

Nonetheless, the university or college does exist as an entity for some purposes and in some contexts, especially when viewed from outside. What it is seen as doing to or for a client is seen usually as a *corporate* responsibility (you have only to experience a vice-chancellor's postbag to understand this (Watson 2005)). Incidentally, one of the things that, in my experience, most infuriates senior managers is when quite senior members of the organisation say 'why doesn't the university do something about x?', as if they have nothing to do with it.

More seriously, if the reification of the university is to have positive effects, it is normally the management who have to take some responsibility for defining and reflecting it, even if they do so by stealth. On stealth, the classic formulation is Eric Ashby's in *Technology and the Academics* (1958), about seeding your best ideas with others, and nodding approvingly when they come back under different ownership. Graeme Davies, vice-chancellor of the University of London, has recently said almost exactly the same thing: 'there is no limit to what you can achieve provided that you are prepared to take no credit for it' (Davies, private communication).

Story-telling

It's fashionable to refer to this process of institutional promotion as story-telling. Story-telling in complex organisations received a big boost at the turn of the century from Steve Denning's book about the World Bank, *The Springboard: How Story-Telling Ignites Action in Knowledge Era Organisations* (further elaborated in Denning 2005). It is, however, quite important not to look at stories in organisations through rose-tinted spectacles. Don't assume that all story-telling in institutions is good (or that the same is true about institutional humour – Rob Cuthbert has written powerfully on this); it can also be corrosive and disruptive. 'The principal is the shepherd of his people; the vice-principal is the crook on his staff' (see Cuthbert 1996: 97). Denning's latest work has an important section on 'taming the grapevine' (Denning 2005: 201–23).

To get back to story-telling, the 'management' trick is probably maintaining the connection between the big story, and all of the little stories that parts of the organisation like to tell (about their students, themselves, and their achievements).

It doesn't mean that the big story and all of the little stories have to be the same. It may even be tolerant of contradictions between the big story and the little stories (i.e. 'tolerance' may be part of the big story itself). From a wider perspective, Gerard Delanty says almost the same thing: 'there is no single legitimizing idea of the university, no grand narrative, but a plurality of ideas and a growing diversity of universities and institutions of higher education' (Chapter 9 above).

Despite this stricture, it is worth thinking about the conditions of a successful big story.

- *Authenticity* is one element. It has to be believable. Of how many claims to be 'world class' is this true?
- Its authors have to be in control. Hence *autonomy* is important.
- It may well have to be *adaptable*. The most successful universities and colleges have always been good at reinventing themselves. Again, as Delanty affirms, the university is a 'process' (or, as I would prefer to call it, a 'work in progress'), rather than a 'form or a structure'.
- Above all, it has to be based on an understanding of what is really going on. It has to be *analytical*. For example, this is what lies behind the reports of the

UUK Longer Term Strategy Group; *Patterns of UK HEIs* (see UUK 2006). The group's mission is about confronting opinion with evidence. What's more the analysis has to be 'inside-out' as well as 'outside-in'. We can spend too much time on what's being done to us, and not enough on what we are doing to ourselves.

• None of this, of course, precludes the story being appropriately *ambitious*.

What can frustrate university leaders is a sense that they are not in control, as they imagine their counterparts in the private corporate world are. On this score there is some reassurance from the Harvard Business School. Jeffrey Pfeffer and Robert Sutton include the illusion that great leaders are in control of their companies among their collection of *Hard Facts, Dangerous Half-Truths and Total Nonsense*. In reality, they conclude, 'believing you are in control can wreck your organisation.' Instead what good leaders should do is to build systems and teams, 'figure out when and how to get out of the way', project confidence, 'be specific about the few things that matter and keep repeating them' and, 'if all else fails, slow the spread of bad practice' (Pfeffer and Sutton 2006: 206–30). The celebrity vice-chancellor who attempts to build an organisation in his or her image is empirically (eventually) doomed. Constructively, Pfeffer and Sutton's final injunction is that leaders should promote curiosity:

Leaders breed such curiosity by having both the humility to be students and the confidence to be teachers (and to know when and how to switch roles).

(ibid.: 234)

To echo Laura Miller, they have responsibilities to create the conditions of a Habermasian 'public space', as well as to share Arendtian 'perplexities'. In this context, Lapworth's conclusion about the absence of a 'culture of critical discourse' about management in HEIs strikes me as perhaps unduly severe.

Evans concludes his Hamburg study with a meta-narrative: '*laissez-faire* liberalism proved incapable of dealing with the problems generated by massive urbanindustrial growth and was forced by the ensuing disaster to give way to "Prussian"-style state interventionism' (Evans 1997: 147). Is there a meta-narrative here? If so, it may be found in the next and final chapter, by our editors.

Coda

Identity and voice in higher education
Making connections

Ronald Barnett and Roberto Di Napoli

Scope and diversity

The contributions to this volume have implicitly raised the following questions: Is there an identity that is characteristic of those who work in higher education? Might we hope even now to uncover a common identity here? Or, amid mass higher education systems, are we now fated to see only 'diversity'?

There is a paradox here; or at least a set of tensions. In higher education, an institution of 'free speech' and 'academic freedom', we may indeed expect to encounter diverse voices and identities. So the *universalism* of free speech and academic freedom will call forth *specificity* and plurality of voice and identity. Plurality is a sign of the university doing its job as a site of universal academic freedom. Plurality and universalism may not be counterposed after all; they may go hand in hand. As a broad principle, then, plurality of identity is to be welcomed and not mistrusted.

However, in the contemporary age, where the state takes an ever closer interest in higher education (even if it promotes the market as a defining and steering mechanism), the possibility arises that voice and identity on campus may be diminishing in their range, even as they may also be changing. So, change amidst diminution; even as voice and identity change, they shrink.

But the tea leaves may be read differently. In an age in which higher education institutions are developing their missions – and just may be developing different missions – voice and identity may be widening. And, surely, we have seen just this in this volume: the several chapters are testimony to the development of diverse 'communities of practice' with their own identity projects, even if some of those communities are struggling to establish a coherent identity. Among the academics alone, some retain scholarly pursuits; some reach out to become pedagogical experts; others become incorporated into change agents; yet others become entrepreneurs (earning more than their vice-chancellors); and others are given space to pursue quasi-ideological missions (of 'access' and 'rights') and evince appropriate modes of voice and identity. So identities widen.

It may be that these different readings are not incompatible with each other. It just may be that we are seeing a narrowing *and* a widening of academic voice and identity all at once. Given (i) the 'neo-liberal' repositioning of higher education, and state policies of (ii) selectivity and (iii) mission diversity, a multiplicity of voices and identities are very likely to emerge. But it may well be both that the fulcrum, the pivotal point, of these voices and identities has shifted and that, in turn, the range of the contemporary voices and identities is restricted. The space for significant scholarship, for the careful crafting of books over a number of years, and for close pedagogical relationships is surely passing. The 'academic scholar' may be an endangered species. At the same, the study of a discipline 'for its own sake' may also be an outmoded form of academic life.

Analogous movements may perhaps be evident among students. The commonplace observation that students are not as radical as they were a generation or more ago is testimony to the displacement of student voice and identity: in the knowledge society, in which very many have degrees, rather little positional advantage attaches to a degree as such (other than access to the labour market). Accordingly, students just focus on getting by, on securing the finances to cover the cost of their studies; many will strive to secure the 'best' degree that they can; some may even resort to purchasing their essays on the private market.

So, it just may be that greater diversity of voice and identity is evident even as the scope of those voices may be lessening. One hundred or more blooms may be flowering in academe but they flower in a somewhat different kind of flower bed, one that both stands in a new place and occupies a smaller plot. The plot is not being tended especially well either.

Voice and identity

Another theme of this volume has been that of identity and voice. Just how might we understand their interrelationships?

For any identity, there is a characteristic voice. The voice is the projection of the identity into the world. But a single academic or a single student (or any other member of any other sub-group in academe) may have several academic identities and, so, have several voices. After all, an academic or a student may be positioned in multiple networks within academe.

A student may take different subjects, especially within a modular course; and may be positioned quite differently as s/he finds him/herself a student within different departments of the one university. The student taking chemistry and Spanish, where the Spanish teaching is provided in a 'service' function by the department of Spanish, may be valued as a person in his/her own right in the chemistry department but may find him/herself having a more distant relationship with the Spanish department, especially if that service function is provided simultaneously to a large and mixed group of students drawn from a number of departments. Or the balance of the relationships may, of course, be entirely round the other way. To take another example, an academic may have run into difficulty in her/his department – perhaps her/his research interests or mode of conducting research are out of keeping with the dominant research interests of the department – but may be well thought of by her/his faculty or even by senior managers in the university (our lecturer has taken on particular responsibilities across the faculty or even across the university, perhaps in relation to learning and teaching or in relation to academic staff development). In either case, student or staff member, the individual may have different personae in different settings in the academy. In turn, the individual will have a different voice and a different identity in the different situations.

Voice and identity are particular to individuals; individuals vary in their voice and identity. But the script of different settings sets the voice; the score is written to a significant extent. In committees, in the vice-chancellor's room, in submitting a paper to a journal, certain voices and identities are encouraged while others are discouraged, if not ruled out of order altogether. Censure may take subtle forms; less excommunication and more a silent boycott. The committee's business is moved on before a particular voice can be heard again. In turn, an individual may sense the norms in place and may censure him/herself and attempt to speak in the expected voice.

Does the individual 'sing'? Or is the individual mute? Is the individual encouraged to try to develop a new voice? Or, indeed, is the individual expected to take on a new identity, for example, as an academic entrepreneur?

Transformation and improvisation

The slide in those questions from 'voice' to 'identity' offers further insight into the relationship between the two terms. An identity may try different voices; some of those voices may be uttered wholeheartedly and others may be voiced with little enthusiasm and even resistance.

Change in identity is more fundamental than change in voice. Change in identity is a matter of change in being, of change in the patterning of the relationships of the individual with the (academic) world around her/him. Change in voice is a weaker notion, for it can – to a significant extent – be enacted at will. The individual takes on the appropriate voice as s/he moves from a committee meeting (in which s/he can invest herself and her/his values in advancing, say, an 'access' agenda) to another meeting held down the corridor (in which her/his course is part of a suite of courses subject to a major course review, which includes one or more external members of the review panel). In this latter case, identity may even be felt to be on trial. To some extent, too, the identity changes at the same time, but it is to a limited extent. The multiple identities held by a single person are as variants on a theme; her/his voices, on the other hand, may be fundamentally different.

The pathologies of identity and voice differ: we speak of an identity being confined and a voice suppressed. An identity is less easily taken away than voice. A voice may be altogether extinguished while the identity, to a large extent, remains;

though, in such circumstances, it is liable to narrow in its range. An intimidating teaching style, or one in which respect for students is just absent (evident in brusque words in the margin of the essay) may lead to the student censuring him/herself so that his/her voice dries up. The voice may go silent even though the identity remains intact; it just lacks the possibility for its expression. Over time, however, if the voice is silenced, the identity itself may wither. On the other hand, if the voice is encouraged, the identity itself may grow and make possible new kinds of voice.

Similar patterns of encouragement and discouragement, of the flowering of voice and the widening of identity – or their respective suppression and withering – may be seen among staff on contemporary campuses. Talk of 'academic freedom', or of 'care' for one's students, or of scholarly research that yields little revenue to the university, may be subtly sensed to be off-message. Voice is not discouraged, provided it is the right kind of voice. The vice-chancellor may come to hear what s/he wants to hear.

The vice-chancellors do not act wilfully here (or very seldom so). An internal management tone – and even occasionally actual policies – emerge largely as a reading of the external environment in which universities are placed. On the one hand, the university is subject to public evaluations on which depend resources and reputation (strains that coalesce in national and even international league tables). On the other hand, the university strives to project itself in different market-places and feels itself subject to the sensitivities of various constituencies. All this 'environmental scanning' can easily and understandably bring a nervousness into the university. Voices had better be softened if not actually modulated. And these forms of personal self-monitoring have quickly to fall into place. The rhythms of the public audits and of the market call not only for identity shifts but now, today. Identity change is accelerated. In their cautions on self-expression, the managers anticipate tomorrow's newspapers

Amid firm management styles characteristic of some universities, and the major shifts that are befalling universities – their marketisation, their growing hierarchy, and the growing intensity of academic life (as academics' roles widen with little in the way of increased resources) – it is too easy to feel that the space for voice and the affirmation of self-developed identity are a relic of a former age. But a dismal countenance can be counter-productive: it can help to bring about the very reduction of voice and the confinement of identity of which it is critical. Declarations that the university is 'in ruins' may bring about that very end.

In fact, all manner of responses are possible that will sustain and even help to develop both voice and identity. Academics, it is often remarked, are often clever people and are well able to find strategies to circumvent perceived attempts 'to cabin, crib and confine' them. An unhappiness within a university may prompt the development of a person's network off-campus; correspondingly, an unease with perceived oppressiveness among an externally driven quality regime can bring about behaviours and stratagems that preserve identities while seeming to play the required part (in maintaining suitable quality systems on campus). Surreptitiously, academics – either as individuals or in concert together – can often outflank pernicious regulatory and managerial regimes. Through imaginative improvisations, identities can be preserved, even if voices are softened. The voices may mimic or 'ventriloquise' the dominant discourses without identifying with them. Sometimes, however, individuals may 'buy in' to the new discourses: students may come to play the part of the consumer that is written for them.

But, if improvisations are readily to hand, there have to be more doubts about transformations. The key issue is: To what extent is there space for transformations of identity and voice that are under the control of academic persons (whether staff or students)? A dominant narrative of contemporary higher education, after all, is precisely one of transformations. So the presence of transformations per se is not at issue. The problem is that those transformations are often a matter of *force majeur*: transformations to a higher education system are not just changes in systems but are changes in ontologies, in modes of academic being. Under these circumstances, the question is precisely whether academic persons may be the authors of their own transformations.

Is self-willed transformation of identity and voice necessary? Why is the status quo not acceptable? The matter is less one of acceptability and more one of pragmatic adjustment. That, worldwide, higher education is caught up in massive changes – of marketisation, of selectivity, of structural change, of the challenge of new knowledges – there can surely be little debate. Accordingly, transformations are taking place in any case. Identities are being refashioned; spaces for new identities open up and that for old-fashioned identities shrinks. But identities are not just given; they are fashioned by individuals. And they can be fashioned with any energy only if there is identification with the identity on the part of the subject. Otherwise, bad faith or psychic distance may result: the behaviours are apparent but they are not exhibited with any zeal.

Another concept presents itself, therefore, that may help these concluding reflections, that of 'being'. In its (original) Heideggerian formulation, 'being' was understood relationally, both in a context of immediate ways of life and in time, backwards and forwards. The being, we might say, is the fundament of identity; it is the anchoring of the self in the world, which in turn furnishes the identity. Accordingly, we may observe that underlying 'academic identity' is 'academic being'; a way of being in the world that owes to the personhood and position that are an individual's. This observation returns us to our opening question: are we here concerned with universal or particular matters? Is academic being universal or particular? Amid diversity, marketisation, and regionalisation as policy imperatives in higher education, it is difficult but not impossible to make out a universal case these days. What can be said, surely, is that there are various modes of permitted academic being these days. A problem with the notion of 'being', if we are not careful, is that it can imply a static or given ontological structure; or one that changes only slowly, with the passing of generations. But academic being may itself be changing quite fast.

The management of identity and voice

A last set of major issues arises, therefore, as we have also seen in the contributions here, over institutional management and perhaps of leadership too; and, more especially, of strategic management and of human resource management. Are there spaces still to be left for many kinds of academic identity on campus or is there a tacit sense of the kind of academic that 'we want here'? Is there a sense that a multiplicity of identities actually adds strength to a university in a turbulent age or is there a sense that one shape fits all?

There are, therefore, issues to hand of both 'structure' and 'agency'; of changing, and permitted spaces for identities but also of the extent to which individuals steer themselves around and through the available spaces, and so determine a trajectory that enables them to live out their own personal hopes with some sense of integrity. And individuals vary in their competence and energies to effect such self-willed transformations.

Here, we may have a clue as to a further difference between identity and voice. *Identity* may be understood to be more a function of structure whereas *voice* may be felt to be more a matter of agency. Identity, indeed, may be understood precisely in structural terms, as a position in a network or number of networks, with the connections between 'individuals' in those networks being stronger or weaker; and those connections are largely given. An identity, in this perspective, is nothing other than a position in networks. An individual may be 'connected' to her/his head of department or the decision-making centres in the university or may have no connection of any substance: the networks vary and the identity varies in turn.

Voice may be understood as the way in which an individual seizes or does not the opportunities that those networks open up. Some are adept at working those networks, in making their voices heard, in becoming visible; others are much more reticent at declaring themselves. Unfortunately for them in this age, for those with softer voices, opportunities and prizes come more rarely. Voice has to be worked at for personal survival.

One way of putting this distinction is to observe that identity is more a sociological concept and voice is more a psychological concept. But the two realms are not tightly separated. The stretching of the voice – the researcher beginning to place her/himself in the public domain by appearing on the television or by writing articles in the press; the scholar who tries her/his hand at running interactive workshops in strange settings – brings in its wake new networks as well as a new academic psychic structure. And so, as the voice is stretched, the identity may also grow. Structure and process turn out to be intertwined, for both voice *and* identity.

Why mention these matters under the heading of 'the management of identity and voice'? Because they place challenges on management and, indeed, on leadership. For now, leadership has surely to be understood as the widening of identity on campus and the enabling and the bringing forth of voice. The role of the university leader is none other than to enable all those at the university to see themselves in an ever-widening aspect and also to encourage a culture that gives encouraging space to the uncovering of the appropriate voices, fitting those new identities. Which identities? In part, at least, the identities of the university's emerging new mission and corporate strategy. If the university is intent on developing as a global player, or is keen to develop its capacities for civic engagement or wishes to become more entrepreneurial (to pick up three emerging institutional identities of our age), then the requisite individual identities will have to be elicited. Individuals will here be invited to be part of new networks – for example, in research or in other countries or in the regional business and commercial communities. And individuals, in taking on those wider identities through those new networks, will also need to be encouraged themselves to give voice to the personas that are in keeping with those new identities.

That is a large enough set of tasks. But the role is by no means exhausted yet. For a multi-faculty university may choose to set about developing all three missions and, in that event, nice questions arise. Is every member of staff expected to take on all three associated identities – a global profile, civic engagement and entrepreneurialism – or are these identities to be clustered? Is it that some units and centres will be expected to specialise in one of those missions, so allowing a specificity of identity? Or are the new missions to be distributed reasonably smoothly across the campus, so that most staff are expected to have something of each of those missions in their own personal identities? Portfolio staff with portfolio identities? If the first task, of encouraging the *emergence* of wider identities and new voice, is properly one of institutional leadership, the second task, of determining the *distribution* of identity and voice, is more properly one for institutional management.

It follows that 'human resource management' needs a theory both of voice and of identity. But that seems a distant prospect. The term 'human resource management' is part of a discourse that takes it for granted that human beings, even in universities, are to be managed (contrast the term with 'academic development'). 'Voice' and 'identity', in contrast, are concepts that at least raise issues about freedom and individuality, as well as about collectivity and sharedness, and so are hardly likely to come within the ken of human resource management.

It follows, too, that, although both identity and voice are proper subjects of a human resource strategy, identity will come into play there more than voice. For the management of voice, individuals must look in the first place to their own resources.

Conclusions

This book can be read as a depiction of, and a set of commentaries on, the fragmentation of the university. Not only are there increasingly disparate sub-communities in the academy – the academic developers, the new managers and the entrepreneurs alongside the academics, the students, and the support staff – but all of these sub-communities themselves are splintering into numerous internal communities. The managers, the academics, the staff developers, the students and all the other groups turn out, on examination, to comprise – within each sub-group – differing identities, different sets of value positions, and different sets of understandings of academic life. (Even the phrase 'academic life' would be difficult for the holders of some of those identities.)

So, for the contemporary story of identity in the academy, we may read also a story about the apparent dissolution of the academy. At least, the academy – on the evidence of this volume – appears to have no centre these days. There seems to be nothing, no idea, no value, no understanding that binds these proliferating identities together. Indeed, the sub-communities are ever smaller on campus, as a result of this proliferation of identity structures.

But then, as we have seen, a new question for academic leadership arises: can the different identities find some kind of bridge or set of bridges between them? Is the role of academic leadership in part to be that of translating between mutually non-comprehending communities? Or can academic leadership identify perhaps a new language, and a new conception of the university, with which the different identities can identify? Perhaps, here, arises a role for voice as distinct from identity.

Crudely, identity may be more associated with 'structure' and voice with 'agency' but the two moments of individuality intersect with each other. A changing identity may encourage or inhibit voice; an enlarging voice may help an identity to widen. The higher education sector in general and also individual institutions have themselves space to determine the space that they will accord different identities; in turn, individuals have space imaginatively to interpret their positions, and to express their voice, and even to widen or change their identities.

Academic being, in turn, is not fixed but itself may undergo subtle but quite rapid changes. If the changes – of being, identity and voice – are too rapid, stress may result and even some kind of personal breakdown. But personal breakdown may be a function of an individual's character: there may be opportunities either for the expression of voice or even for the framing of a personal identity that are simply being missed. Transformations on one's own terms may still yet be possible, even if daunting.

Bibliography

Abbas, M. and McLean, M. (2001). Becoming sociologists: professional identity for part-time teachers of sociology, *British Journal of Sociology of Education*, 22(3): 339–352.

Abrams, P. (1981). Visionaries and virtuosi: competence and purpose in the education of sociologists, *Sociology*, 15(4): 530–538.

Allen, D. and Newcomb, E. (1999). University management in the 21st century, *Perspectives: Policy and Practice in Higher Education*, 3(2): 38–43.

Allen Collinson, J. (2004). Occupational identity on the edge: social science contract researchers in higher education, *Sociology*, 38: 313–329.

Anderson, D., Johnson, R. and Saha, L. (2002). *Changes in Academic Work: Implications for Universities of the Changing Age Distribution and Work Roles of Academic Staff*, available online at http://www.dest.gov.au/sectors/higher_education/publications_resources/.

Apple, M. (2001). Comparing neo-liberal projects and inequality in education, *Comparative Education*, 37(4): 409–423.

Arendt, H. (1978). *The Life of the Mind*, New York: Harcourt Brace.

Arfwedsson, G. (1983). *Varför är skolor olika? En bok om skolkoder*, Stockholm: Liber Utbildningsförlaget.

Aristotle, trans. Ross, D. (1998). *The Nicomachean Ethics*, Oxford: Oxford University Press.

Ashby, E. (1958). *Technology and the Academics*, London: Macmillan.

Ashford, P., Handal, G., Hole, C., Land, R., Orr, M. and Phipps, A. (2004). Who are 'we'? Who are 'you'?, Who are 'they'? Issues of role and identity in academic development, in Elvidge, L. (ed.) *Exploring Academic Development in Higher Education: Issues of Engagement,* Cambridge: Jill Rogers Associates, pp. 71–82.

Barnett, R. (1992). *Improving Higher Education: Total Quality Care*, Buckingham: Society for Research into Higher Education.

Barnett, R. (1993). The idea of academic administration, *Journal of Philosophy of Education*, 27(2): 179–192.

Barnett, R. (2000). *Realizing the University in an Age of Supercomplexity*, Buckingham: Society for Research into Higher Education.

Bauman, Z. (2001). *Liquid Modernity*, Cambridge: Polity Press.

Bauman, Z. (2005). The liquid modern challenges to education, in Robinson, S. and Katulushi, C. (eds) *Values in Higher Education*, Vale of Glamorgan: Aureus Publishing, pp. 36–50.

Bayne, S. (2004). *Learning Cultures in Cyberspace*, unpublished PhD thesis, Edinburgh: Queen Margaret University College.

Becher, T. (1989). *Academic Tribes and Territories*, Buckingham: Society for Research into Higher Education.

Becher, T. and Trowler, P.R. (2001). *Academic Tribes and Territories: Intellectual Enquiry and the Culture of Disciplines*, Buckingham: Society for Research into Higher Education.

Beck, U. (1992). *Risk Society: Towards a New Modernity*, Thousand Oaks, CA: Sage.

Belsey, C. (1980). *Critical Practice*, London: Routledge.

Benwell, B. and Stokoe, E. (2002). Constructing discussion tasks in university tutorials: shifting dynamics and identities, *Discourse Studies*, 4(4): 429–453.

Bernstein, B. (2000). *Pedagogy, Symbolic Control and Identity*, Oxford: Rowman and Littlefield.

Blackler, F. (1993). Knowledge and the theory of organizations: organizations as activity systems and the reframing of managements, *Journal of Management Studies*, 30(6): 863–884.

Bosworth, S. (1986). *Beyond the Limelight*, Manchester: Conference of University Administrators.

Bourdieu, P. (1988). *Homo Academicus*, Cambridge: Polity Press.

Bourdieu, P. (1993). *The Field of Cultural Production*, New York: Columbia University Press.

Bourdieu, P. (1996). *The State Nobility*, Cambridge: Polity Press.

Bourdieu, P. and Passeron, J.-C., trans. Nice, R. (1979). *The Inheritors: French Students and their Relation to Culture*, Chicago: University of Chicago Press.

Bouton, J. (1970). *Ball Four: My Life and Hard Times Throwing the Knuckleball in the Big Leagues*, New York: Dell.

Brenneis, D. (1994). Discourse and discipline at the National Research Council: a bureaucratic bildungsroman, *Cultural Anthropology*, 1: 23–36.

Brew, A. (2002). The changing face of academic development, *International Journal for Academic Development*, 7: 1, 5–6.

Brown, S. (1993). Postmodern marketing?, *European Journal of Marketing*, 27(4): 19–34.

Bruner, J. (1990). *Acts of Meaning*, Cambridge, MA: Harvard University Press.

Burgess, R.G. (ed.) (1994a). *Postgraduate Education and Training in the Social Sciences: Processes and Products*, London: Jessica Kingsley.

Burgess, R.G. (ed.) (1994b). Debates on doctoral training in the United Kingdom, in Burgess, R.G. and Schwartz, M. (eds) *International Perspectives on Postgraduate Education and Training*, Vienna: Zeitschrift für Hochschuldidaktik, pp. 166–174.

Burgess, R.G. (1999). Patterns of inequality in education, in Benyon, H. and Glavanis, P. (eds) *Patterns of Social Inequality*, London: Longman, pp. 74–96.

von Busekist, A. (2004). Uses and misuses of the concept of identity, *Security Dialogue*, 35(1): 81–98.

Callon, M. (1998). An essay on framing and overflowing: economic externalities revisited by sociology, in *The Laws of the Markets*, Oxford: Blackwell Publishers/Sociological Review, pp. 244–269.

Carr, W. and Kemmis, S. (1986). *Becoming Critical: Education, Knowledge and Action Research*, Barcombe: The Falmer Press.

Castells, M. (1996). *The Rise of the Network Society*, Oxford: Blackwell.

Castells, M. (1997). *The Information Age Economy, Society and Culture, Volume II: The Power of Identity*, Oxford: Blackwell Publishers.

Centra, J.A. (1989). Faculty evaluation and faculty development in higher education, in

Smart, J.C. (ed.), *Higher Education: Handbook of Theory and Research*, New York: Agathon Press, pp. 155–179.

Chaudhary, N. (2003). Speaking the self into becoming?, *Culture & Psychology*, 9: 471–486.

Clark, B. (1995). Leadership and innovation in universities: from theory to practice, *Tertiary Education and Management*, 1(1): 7–11.

Clark, B. (1998). *Creating Entrepreneurial Universities: Organisational Pathways of Transformation*, Paris: International Association of Universities Press.

Clark, B. (2004). *Sustaining Change in Universities: Continuities in Case Studies and Concepts*, Maidenhead: Society for Research into Higher Education.

Clarke, T. and Rollo, C. (2001). Capitalising knowledge: corporate knowledge management investments, *Creativity and Innovation Management*, 10: 177–188.

Clegg, S., Rowland, S., Mann, S., Davidson, M. and Clifford, V. (2004). Reconceptualising academic development: reconciling pleasure and critique in safe spaces, in Elvidge, E. (ed.) with Fraser, K., Land, R., Mason, C. and Matthew, B., *Exploring Academic Development in Higher Education: Issues of Engagement*, Cambridge: Jill Rogers Associates, pp. 29–39.

Connor, H., La Valle, I., Tackey, N.D. and Perryman, S. (1996). *Ethnic Minority Graduates: Differences by Degrees*, Institute for Employment Studies Report 309.

Considine, D. (1994). The loose cannon syndrome: university as business and students as consumers, *Australian Universities' Review*, 37(1): 36–40.

Conway, M. (2000). Defining administrators and new professionals, *Perspectives: Policy and Practice in Higher Education*, 4(1): 14–15.

Corsín Jiménez, A. (2004). Teaching the field: the order, ordering and scale of knowledge, in Mills, D. and Harris, M. (eds) *Teaching Rites and Wrong: Universities and the Making of Anthropologists*, Birmingham: Higher Education Academy Network, pp. 145–162.

Currie, G. and Knights, D. (2003). Reflecting on a critical pedagogy in MBA education, *Management Learning*, 34(1): 27–49.

Cuthbert, R. (1996) (ed.) *Working in Higher Education*, Buckingham: Society for Research into Higher Education.

Dearing, R. (1997). *Higher Education in the Learning Society*, London: HMSO.

Dearlove, J. (1998). The deadly dull issue of university 'administration'? Good governance, managerialism and organizing academic work, *Higher Education Policy*, 11: 59–79.

Deem, R. (1998). 'New managerialism' and higher education: the management of performances and cultures in universities in the United Kingdom, *International Studies in Sociology of Education*, 8(1): 47–70.

Delanty, G. (2001). *Challenging Knowledge: The University in the Knowledge Society*, Buckingham: Open University Press.

Delucchi, M. (2000). Don't worry, be happy: instructor likability, student perceptions of learning, and teacher ratings in upper-level sociology courses, *Teaching Sociology*, 28(3): 220–231.

Denning, S. (2005). *The Leader's Guide to Storytelling: Mastering the Art and Discipline of Business Narrative*, San Francisco: Jossey-Bass.

DfES (2003). *The Future of Higher Education*, London: The Stationery Office.

Engeström, Y. (1987). *Learning by Expanding: An Activity-Theoretical Approach to Developmental Research*, Helsinki: Orienta-Konsultit Oy.

Engeström, Y. (2001). Expansive learning at work: toward an activity theory reconceptualization, *Journal of Education and Work*, 14(1): 133–156.

Engeström, Y., Miettinen, R. and Punamäki, R.-L. (eds) (1999). *Perspectives on Activity Theory*, Cambridge: Cambridge University Press.

Ericson, R. (2005). Governing through risk and uncertainty, a review of P. O'Malley, *Risk, Uncertainty and Government, Economy and Society*, 34: 659–672.

Errante, A. (2000). But sometimes you're not part of the story: oral histories and ways of remembering and telling, *Educational Researcher*, 29(2): 16–27.

Evans, R.J. (1997). *In Defence of History*, London: Granta Books.

Ferlie, E. (2001). Quasi strategy – strategic management in the public sector, in Pettigrew, A., Thomas, H. and Whittington, R. (eds) *Handbook of Strategy and Management*. London: Sage, pp. 279–298.

Finlayson, A. (1999). Language, in *Contemporary Social and Political Theory: An Introduction*, Buckingham: Open University Press.

Foucault, M., trans. Sheridan Smith, A. M. (1975) *The Birth of the Clinic: An Archeology of Medical Perception*, New York: Vintage Books.

Fraser, K. (1999). Australian academic developers: entry into the profession and our own professional development, *The International Journal for Academic Development*, 4: 1, 89–101.

Fraser, K. (2001). Australian academic developers' conception of the profession, *International Journal for Academic Development*, 6: 54–64.

Fuller, S. (2000). *The Governance of Science*, Buckingham: Open University Press.

Gibbons, M. (2000). Changing patterns of university–industry relations, *Minerva*, 38: 352–361.

Gibbons, M., Limoges, C., Nowotny, H., Schwartzman, S., Scott, P. and Trow, M. (1994). *The New Production of Knowledge, the Dynamics of Science and Research in Contemporary Societies*, London: Sage.

Gibbs, G. and Coffey, M. (2004). The impact of training of university teachers on their teaching skills, their approach to teaching and the approach to learning of their students, *Active Learning in Higher Education*, 5: 1, 87–100.

Giddens, A. (1984). *The Constitution of Society*, Cambridge: Polity Press.

Giddens, A. (1991). *Modernity and Self-Identity: Self and Society in the Late Modern Age*, Cambridge: Polity Press.

Giroux, H. (2002). Neoliberalism, corporate culture, and the promise of higher education: the university as a democratic public sphere, *Harvard Educational Review*, 72(4): 425–4633.

Glaister, Dan (2006). Rightwing group offers students $100 to spy on professors, *The Guardian*, 19 January (http://education.guardian.co.uk/higher/worldwide/story/0,,1689657,00.html, accessed 24 March 2006).

Goffman, E. (1967). *Interaction Ritual: Essays on Face-to-Face Behaviour*, Garden City, NY: Anchor/Doubleday.

Gornall, L. (1999). New professionals: change and occupational roles in higher education, *Perspectives: Policy and Practice in Higher Education*, 3(2): 44–49.

Gosling, D. (2001). Educational development units in the UK – what are they doing five years on?, *International Journal for Academic Development*, 6: 1, 74–90.

Gozzer, G. (1982). Interdisciplinarity: a concept still unclear, *Prospects*, 12(3): pp. 281–292.

Graff, G. (2003). *Clueless in Academe: How Schooling Obscures the Life of the Mind*, New Haven, CT: Yale University Press.

Gray, J. (2002). *Straw Dogs: Thoughts on Humans and Other Animals*, London: Granta Books.

The Guardian (2006). US university spying scandal prompts resignations, 20 January (http://education.guardian.co.uk/higher/news/story/0,9830,1691266,00.html?gusrc=rss. accessed 24 March 2006).

Gumport, P.J. (2000). Academic restructuring: organizational change and institutional imperatives, *Higher Education*, 39(1): 67–91.

Habermas, J., transl. McCarthy, T. (1984). *The Theory of Communicative Action, Volume One: Reason and the Rationalisation of Society*, Boston, MA: Beacon Press.

Hall, D.E. (2004). *Subjectivity*, London: Routledge.

Hall, D.T. (1987). Careers and socialization, *Journal of Management*, 13: 301–321.

Hall, S. (1992). The question of cultural identity, in Hall, S. Held, D. and McGrew, T. (eds) *Modernity and its Futures*, Cambridge: Polity Press, pp. 273–326.

Hall, S. (2000). Who needs identity, in Reader, A., du Gay, P., Evans, J. and Redman, P. (eds) *Identity*, London: Sage, pp. 15–30.

Halsey, A.H. (1992). *The Decline of Donnish Dominion: The British Academic Professions in the Twentieth Century*, Oxford: Clarendon Press.

Handal, G. (1999). Consultation using critical friends, in Knapper, C. and Piccinin, S. (eds) *Using Consultants to Improve Teaching, New Directions for Education and Learning*, San Francisco: Jossey Bass Inc. 79: 59–70.

Handal, G. (2000). The professional context and the professional role of the faculty developer: the case for 'the critical friend', keynote speech at the Third International ICED Conference in Bielefeld, Germany, 22–26 July.

Handal, G. and Lauvås, P. (1987). *Promoting Reflective Teaching: Supervision in Action*, Milton Keynes: Society for Research into Higher Education.

Harris, S. (2005). Rethinking academic identities in neo-liberal times, *Teaching in Higher Education*, 10(4): 421–433.

Harvey, L., Locke, W. and Morey, A. (2002). *Enhancing Employability, Recognising Diversity: Making Links Between Higher Education and the World of Work*, London: Universities UK, available online at http://bookshop.universitiesuk.ac.uk/downloads/employability.pdf.

Hauser, G.A. and Grim, A. (eds) (2004). *Rhetorical Democracy and Civic Engagement*, Mahwah, NJ: Erlbaum.

HEFCE (2003). Leadership, governance and management fund, *HEFCE 2003/55*, Bristol: HEFCE.

Hegel, G.W.F., trans. Petry, M.J. (1978). *Philosophy of Subjective Spirit, Volume 2: Anthropology*, Dordrecht: D. Reidel Publishing Company.

Henkel, M. (2000). *Academic Identities and Policy Change in Higher Education*, London: Jessica Kingsley.

HESA (2006). *Students in Higher Education Institutions 2004/05*, Cheltenham: HESA

HESDA (2001). *Higher Education: Sector Workforce Development Plan*, Sheffield: Higher Education Staff Development Agency.

HMSO (2003). *The Future of Higher Education*, London: HMSO.

Ho, A. (2000). A conceptual change approach to staff development: a model for programme design, *International Journal for Academic Development*, 5(1): 30–41.

Holmes, D. (1998). Some personal reflections on the role of administrators and managers in British universities, *Perspectives: Policy and Practice in Higher Education*, 2(4): 110–115.

Hughes, G.W. (2005). Obituary for Michael Ivens, *The Tablet*, 8 October, p. 40.

Hyland, K. (2004). *Disciplinary Discourses: Social Interactions in Academic Writing*, Ann Arbor, MI: University of Michigan Press.

Ibarra, H. (1999). Provisional selves: experimenting with image and identity in professional adaptation, *Administrative Science Quarterly*, 44(4): 764–791.

Institute of Education (2006). *MBA in Higher Education Management 2006–07*, London: IoE, available online at http://k1.ioe.ac.uk/courses/MBAHEMbrochure06.pdf.

Institute of Higher Education, Shanghai Jiao Tong University (2005). Academic ranking of world universities (http://ed.sjtu.edu.cn/rank/2005/ARWU2005_Top100.htm, accessed June 2006).

Johannessen, K.S. (1988) *Tankar om Tyst kunnskap*, Stockholm: Dialoger, 6.

Kemerling, G. (2001). *Heidegger: Being-There (or Nothing)*, available online at http://www.philosophypages.com/hy/7b.htm.

Kerr, C. (1963). *The Uses of the University*, Cambridge, MA: Harvard University Press.

Knight, P. and Trowler, P. (2001). *Departmental Leadership in Higher Education*, Buckingham: Society for Research into Higher Education.

Kogan, M., Moses, I. and El-Khawas, E. (1994). *Staffing Higher Education – Meeting New Challenges*, London: Jessica Kingsley.

Lacan, J., trans. Sheridan, A. (1977). *Ecrits: A Selection*, London: Tavistock.

Lago, C. and Shipton, G. (1995). *Personal Tutoring in Action*, Sheffield: Sheffield University Counselling Service.

Lambert, P. (2003). Promoting developmental transfer in vocational teacher education, in Tuomi-Grohn, T. and Engeström, Y. (eds) *Between School and Work: New Perspectives on Transfer and Boundary-Crossing*, Amsterdam: Pergamon, pp. 233–254.

Lambert, R. (2003). *Lambert Review of Business–University Collaboration, Final Report*, London: HMSO.

Land, R. (2000). Orientations to educational development, *Educational Developments*, 1: 19–23.

Land, R. (2001). Agency, context and change in academic development, *International Journal for Academic Development*, 6: 4–20.

Land, R. (2004). *Academic Development: Discourse, Identity and Practice*, Maidenhead: Society for Research into Higher Education.

Land, R. (2006). Paradigms lost: academic practice and exteriorising technologies, in Bayne, S., Land, R. and Oliver, M. (eds) *Learning in the Digital Age: Papers from the Second Ideas in Cyberspace Education Symposium. Part 2, E-Learning*, 3(1): 101–111.

Lave, J. and Wenger, E. (1991). *Situated Learning: Legitimate Peripheral Participation*, Cambridge: Cambridge University Press.

Leadership Foundation (2006). http://www.lfhe.ac.uk/about/.

Leckie, G.J. (1996). Desperately seeking citations: uncovering faculty assumptions about the undergraduate research process, *Journal of Academic Librarianship*, vol.: 201–208.

Light, R. J. (2001). *Making the Most of College: Students Speak their Minds*, Cambridge, MA: Harvard University Press.

Lindsay, R. (2004). (Book review), *Studies in Higher Education*, 29(1): 279–286.

Lycke, K.H. (1999). Faculty development: experiences and issues in a Norwegian perspective, *International Journal for Academic Development*, 4: 2, 124–133.

Lycke, K.H. and Handal, G. (2005). Faculty development programs in Norway: status, design and evaluation, in Bredel, S., Kaiser, K. and Macke, G. (eds) *Hochschuldidaktische Qualifizierung. Strategien und Konzepte im internationalen Vergleich. Bielefeld, W.*, Arbeitsgemeinschaft für Hochschuldidaktik: Bertelsmann Verlag GmbH & Co, pp. 53–70.

Lyotard, J.-F. (1984). *The Postmodern Condition: A Report on Knowledge*, Manchester: Manchester University Press.

McCluskey-Titus, P. (2005). The housing professionals' challenge: to involve faculty members meaningfully in our residence programs, *Journal of College and University Student Housing*, 33(2): 10–13.

McInnis, C. (1998). Academics and professional administrators in Australian universities: dissolving boundaries and new tensions, *Journal of Higher Education Policy and Management*, 20(2): 161–173.

McMaster, M. (2005). A theory of the university organisation as diarchy: understanding how deans and faculty managers in Australian universities work together across academic and administrative domains, Melbourne: Centre for the Study of Higher Education, Faculty of Education, Melbourne.

McNay, I. (2005). Higher education communities: divided they fail?, *Perspectives: Policy and Practice in Higher Education*, 9(2): 39–44.

McWilliam, E. (2002). Against professional development, *Educational Philosophy and Theory*, 34(3): 189–299.

McWilliam, E. (2005). Managing 'nearly reasonable' risk in the contemporary university, keynote paper presented at the Society for Research in Higher Education Conference, University of Edinburgh, 13–15 December.

Madden, M.M. (2005). 2004 division 35 presidential address: gender and leadership in higher education, *Psychology of Women Quarterly*, 29(1): 3–14.

Manathunga, C., Peseta, T. and Juwah, C. (2006). Theorising resistance to/in educational development: towards a productive conceptual framework, paper presented to the 6th Conference of the International Consortium for Educational Development, Sheffield, UK, 11–14 June.

Manicas, P. and Odin, J. (eds) (2004). *Globalization and Higher Education*, Honolulu: University of Hawai'i Press.

Mansilla, B.V. and Gardner, H. (2003). *Assessing Interdisciplinary Work at the Frontier: An Empirical Exploration of 'Symptoms of Quality'*, *Rethinking Interdisciplinarity*, available online at http://www.interdisciplines.org.

Marcuse, H. (1972). *Negations*, Harmondsworth: Penguin University Books.

Marginson, S. (1997). Investment in the self: the government of student financing in Australia, *Studies in Higher Education*, 22(2): 119–131.

Marshall, V.W. (2000). Agency, structure and the life course in the era of reflexive modernization, paper presented at the American Sociological Association Conference, Washington, DC, 12–16 August, available online at http://www.aging.unc.edu/infocenter/resources/2000/marshallv.pdf.

Martin, B. (1998). *Tied Knowledge: Power in Higher Education*, available online at www.uow.edu.au/arts/sts/bmartin/pubs/98tk/tk04.html.

Messmer, M.W. (1978). The vogue of the interdisciplinary, *Centennial Review*, 22(4): 467–478.

Meyer, J.H.F. and Land, R. (2006). *Overcoming Barriers to Student Understanding: Threshold Concepts and Troublesome Knowledge*, London and New York: Routledge.

Meyer, J.H.F. and Land, R. (2005). Threshold concepts and troublesome knowledge (2): epistemological considerations and a conceptual framework for teaching and learning, *Higher Education*, 49(3): 373–388.

Middlehurst, R. (2004). Changing internal governance: a discussion of leadership roles and management structures in UK universities, *Higher Education Quarterly*, 58(4): 258–279.

Mills, D. (2004). Disciplinarity and the teaching vocation, in Mills, D. and Harris, M. (eds), *Teaching Rites and Wrong: Universities and the Making of Anthropologists*, Birmingham: Higher Education Academy Network, pp. 20–39.

Miyazaki, H. (2004). *The Method of Hope: Anthropology, Philosophy, and Fijian Knowledge*, Stanford: Stanford University Press.

Miyazaki, H. and Riles, A. (2005). Failure as endpoint, in Ong, A. and Collier, S. (eds) *Global Assemblages: Technology, Politics, and Ethics as Anthropological Problems*, New York: Blackwell Publishers, pp. 320–331.

Moodie, G.C. and Eustace, R. (1974). *Power and Authority in British Universities*, London: Allen and Unwin.

Moran, J. (2001). *Interdisciplinarity*, London: Routledge.

Naylor, A. (1997). Lend me your ears: learning how to listen properly can be good for business, *Accountancy*, December: 75.

NCES (2004). Fall staff 2004 survey form, *Integrated Postsecondary Education Data Set (IPEDS)*, Washington, DC: National Center for Education Statistics, US Department of Education, available online at http://nces.ed.gov/ipeds/pdf/webbase2004/fs_long_form.pdf.

NCIHE (National Committee of Inquiry into Higher Education) (1997). *Higher Education in the Learning Society*, London: HMSO.

Nelson, C. and Watt, S. (1999). *Academic Keywords: A Devil's Dictionary for Higher Education*, New York and London: Routledge.

Neuman, R. (2001). Disciplinary differences and university teaching, *Studies in Higher Education*, 26(2): 135–146.

Newman, J.H. (1920). *On the Scope and Nature of University Education*, London and Toronto: J.M. Dent & Sons Ltd.

Newman, J., ed. Turner, F. (1996). *The Idea of the University*, New Haven, CT: Yale University Press.

van Oers, B. (1998). From context to contextualising, *Learning and Instruction*, 8(6): 473–488.

Office of the Independent Adjudicator (2006). Resolving student complaints, *Annual Report 2005*, Reading: OIA.

Parker, M. and Jary, D. (1995). The McUniversity: organisation, management and academic subjectivity, *Organisation*, 2(2): 319–338.

Parsons, T. and Platt, G. (1973). *The American University*, Cambridge, MA: Harvard University Press.

Perkins, D. (2006). Constructivism and troublesome knowledge, in Meyer, J.H.F. and Land, R. (eds) *Overcoming Barriers to Student Understanding: Threshold Concepts and Troublesome Knowledge*, London and New York: Routledge, pp. 33–47.

Peseta, T. (2005). *Learning and Becoming in Academic Development: An Autoethnographic Inquiry*, unpublished PhD thesis, Sydney: University of Sydney.

Pfeffer, J and Sutton, R.I. (2006). *Hard Facts, Dangerous Half-Truths and Total Nonsense: Profiting from Evidence-Based Management*, Boston, MA: Harvard Business School Press.

Polanyi, M. (1958). *Personal Knowledge*, London: Routledge & Kegan Paul.

Polanyi, M. (1966). *The Tacit Dimension*, New York: Doubleday & Co.

Pole, C. (1992). *Assessing and Recording Achievement: Implementing a New Approach in School*, Buckingham: Open University Press.

Poster, M. (2001). *What's the Matter with the Internet?*, Minneapolis, MN: University of Minnesota Press.

Powell, W.W. and DiMaggio, P.J. (1991). *The New Institutionalism in Organizational Analysis*, Chicago: University of Chicago Press.

Power, M. (1997). *The Audit Society: Rituals of Verification*, Oxford: Oxford University Press.

Power, M. (2004). *The Risk Management of Everything: Rethinking the Politics of Uncertainty*, London: Demos.

Prichard, C. and Willmott, H. (1997). Just how managed is the McUniversity?, *Organization Studies*, 18(2): 287–316.

Ralston Saul, J. (2001). *On Equilibrium*, Ringwood, Vic.: Penguin Books.

Ramsden, P. (1998). *Learning to Lead in Higher Education*, London: Routledge.

Readings, B. (1996). *The University in Ruins*, Cambridge, MA: Harvard University Press.

Rée, J. (2000). *I See a Voice: Deafness, Language and the Senses – a Philosophical History*, London: Flamingo.

Rhoades, G. (2005). Capitalism, academic style, and shared governance, *Academe*, 91(3), available online at: www.aaup.org/publications/Academe/2005/05mj/05mjrhoa.htm.

Riesman, D. (1998). *On Higher Education: The Academic Enterprise in an Era of Rising Student Consumerism*, Somerset, NJ: Transaction Publishers.

Robbins, L. (1963). *Higher Education*, London: HMSO.

Robins, K. and Webster, F. (eds) (2002). *The Virtual University*, Oxford: Oxford University Press.

Rogers, C.R. (1983). *Freedom to Learn for the 80's*, Columbus, OH: Charles E. Merrill Publishing Company.

Rowland, S. (2000). *The Enquiring University Teacher*, Buckingham and Philadelphia, PA: Society for Research into Higher Education and Open University Press.

Russell, T. (1996). Institutions, professional societies and associations as partners in lifelong learning for higher education faculty and staff, presentation to the General Meeting of OECD Institute for Higher Education Management, Paris, France, August.

Ryle, G. (1949) *The Concept of Mind*, London: Hutchinson.

Schrag, C.O. (1997). *The Self after Postmodernity*, New Haven, CT: Yale University Press.

Scott, P. (ed) (1998). *The Globalization of Higher Education*, Buckingham: Open University Press.

Self, P. (1972). *Administrative Theories and Politics: An Inquiry into the Structure and Processes of Modern Government*, London: Allen and Unwin.

Selwood, S. (2002). *Measuring Culture: Spiked Culture*, available online at http://www.spiked-online.com/printable/00000006DBAF.htm.

Senge, P. (1990). *The Fifth Discipline: The Art and Practice of the Learning Organisation*, London: Random Century Group.

Senge, P., Scharmer, C.O., Jaworski, J. and Flowers, B.S. (2004). *Presence: Exploring Profound Change in People, Organizations, and Society*, London: Nicholas Brealey Publishing.

Sennett, R. (1998). *The Corrosion of Character: The Personal Consequences of Work in the New Capitalism*, New York and London: W.W. Norton & Company.

Sharman, A. and Sekhon, P. (1996). *Australian Professional Doctorates*, Graduate School Discussion Paper 6, Sydney: UTS.

Shore, C. and Wright, S. (2000). Coercive accountability: the rise of audit culture in higher education, in Strathern, M. (ed.) *Audit Cultures: Anthropological Studies in Accountability, Ethics and the Academy*, London and New York: Routledge.

Showalter, Elaine (2005). *Faculty Towers: The Academic Novel and its Discontents*, Oxford: Oxford University Press.

Simons, H. (1987). *Getting to Know Schools in a Democracy: The Politics and Process of Evaluation*, London: The Falmer Press.

Sinaceur, M.A. (1977). What is interdisciplinarity?, *International Social Science Journal*, 29(4): 571–579.

Slaughter, L. and Lesley, L. (1997). *Academic Capitalism: Politics, Policies and the Entre- preneurial University*, Baltimore, MD: Johns Hopkins University Press.

Smith, A. and Webster, F. (eds) (1996). *The Postmodern University?*, Buckingham: Open University Press.

Stenhouse, L. (1979). Research as a basis for teaching, inaugural lecture at the University of East Anglia, 20 February. Subsequently published in Rudduck, J. and Hopkins, D. (eds) (1985) *Research as a Basis for Teaching: Readings from the Work of Lawrence Stenhouse*, London: Heinemann Educational, pp. 113–128.

Stets, J.E. and Burke, P.J. (2000). Identity theory and social identity theory, *Social Psycho- logy Quarterly*, 63(3): 224–237.

Stets, J.E. and Harrod, M.M. (2004). Verification across multiple identities: the role of status, *Social Psychology Quarterly*, 67(2): 155–171.

Strathern, M. (2004). Accountability across disciplines, in *Commons and Borderlands: Working Papers on Interdisciplinarity, Accountability and the Flow of Knowledge*, Wantage: Sean Kingston Publishing, pp. 68–86.

Surridge, P. (2006). *The National Student Survey 2005*, Bristol: HEFCE.

Szekeres, J. (2004). The invisible workers, *Journal of Higher Education Policy and Man- agement*, 26(1): 7–22.

Szekeres, J. (2006). General staff experiences in the corporate university, *Journal of Higher Education Policy and Management*, 28(2): 133–145.

Taylor, C. (1999). *Hegel*, Cambridge: Cambridge University Press.

Taylor, M. (1987). Self-directed learning: more than meets the observer's eye, in Boud, D. and Griffin, V. (eds.) *Appreciating Adults Learning: From the Learners' Perspective*, London: Kogan, Page, pp. 179–196.

Taylor, P.G. (1999). *Making Sense of Academic Life: Academics, Universities and Change*, Buckingham: Society for Research into Higher Education.

THES (2006a). Table from a paper by Ken Roberts given at the 2006 British Sociological Conference entitled Sociology and the Present-Day University Student Experience in the UK, extract appeared *Times Higher Education Supplement*, 21 April, p. 4.

THES (2006b). Head for business, heart for academe? (letters on what makes a good Vice- Chancellor), *Times Higher Education Supplement*, 25 August, p. 14.

Tiller, T. (1990). *Kenguruskolen – det store spranget*, Oslo: Gyldendal.

Trow, M. (1993). Managerialism and the academic profession, *Studies of Higher Educa- tion and Research*, 4: 2–23.

Trowler, P. and Bamber, R. (2005). Compulsory higher education training: joined-up policies, institutional architectures and enhancement cultures, *International Journal for Academic Development*, 10: 2, 79–93.

Tuomi-Grohn, T., Engeström, Y. and Young, M. (2003). From transfer to boundary-cross- ing between school and work as a tool for developing vocational education: an intro- duction, in Tuomi-Grohn, T. and Engeström, Y. (eds) *Between School and Work: New Perspectives on Transfer and Boundary-Crossing*, Amsterdam: Pergamon, pp. 1–15.

Universities UK (UUK) (2006). *Patterns of Higher Education Institutions in the UK: Sixth Report*, London: UUK.

Usher, R. and Edwards, R. (1994). *Postmodernism and Education*, London: Routledge.

Van Huizen, P., van Oers, B. and Wubbels, T. (2005). A Vygotskian perspective on teacher education, *Journal of Curriculum Studies*, 37(3): 267–290.

Vignoles, V.L., Golledge, J., Regalia, C., Manzi, C. and Scabini, E. (2005). Beyond self-esteem: influence of multiple motives on identity construction, *Journal of Personality and Social Psychology*, 90(2): 308–333.

Waquet, F. (2003). *Parler comme un livre: l'oralité et le savoir (XVIe–XXe siècle)*, Paris: Albin Michel.

Watson, D. (1989). *Managing the Modular Course: Perspectives from Oxford Polytechnic*, Buckingham: Society for Research into Higher Education.

Watson, D. (2000). *Managing Strategy*, Buckingham: Open University Press.

Watson, D. (2005). You've got mail, *Engage*, 4 (October): 12.

Watson, D. (2007). *Managing Civic and Community Engagement*, Maidenhead: Open University Press.

Webb, G. (1996). *Understanding Staff Development*, Buckingham: Society for Research into Higher Education.

Weil, S. , trans. Price, H. (1990). *Lectures on Philosophy*, Cambridge: Cambridge University Press.

Wellington, B. and Austin, P. (1996). Orientations to reflective practice, *Educational Research*, 38(3): 307–316.

Welsford, E. (1968). *The Fool: His Social & Literary History*, London: Faber and Faber.

Wenger, E. (1998). *Communities of Practice: Learning, Meaning and Identity*, Cambridge: Cambridge University Press.

Whitchurch, C. (2004). Administrative managers – a critical link, *Higher Education Quarterly*, 58(4): 280–298.

Whitchurch, C. (2005). Administrators or managers? The shifting roles and identities of professional administrators and managers in UK higher education, in McNay, I. (ed.) *Beyond Mass Higher Education*, Maidenhead: Society for Research into Higher Education, pp. 199–208.

Whitchurch, C. (2006a). *Professional Managers in UK Higher Education: Preparing for Complex Futures*, London: Leadership Foundation for Higher Education, available online at www.lfhe.ac.uk/projects.

Whitchurch, C. (2006b). Who do they think they are? The changing identities of professional administrators and managers in UK higher education, *Journal of Higher Education Policy and Management*, 28(2): 159–171.

White, C. (2004). *The Middle Mind: Why Americans Don't Think for Themselves*, San Francisco: Harper.

Woodward, K. (ed.) (1997). *Identity and Difference*, London: Sage.

Woodward, K. (2002). *Understanding Identity*, London: Arnold.

Ylijoki, O.-H. (2005). Academic nostalgia: a narrative approach to academic life, *Human Relations*, 58: 555–576.

Index

Abbas, M. and McLean, M. 105
about this book: co-construction 7;
    communities of identity 5–6; framing
    of the book 5–6; genesis of 3–4;
    historical background 4–5; identity
    of 3; knowledge, conceptions of 7;
    structure of 6–7; student voices 7;
    synoptic view of 8, 187–93; voice,
    concept of (and voices in the book) 6
Abrams, P. 100
academic administration model 70–1
academic context: of academic
    development 61–2; changes in
    academic work today 104–6
academic developers 191; activities of
    56–7; aspects of development 122–3;
    'communities of practice', relation
    to 58–9, 67; competing tensions for
    123; 'court jester' role 63–4, 143–4; as
    critical friends 64–5, 66; educational
    backgrounds of 59–60; Fool,
    developers in role of 63–4, 143–4;
    identities of 115, 134–6; orientations
    and identities of 57; professional
    backgrounds of 59–60; teacher and
    developer, complementary role-
    relationship 64, 67; vulnerability of
    61–2; wider role for 122–3
academic development 55–6; academic
    context of 61–2; activities of
    developers 56–7; allegiance 139;
    change agent orientation in 62, 63;
    'communities of practice', relation of
    developers to 58–9, 67; community
    and identity, relation between 135;
    complexity of task 136–7; court
    jester, developer in role of 63–4,
    143–4; critical forms 66–7; critical

friend, role of developer as 64–5, 66;
    criticism as academic virtue 65–7;
    disciplinary identities, threat to 138;
    domestication and critique 136–7;
    educational backgrounds of developers
    59–60; endo-paradigmatic criticism
    67; evidence base of development
    practice 134; Fool, developer in role
    of 63–4, 143–4; fruitful role for 64;
    identity and 'communities of practice'
    58; identity and misrecognition 141–2;
    identity and paradox 134–44; identity
    and resistance to 137–8; identity and
    subjectivity 140–1, 142; identity
    formation, perspective on 57–8, 59,
    67–8; international professional group
    61; knowledge, 'alien' or 'troublesome'
    134–5; liminality 140; midwife
    orientation in 62–3; moral economy
    and insider resistance 142–3; mutual
    engagement in 58; organisation of
    units 60; orientations and identities
    of developers 57; orientations to
    136–7; participation process 58, 59,
    67; pedagogical research, contested
    nature of 139–40; placement of
    units 60; privacy, threat to 138–9;
    professional backgrounds of developers
    59–60; reification process 58, 59, 67;
    reorientation 139; resistances 137–40;
    self-alignment with change 138;
    subjectivities, manipulation of 143;
    subjectivity 135; teacher and developer,
    complementary role-relationship 64,
    67; teaching, denigration of 139; trust
    and rebuke, treading the line between
    143–4; undergraduate identity 177;
    vulnerability of developers 61–2

market forces 111
market values 131–2
marketplace and entrepreneurial voice 43–4, 54
Marshall, V.W. 152
Martin, B. 105
Messmer, M.W. 109
meta-narratives 193
Meyer, J.H.F. and Land, R. 140
Middlehurst, R. 82, 96
Miller, Laura 91, 92, 104–12, 191, 193
Mills, D. 14
Milton, John 139
Miyazaki, H. 16–17, 18, 19
Miyazaki, H. and Riles, A. 19
Montaigne, Michel de 47
Moodie, G.C. and Eustace, R. 74
moral economy and insider resistance 142–3
Moran, J. 108
multi-positionality 129
multi-vocality 76
multidisciplinarity 17, 98
multiple analyses, technique of 187–8, 189
multiple systems, identity within 120–2
multiplicity of professional identities 167–8
'multiversity' 126–7
Murray, C. and Herrnstein, R.J. 110n5
mutuality 80–1

National Academic Advising Association (NACADA) 155
National Association for College Admission Counselling (NACAC) 155
National Association of College and University Attorneys (NACUA) 155
National Association of College and University Business Officers (NACUBO) 156
National Association of College and University Food Services (NACUFS) 156
National Association of College Auxiliary Services (NACAS) 156
National Association of College Stores (NACS) 156
National Association of Student Financial Aid Administrators (NASFAA) 156
National Association of Student Personnel Administrators (NASPA) 151, 156
National Career Development Association (NCDA) 156
National Orientation Directors Association (NODA) 157
Naylor, A. 50–1
NCES (National Center for Education Statistics) 149
negative climate in academic work 27, 30–1, 34
Nelson, C. and Watt, S. 188
neo-institutionalism 126, 133
neo-liberal reform 116
networks and identities as flows 132
Neuman, R. 105
new public management (NPM) 169, 170
Newman, John Henry, Cardinal 46, 125, 129, 161
niche building 83–4

van Oers, B. 87
open dialogue, denial of 109–11
organisational liquidity 126–7
organisational practices 14
orientations: to academic development 136–7; in academic work today 106–7; and identities of developers 57
overlapping identities 126
overlapping territories 80–2

Paradise Lost (Milton, J.) 139
Parker, M. and Jary, D. 77
Parsons, T. and Platt, G. 126
participation 58, 59, 67, 94–5, 101–2
partnership: in leadership 96–7; service meets 78–80
pathfinding 84–6
Pauling, Linus 110n6
pedagogical research, contested nature of 139–40
peer review 102
performance indicators, skills and 14–15
performativity, identity and 126
Perkins, D. 134
personal agency 118
personal development 176–7
personal experiences, work arrangements and 36–7
personal identity, narrative and 187
personal loss, sense of 27, 31–3, 34–5
personal tutorials 52–3
personal view, management and institutional research 146–8
personhood and entrepreneurial values 44
Peseta, T. 135, 142
planning arrangements, devolution of 76
plurality 197–8